SCOTTISH GODS

SCOTTISH GODS

RELIGION IN MODERN SCOTLAND, 1900–2012

· · ·

STEVE BRUCE

EDINBURGH
University Press

Edinburgh University Press Ltd
The Tun – Holyrood Road
12 (2f) Jackson's Entry
Edinburgh EH8 8PJ
www.euppublishing.com

First published in hardback by Edinburgh University Press 2014

This paperback edition 2016

Typeset in 10/12.5 Sabon by
Servis Filmsetting Ltd, Stockport, Cheshire,
and printed and bound in Great Britain by
CPI Group (UK) Ltd, Croydon CR0 4YY

A CIP record for this book is available from the British Library

ISBN 978 0 7486 8289 8 (hardback)
ISBN 978 1 4744 0840 0 (paperback)
ISBN 978 0 7486 8291 1 (epub)
ISBN 978 0 7486 8290 4 (webready PDF)

CONTENTS

PREFACE

A few preliminary words about the history and style of this book may help the reader make sense of it. Having spent much of my life writing rather abstractly about competing explanations of religious change, I wanted to end my career by writing something more concrete. In particular I wanted to keep in more of the observational detail from my research: the stuff that makes field research interesting but which usually gets ditched as that material gets processed into sociologese. The intention was to write a very detailed account of religion in modern Britain but, because there are so many differences in the religious cultures of Scotland, Wales and England that many points had to be made three times in slightly different ways, British Gods became too long and too complex. So I decided to take each part separately. Hence Scottish Gods.

This is not a partisan account. Whether Christianity (or any other religion for that matter) is a good thing is a race in which I have no horse. Readers of drafts of various sections have sometimes objected to my tone but, if there is still anything which offends, it is more likely a result of wishing to lighten what can be a dull subject than a subconscious expression of anti-religious animus. Probably because my day job requires me to hold the attention of large audiences of dozy undergraduates (and a few alert ones), I have developed a by-now-incurable tendency to flippancy. I can only apologise in advance to readers who expect sociologists to be perpetually po-faced.

A second note on style. I have deliberately refrained from naming academics in the text because I want to keep the focus firmly on religion in modern Scotland, not on which commentators have said what about religion in Scotland. However, I hope it is clear from the acknowledgements and the endnotes that I am very deeply indebted to those who have gone before. Scholarship is a collective enterprise and, as Isaac Newton put it: 'If I have seen further it is by standing on ye sholders of Giants'.

Finally I would like to enter a plug for the website British Religion in Numbers or BRIN. Initially the work of David Voas, Clive Field and Siobhan McAndrew, BRIN provides an unprecedentedly useful collection of statistics about religion in the UK. I had originally planned to include a lengthy appendix of the statistics on religion in Scotland but concluded that the future is digital.

ACKNOWLEDGEMENTS

As I have been researching religion in Scotland sporadically for forty years, I have gathered an impossibly long list of obligations. I have tried to recall them here but I apologise to the very many I will have forgotten.

My major debt, as ever, is to my employers – the Queen's University of Belfast from 1978 to 1991 and the University of Aberdeen subsequently – who gave me ample opportunity to pursue my research interests.

Next must come the funders of my research. The Economic and Social Research Council (grant R000223485) funded the insertion of a module of questions on religion in the 2001 Scottish Social Attitudes Survey (which was very efficiently managed by Alison Park and the staff of the National Centre for Research). The Leverhulme Trust awarded me a fellowship that allowed me to research fulltime from 2007 to 2009. The Carnegie Trust for the Universities of Scotland gave me a small grant to cover travel expenses.

I am obliged to three postgraduate students for heightening my interest in three topics covered here: Iain Paterson (sectarianism); Liz Dinnie (Findhorn) and John Mackenzie (Samye Ling).

A particular debt is owed to two colleagues: Tony Glendinning of the University of Aberdeen and David Voas of the University of Essex. Without Glendinning's expertise, I would never have dared enter the technical swamps of survey research and statistical analysis. Voas has also been a patient guide to the world of numbers and his work, particularly with the late Alasdair Crockett, has been an inspiration. I have now co-written a great deal with both and can testify that the experience has been educational and pleasant.

Much of Chapter 3 draws on Sectarianism in Scotland, which I co-authored with Glendinning, Paterson and Michael Rosie of Edinburgh University, and I am grateful to them for what they brought to that project and for their permission to draw on that research subsequently. The Chief Executive's Office of Glasgow City Council gave me permission to analyse the data collected by NFO Social Research as part of the council's study of sectarianism. Chris Martin of NFO assisted with some technical advice.

Perhaps because much of what academic social scientists do is, well, academic, scholarly exchanges are tetchy and even vicious. In that context, it is humbling to reflect on the very large number of colleagues who have assisted me in many small ways, even when they knew that I disagreed with them about some interpretation or argument. To those already named I should add Eileen Barker, David Bebbington, Jim Beckford, Harold Bowes, Callum Brown, Stewart J. Brown, Grace Davie, Neil Dixon, Lynn Eldershaw, Clive Field, Tom Gallagher, Paul Heelas, Eric Kaufmann, Peter Lynch, David McCrone, Hugh McLeod, James Mitchell, Robert Mochrie, Tariq Modood, Lindsay Patterson, Gillian Robinson, John Sawkins, Corey Sparks, Marta Trzebiatowska, Bryan Turner, Graham Walker and Linda Woodhead.

The staff of the General Register Office of Scotland very helpfully provided detailed breakdowns of the religion data in the 2001 census; a particular thanks is owed to Frank Morris. I also owe a great deal (especially for the data informing Chapter 2) to the staff of the library of Aberdeen University and the Mitchell Library, Glasgow. I am also grateful to the staff of the local record offices in Dumfries, Kirkwall, Lerwick and Stornoway; they do a fantastic job of helping the ignorant and curious find their way to obscure historical materials. Even larger is the number of church headquarters staff who provided information on church membership and the like. I should also thank the hundreds of clergy, church stewards and ordinary churchgoers who have accepted my presence at their services and humoured my questions.

I am also obliged to journalist John MacLeod for his corrections to an early draft of Chapter 7 and to his father Professor Donald Macleod for his comments on chapters 1 and 2, to Mark Smith of the River of Life, Dumfries, for his assistance with Chapter 8, and to the anonymised 'Tim Harris' for his help with my Eskdalemuir research.

It is common for academics to warn their students off internet research. It is certainly no substitute for reading original documents and detailed scholarly histories but I have often found Wikipedia's summaries helpful as aids to recovering memories of subjects I have not considered since my undergraduate days and I would like to thank all the anonymous contributors to its entries. I would also like to acknowledge the value of Amazon as a source of bibliographic details and to Google as a rapid way of checking names and dates. In this list of small things that improve the scholar's life, I should also acknowledge the Findhorn Foundation cafe, the Tibetan Tearoom at Samye Ling and the numerous providers of after-church service coffee and cakes for their contribution to my waistline.

Finally I would like to acknowledge the debt that I (and every other student of religion in modern Britain) owes to Peter Brierley. Trained in both statistics and theology, Brierley followed eleven years as a government statistician with over thirty years (under a variety of titles such as MARC Europe and Christian Research) as a collector, compiler and analyst of statistical data on British church life. He was responsible for the annual *UK Christian Handbook* which hived off its statistical sections as *Religious Trends* and for a large number of censuses of church attendance. As well as providing these vital public sources of information, he has always been extremely helpful in responding to private queries. If he has been as helpful to others as he has been to me, he is both extraordinarily generous and hard-working.

TABLES

CHAPTER

1

THE CAST LIST

My father was born in 1913 in a Christian country. The village school he attended began each day with Bible study and made no apology for regarding other religions as mistakes which Scotland's missionaries, supported by the school's collecting box, would soon correct.[1] Most Scots were Presbyterian Protestants. Though Catholics were a substantial presence in the industrial lowlands, the national Church of Scotland still claimed to represent the Scottish people. The country into which my son was born in 1994 was a very different place. It still had the national Kirk but churchgoers were a minority and as likely to be Catholic as Presbyterian. My father was delivered at home by the local midwife: a bastion of the parish church. My son was delivered in Aberdeen's maternity hospital by a Bahraini Muslim; just one of the many immigrants who have added new colours to Scotland's religious complexion.

Stereotypes outlive their realities as much as they exaggerate them. The image of 'Scotland as a land where people and church are in unique alliance' remained current long after that alliance had collapsed.[2] At the end of the twentieth century, the Queen's summer holiday attendances at Crathie Kirk were still reported on the evening news, the popular magazine the *People's Friend* as often as not featured a rural church on its front cover, and every profile of the Labour government's chancellor Gordon Brown mentioned that he was 'a son of the manse'. Minority religious communities could, with little difficulty, be squeezed into the same stereotype. The highlands and islands were either the last stronghold of the pure gospel or a puritan wasteland where nothing moved on a Sunday, but their eccentricity was distinctly Scottish. And even the much-exaggerated sectarian conflict of Catholics and Orangemen in Glasgow could be treated under the same general rubric: England's hooligans were modern; Scotland's re-fought the Reformation.

It is common for the edges of countries to be more religious than their cosmopolitan centres.[3] The social forces that undermine religion strike the industrialised, wealthy and socially diverse core first and most forcefully. The people of the peripheries then compensate for their supposed backwardness by emphasising godliness as a claim to moral superiority over the decadent centre. It is certainly the case that for most of the twentieth century Scotland, like Wales, was markedly more churchgoing than England. In 1980 only 13 per cent of English adults were church members; the comparable figures for Wales and Scotland were 23 per cent and 37 per cent. By the end of the century English church membership had fallen to 9 per cent but the Welsh and Scottish figures had fallen faster, to 12 and 25 per cent respectively. And if we consider church attendance rather than nominal membership we find the differences further eroded. In 2000 both Welsh and English church attendance was at 8 per cent and the proportion of adult Scots who attended church was 13 per cent.[4]

This chapter will introduce the themes and the characters that are later explored in greater detail. First the general nature and condition of contemporary religion in Scotland at the start of the twenty-first century will be sketched. Then a condensed history of religion in Scotland will introduce the main players and the differences between them.

Current Affiliations and Attitudes

When the British government decided that the 2001 census would, for the first time, ask people their religion, the Registrar-General for Scotland initially declined on the contradictory grounds that religion was not important enough to justify the space taken on the form and that the data produced by such a question might be controversial. Under pressure from academics and the Scottish Parliament, he relented and the 2001 Scottish census asked, 'What religion, religious denomination or body do you belong to?' Just under two-thirds of Scots identified with some Christian church. Just under a third disclaimed any religion or declined the opportunity to claim any. Non-Christians accounted for the small gap between those figures. The largest group of Christians (43.4 per cent) identified with the national Church of Scotland. Roman Catholic identifiers were 15.9 per cent and the smaller Christian bodies amounted to 6.8 per cent.

A major survey of the same year asked the slightly more specific 'Do you regard yourself as belonging to any particular religion?' and produced the same order but with slightly lower figures.[5] Now 36 per cent chose Church of Scotland, 14 per cent chose Roman Catholic, 5 per cent chose 'Christian, but of no specific denomination' and 3 per cent chose Episcopalian. No other shared identity describes more than 1 per cent of the sample. More than a third declined to nominate any religion; the 'No Religion' option (37 per cent) even outstripped that for the national church (see Appendix Table A1.1). Such data flatter because there is still something of what survey experts call a 'compliance effect'. Especially among older people, having a church connection may still be a mark of respectability, and claiming a religious identity may well signify respect for one's heritage. Hence these survey-based estimates are higher than the membership counts which churches derive from their records but the order of relative size is the same. Strictly speaking, Scotland is not a multi-faith or a multi-cultural society. It is a formerly Christian society with a large minority of active Christians and very small representations of other faiths.

The appearance of mosques in Glasgow, Edinburgh and Dundee may be the most striking visual sign of change in Scotland's religious culture, but the biggest change has been the growth of indifference. Even in the 1960s a church affiliation was assumed. When I was enlisted in a military boarding school in 1963 I was asked my religion and being unable to provide one was recorded as 'Church of Scotland'. Every day began with a fifteen-minute church service in the chapel; on Sunday we had a full hour. And no parents objected to such imposed observance. By 1974, 24 per cent of Scots described themselves as having no religion; in 2001 it was 37 per cent, and in 2011 just over half of Scots said they had no religion.[6]

The growth of indifference has not been haphazard or erratic. The 2001 census, and the large-sample survey conducted the same year, asked both for current religious identification and for religion of upbringing. We can thus map the general patterns of change over the second half of the twentieth century (see Appendix Table A1.1). The Catholic Church was most successful in retaining at least the nominal attachment of its people: three-quarters of those raised as Catholic still described themselves as such; of the rest almost all were 'No religion'. Two-thirds of those raised in mainstream Protestant churches (such as the Kirk) still described themselves as such: almost all the defectors had gone to 'No religion' and none of them had joined more conservative churches (such as the Free Churches or the Baptists). The conservative Protestant churches had apparently fared worst: they had lost two-thirds of their children, with one-third to 'No religion' and one-third to mainstream churches. Before we take this to mean that the Catholic Church was vastly more successful at retaining its children, we should note that we are comparing nominal attachment, which is always more popular for the large mainstream churches than for the small and marginal ones: few people will claim to be Baptist or Brethren unless they still regularly attend. But that complexity does not cloud two clear observations. First, adult conversion is rare: only 7 per cent of those raised with no religion later claimed a religious identity. Second, almost all the movement between childhood and adulthood had been in a liberal direction: either from conservative to more mainstream churches or from some religion to none. There was almost no flow in the other direction.

Another way to see change over time is to compare different age cohorts.

By every measure, young Scots were less likely to be religious than older Scots. Indeed, the most popular religion among Scots under 35 was 'None'. Just over a third of the sample were 55 or older but more than half of those who described themselves as Church of Scotland fell into that age bracket. The imbalance was even greater among churchgoers, of whom nearly two-thirds were 55 or older. This might be seen as evidence of an ageing effect: that as people get older, perhaps because they are confronted with their own mortality, they become more religious. This is unlikely. As we have already seen, more than 90 per cent of Scots raised with no religion did not later become religious. Hence if older people are more likely to be church-going now, this is almost certainly because they always were.

A slightly better sense of religious attachment can be gained from church membership figures, although for Catholics such a number has to be estimated because the Catholic Church regards everyone it has baptised as part of its people. In 2000, 40 per cent of Scots aged 16 and over were members of some Christian church, with the Catholic Church (at 20 per cent) and the Church of Scotland (at 15 per cent) accounting for most of them. This represents a major decline since 1950, when some 60 per cent of Scots adults were church members.

If those figures seem high it is because we are still looking at what may be quite nominal identification. As all Christian churches require their people to gather together to worship God, church attendance is a more acute measure of allegiance. The compliance effect problem means that asking people in a social survey 'Have you attended church in the last seven days?' produces higher figures than we would get if we stood at the doors and counted.[7] Fortunately we do have the evidence of a national census, conducted by asking every church and chapel to note attendance on a particular Sunday in 1994.[8] That shows that about 16 per cent of adult Scots then attended church: 6 per cent in Catholic churches and 5 per cent in the Church of Scotland. This represents a considerable change from the middle of the nineteenth century. In 1851, when between 40 and 60 per cent of Scots were churchgoers, more people attended church than were members.[9] This is still true of the smaller Protestant groups such as the Baptists and the Brethren but for the larger churches attendance declined faster than membership and now only about half of those who are interested enough to keep their names on some church roll of members actually attend.

One way in which churches connect with people beyond their core adherents is by providing religious offices to mark rites of passage. In 1900 almost all Scots were baptised, married and buried by a Christian church. By the end of the century the churches had lost a considerable part of their 'hatch, match and dispatch' functions. In 1930 the Church of Scotland baptised about 40 per cent of children aged 0 to 1. The Catholic Church and the smaller Protestant churches would have accounted for a large part of the rest. In 1970, the

Church of Scotland baptised only a third of children aged 0 to 1. In 2010, only 5,382 children were baptised by the Church: a mere 7 per cent of children in their first year of life.[10] Even allowing for the growth of the Catholic and non-Christian populations, this is a considerable decline.

The changes in weddings is also notable. In the years immediately after the Second World War, 84 per cent of Scots weddings were religious. By the late 1960s this had fallen to 74 per cent. In 2010 it was less than 40 per cent.[11] Baptism and marriage are optional but we will all die. Funerals are almost invariably occasions of great sadness and, even for those who cannot really believe it beyond the context of the service, the promise of 'the sure and certain hope of resurrection into eternal life' can be a great consolation, as can the assertion that 'God is our refuge and strength, a very present help in trouble. Therefore we will not fear'.[12] Hence we would expect that the disposal of the dead is more likely than welcoming new members into society or celebrating marriages to remain church business but even here we see a considerable change over the twentieth century. There are no reliable statistical records but there is no doubt that the rapid rise in cremations has, especially since the 1980s, been accompanied by a clear shift from traditional religious services which commend both the dead and the mourning to the care of God to secular celebrations of the life and personality of the deceased.

Thus far we have been looking at Scots in general. One of the most striking changes in Scottish religion has been the disappearance of men. In thoroughly religious societies men and women are equally likely to be religious because being religious is more a property of the society and its shared culture than an individual preference. In largely secular societies such as those of the Nordic countries, few people of either gender are religious. But between the two extremes there is a pattern common to all cultures of women being more religious than men. As churchgoing has declined, women have come to make up an ever-greater part of the congregations. By the 1960s, women were between 60 and 70 per cent of most congregations. By the end of the century 80/20 splits were not uncommon.[13]

The decline in church involvement is uncontentious. We may quibble about a few percentage points in either direction or argue about precisely when any particular index of church interest started to decline but there is no doubt that the Christian churches were markedly less popular at the end than at the start of the twentieth century. What is less easily agreed is the significance of that decline. The obvious reading is that we are less religious than our forebears but it could be that modern Scots are really as religious as ever they were and that the change represents simply a decline in confidence in the churches as institutions. That is, Scots may now be 'believing but not belonging'.[14] The decline of one or two churches might be explained by the unpopularity of some feature (such as ordaining women or not ordaining women) but it seems unlikely that the widespread alienation described above can be explained by

some institutional failing. After all, as we will see shortly, Scotland has long
had such a variety of churches on offer that people who become disillusioned
with one could easily find another more congenial expression of their faith.

Fortunately we do not need to argue about this in the abstract because we
have plenty of information about the religious beliefs of Scots. A large majority
of Scots – almost three-quarters in 2001 – still say they believe in God but only
a quarter choose the conventional Christian God. Roughly similar numbers
preferred 'There is some sort of spirit or life-force' or the remarkably vague
'There is something there' (see Appendix Table A1.2). Taking together a very
large number of surveys, we can conclude two things: that traditional Christian
beliefs (for example, about the nature of the Bible, or about Jesus, or heaven
and hell) have been declining steadily and that holding such beliefs is closely
related to both churchgoing and to age.[15] Churchgoers and those who are old
enough to have been children in the heyday of Sunday School are much more
likely than non-church young people to hold conventional religious beliefs.

Unconventional Beliefs

As Christianity has declined there has been a coincidental (but not compen-
sating) rise in the popularity of claiming to be spiritual rather than religious.
Quite what we should make of that is discussed in detail in Chapter 9. In some
cases it represents a sincere commitment to non-Christian forms of spiritual
enlightenment. In more it is a rhetorical device designed to pre-empt an unwel-
come alternative. When I was young many non-churchgoers would describe
themselves as 'Christian' and mean by it no more than that they were kind and
decent people. What they were pre-empting was the accusation that, because
they were not regular churchgoers, they were dishonest or untrustworthy and
what they were claiming was respectability. Much of the contemporary use
of the term 'spiritual' has a similar purpose but the implied criticism being
pre-empted is interestingly different. We are much more concerned with feel-
ings and emotions than with social rules. It is not respectability we claim if we
describe ourselves as spiritual: it is sensitivity. It means 'I am not a shallow
person with no interests beyond football and grouting the bathroom tiles'.

The decline of Christianity in Scotland may dismay the Christian but
a close look at what people do believe may equally dismay the committed
atheist. While religion in the sense of coherent packages of beliefs about the
supernatural, embedded in organisations and expressed through group rituals,
has declined, many Scots continue to hold supernaturalist (or at least non-
materialist) beliefs. Many of those who have given up the churches have also
given up belief in an afterlife and other non-material entities but, as we can
see from Table 1.1, more Scots than attend church still entertain the sorts of
ideas that were traditionally packaged and presented by the churches: they just
freestyle.

Table 1.1 Non-materialist Beliefs, Scottish Social Attitudes Survey 2001

	Yes %	No %	Can't choose %	Total %
Have you ever . . .				
Experienced getting an answer to prayer?	34	55	11	100
Felt a sense of living a previous life?	17	76	7	100
Had the feeling of being in contact with someone who has died?	23	71	6	100
And, do you think we cease to exist at death (YES), or is there another existence after death (NO)?	27	47	27	101

Just over a third of our 2001 survey respondents claimed to have had an answer to prayer and more than a quarter thought there was some sort of life after death. We need to be cautious of making too much of survey data on beliefs. Questionnaires are always more useful the more concrete the matter in hand. There is little ambiguity in the question 'How many televisions are there in your house?' and, unless we can think of a good reason why respondents should lie, no difficulty in interpreting the replies. Obviously what is heard in the question 'Have you ever experienced an answer to prayer?' and what is meant by a positive answer are not so simple. When we analyse such answers by church attendance (see Appendix Table A1.3) we find the expected. Regular churchgoers are much more likely to assent (68 per cent) than those who never attended regularly (18 per cent) or who say they have no religion (8 per cent). Nonetheless, that 8 per cent of the avowedly non-religious have had an answer to prayer raises an interesting question as to whom they were praying.

On the question of whether we cease to exist at death, or have some sort of further existence, we again find a strong patterning according to church adherence or background: 68 per cent of regular churchgoers and 63 per cent of those who once attended regularly and then quit but have considered going back believe that there is another existence after death. What might be surprising is that a third of each of the other categories (including those people who disclaim any religious identification) also believe in some sort of life after death. Equally significant is the high proportion of these respondents who believe they have lived a previous life: 19 per cent of the non-religious, 17 per cent of those who have never attended church regularly and 16 per cent of those who were socialised in a church but then quit. Even more noteworthy is the high proportion of respondents who feel they have had contact with the dead: about a fifth of people in all categories of religious practice, from those who attend church regularly to those who say they have no religion, claim to have had such an experience.

One further observation reinforces the point that the decline in religion has not been caused by wholesale conversion to atheism. Indeed, most Scots have a considerable sympathy for religion in the abstract. The 2001 survey asked if people were in favour of daily prayers in state schools: 48 per cent were in favour; 40 per cent were against (for details broken down by age cohort, see Appendix Table A1.4). Note that those who favoured public prayers outnumbered the 25 per cent of respondents who believed in a God: to whom or what did they want schoolchildren to pray? As a condition of their licences British television companies are required to produce religious programmes: a reflection of the power of the vision of John Reith, the founder of the BBC. The survey explained this requirement and asked if it should be continued or phased out. Just over half the respondents did not mind either way, 40 per cent were in favour of it continuing and only 6 per cent were against. What makes those responses intriguing is that the audiences for religious programming are tiny, which is why broadcasters want to be rid of the requirement. In 2000, I helped run a Glasgow focus group organised by the Independent Television Commission to discuss the issue.[16] All twenty members of the group declared themselves strongly in favour of religion continuing to enjoy this privileged position in broadcasting. Yet when pressed to name their favourite religious programmes no one claimed to watch such programmes and very few could name any. The panel members thought religion was a good thing because morals were important and religion taught morals. Put more abstractly, the views of that focus group can stand for the attitude of most Scots to religion. So long as faith is relatively undemanding it is a good thing because it makes people nicer. Just so long as religious people are not interfering with me.

Historical Background

To make sense of Scotland's current religious culture we need some knowledge of the key players and the arguments that divide them. The first big split in Christendom began in 1084 when the churches of the East, which took their lead from Constantinople, refused to accept the primacy of Rome. The next great divide – the Reformation that began in the sixteenth century – split the Western Christian church into the Roman Catholic Church and very many Protestant churches. Central to Protestant innovations were rejection of the idea that a professional clergy was necessary to represent humankind to God and vice-versa; rejection of the notion that religious merit could be transferred from one person to another (as when the living pray for the dead); denial of the claim that the clergy had the power to forgive sins (so out goes confession, penance and absolution); and rejection of the Pope's claim to the spiritual direction of the church. In came an insistence that all people had to be equally pious: it was no longer enough for lay people to support a small core of religious professionals who placated God on their behalf. So that ordinary people could know what God required of them, the reformers translated the Bible and the texts spoken in rituals into local languages and taught the people how to read.

In England the Reformation initially owed more to elite interests (Henry's VIII's marriage problems, for example) than to popular sentiment. In Scotland the Reformation was a genuinely popular movement. Small pockets of Catholicism survived in Moray and Aberdeenshire where local magnates were powerful enough to resist change and in the western highlands and islands. But the most modern parts of the country – the English-speaking lowlands – were entirely converted. For a period the national Church of Scotland oscillated between presbyterian government (that is, rule by elders or 'presbyters' elected by members) and the episcopalian model of rule by bishops favoured by the Church of England, but the presbyterian form eventually triumphed and the loser became the Scottish Episcopal Church: largely reformed Protestant in doctrine but episcopal in structure and retaining liturgies for worship that were similar enough to those of the Church of England for it to be the natural home for English visitors and migrants.

Not all Presbyterians were in the national Church. The Covenanters were radical Presbyterians who rejected the national Church on the issue of imposition.[17] In the seventeenth century religion was not a matter of personal choice. Almost everyone supposed that there was one correct way of pleasing God and that the entire nation should support the true church. The Covenanters did not object in theory to coercing people into religious conformity; they just did not think the Church of Scotland was close enough to being the proper God-pleasing church to deserve to be the form that was imposed. Eventually the Covenanting ethos largely prevailed in the national Church but the distinctly rebellious element was successfully crushed and reduced to a small number of congregations mostly in the south-west of Scotland.

Over the century from the 1730s to the 1840s there were a number of Presbyterian departures from the national Church of Scotland, most over the principle of patronage. A national reformed Protestant church was always something of an anomaly because its core principle of organisation was inconsistent with the way it was funded. In Presbyterian theory all believers are equally able to discern the will of God, which translates into the claim that all members of a congregation should have an equal say in the choosing of their minister. The funding principle was dependence on national taxation. The entire country was divided into parishes and the social institutions of those parishes were to be funded by a tax on their landowners (known as 'heritors'). The heritors were bound, among other now-obscure obligations, to fund a church, manse and school and to make some provision for the support of the poor. Not surprisingly, those who paid the piper wanted to call the tune and the idea that the heritors should, as patrons, have the right to select the minister was reinforced by that model being the standard in the rest of the United Kingdom.

The issue was compounded by its political significance. A state church was assumed to be an important source of national identity and social stability. By promising reward in the next life to people who accepted their conditions in this world, the national church bolstered the status quo. After the laird or his resident agent, the minister was often the best-educated and most influential person in any parish so those who had a large stake in the status quo had good reason to wish to control church appointments. Hence Presbyterian democracy and the right (or burden) of patronage enjoyed by the heritors were always in tension. Ironically, absentee landlords who left their factors to manage their affairs were often better at avoiding clashes over patronage than those who actively managed their own lands because the factors, looking for a quiet life, generally consulted congregations and tried to match ministerial choices to their preferences.

In 1733 Ebenezer Erskine, a popular Stirling minister, began to object to the principle of patronage and in 1740 he and a number of like-minded ministers were ejected from the Church of Scotland and founded what became the Secession Church. Like English dissent, the Seceders attracted the growing middle classes and the top end of the working class: the people who matched independence of mind with financial independence. And like the English Methodists, they soon split into a variety of factions. In 1747 they divided over the Burgher Oath, which required holders of public offices to affirm the religion 'presently professed in this kingdom'. With the mental equivalent of holding their noses, some Seceders accepted the oath. Others felt that it compromised their criticism of the Kirk. Eventually both the Burgher and Anti-Burgher factions divided, this time over theology. In both churches, there was a gradual move away from the strict Calvinism of Presbyterianism's founding Westminster Confession of Faith (in which only some people had been 'pre-destined' since eternity to salvation) and toward a more generous (or Arminian) view of the offer of salvation.[18] One minister who was a little ahead of his time suggested that 'Christ died for all and every one of mankind's sinners' and was excommunicated for his troubles, but in the last quarter of the eighteenth century the tide was running his way. In 1798 the Burghers split into Auld Licht and New Licht factions; eight years later the Anti-Burghers did the same. In the first sign that the rise of religious toleration was making the strict impositionist view of church and state increasingly irrelevant, the New Licht Anti-Burghers and the New Licht Burghers united as the United Secession Church in 1820. In turn they united with the Relief Church (which had been founded in 1761 on the principle that religious affiliation should be voluntary rather than state-imposed) to form the United Presbyterian Church of Scotland (or UPC).[19]

The largest split in the Kirk came in 1843 and again involved the principle of patronage. In what was rather euphemistically called 'the Disruption', one-third of the Church of Scotland's clergy left to form the Free Church.

There was also a theological element to this split. Had the patrons consistently appointed evangelical clergy, the dissenters would not have been so troubled by the principle but theological qualms were reinforced by the fact that the patrons tended to appoint 'Moderates': ministers who preferred quietly (or, as their critics would have it, perfunctorily) performing their duties over disturbing their people with prophetic denunciations of sin (especially the sins of inconsiderate landlords). At the time of the split, the Free Church was classically Presbyterian in believing that the state should impose the true religion on the people but, because it had to be self-funding, it gradually came round to the idea that religious affiliation should be a matter of free choice.

That shift was no more than a recognition of social change. A publicly funded state church that managed the nation's education system and disciplined people's behaviour made perfect sense when everyone belonged to the same church. But as well as Catholics and Episcopalians and Reformed Presbyterians and small numbers of English or English-inspired imports such as Baptists and Methodists, there was the large body of United Presbyterians (aka Seceders) to consider. The state had tried to maintain religious conformity with the bayonet and that had failed. It then tried to coerce conformity with legal disabilities, such as barring dissenters from public office, and that had failed. Accepting the inevitable was made easier by the gradual realisation that religious uniformity was not a necessary condition for political stability. The British state did not collapse as ever-larger numbers of its subjects decided that their faith should be a personal choice rather than a condition of citizenship. And the Disruption itself hastened the separation of church and state because after 1843 there were more Scots outside the Kirk than in it.

At the same time as the notion of choosing one's religion was becoming more popular, the tone of the religions that were chosen was changing. Culture – what people believe and value – is never just a reflection of social conditions but ideas do generally alter with people's circumstances. Theologians will object to this simplification but we can think of Calvinism as being well suited to harsh times when most people had little or no say over anything and ill suited to a world in which material conditions were improving and ordinary people were gaining more control over their lives. Impoverished and impotent serfs may find reasonable the idea of a dreadful all-powerful God whose providence is as likely to mean pain as comfort: that just reflects their lives. Skilled tradesmen and affluent businessmen think better of themselves and will prefer a more benign faith which flatters more than it challenges the believer.

It is important for our understanding of Scotland to appreciate the extent to which its regions were out-of-step with each other. When the lowlands (which includes the north-east and the eastern seaboard north of Inverness) became Protestant in religion, Anglophone in language and capitalist in economic organisation, the western highlands and islands, insulated from modernisation by geography and geology, remained Catholic, Gaelic and feudal. A number of related changes radically altered the highlands after 1745. The near success of the second Jacobite rebellion gave the state good reason to suppress the clans and to open up the highlands. In the old order, a clan chief's power rested on the number of men he could mobilise to fight. With the British state determined to pacify its peripheral badlands, the chiefs gave up their military pretensions and recast themselves as landlords pure and simple, converting rents into cash that would buy them status in Edinburgh and London. Now large numbers of subsistence farming followers were a liability rather than an asset and the agricultural changes that had occurred very slowly in England and the Scottish lowlands were imposed on the highlands and islands in a few decades. The clearance of people from their traditional homelands to the barren fringes, where they were set to fishing and, for the short time in which it remained profitable, to converting kelp into the soda ash that was used in glass-making, created great hardship and resentment. It also coincided with vigorous attempts to convert the highlanders to evangelical Protestantism: an endeavour that worked spectacularly well. A few pockets of Catholicism remained (Barra, South Uist and Benbecula, for example) but at the same time as the people of the lowlands were giving up enthusiastic religion, large parts of the highlands and islands were embracing it.

That division between highlands and lowlands explains the contours of subsequent divisions in Scottish Christianity. In 1892 the Free Church, following the example of the UPC and the Kirk, passed a 'Declaratory Act', a clever device which purported to offer principles for interpreting the Westminster Confession of Faith while actually ditching much of it. A small number of ministers and congregations, mostly in the highlands, severed their connection with the Free Church and formed the Free Presbyterian Church of Scotland.

With nothing of importance now distinguishing the three main Presbyterian churches, they united: the Free Church and United Presbyterians merged in 1900 to form the United Free Church and that body then joined the Kirk in 1929. Some conservatives (again mostly found in the highlands), who had nearly split in 1893 but then lost their nerve, now re-formed the Free Church. At its 1901 Assembly it had twenty-five ministers and around sixty-five congregations, mostly in the Gaelic-speaking parts of Scotland. Within two years the Free Church had more than quadrupled in size but it made no serious inroads into the religious culture of lowland Scotland. Though its Glasgow and Edinburgh congregations were among its largest, they were émigré churches: a home-from-home for exiles from Lewis and Assynt.

To summarise, the first century after Erskine's complaints against patronage in 1733 saw Scottish Presbyterianism fragment and the second century saw it re-unite. But every reunion left behind one dissident minority and sometimes two. After 1929 the Church of Scotland was again the national

Church in reality as well as name. But there was also the Free Church and the Free Presbyterian Church in the highlands and islands and a number of very small Presbyterian alternatives in the lowlands. The Scottish Episcopal Church persisted, often as the option for the English in Scotland.[20] One might have thought Scotland amply supplied with competing versions of Protestantism but branches of every Protestant sect found in England also found a foothold in Scotland. The Baptists were conservative in theology but distinguished from conservative Presbyterians by their commitment to adult baptism. Where Presbyterians have seen baptism as a sign of God's freely given grace (and were called paedo-baptists before 'paedo' acquired its unfortunate current connotations), Baptists have taken the view that it marks the believer's realisation of that grace and thus can only be administered to people old enough to understand what any of it means. The Brethren differ mainly in rejecting a professional ministry. No Protestant thinks the clergy have powers denied to the common believer but most Protestant churches have found it convenient to have full-time trained workers in charge of congregations. The Brethren reject this as the thin end of a Romanist wedge.

The Methodists' main appeal in the early nineteenth century (they were hardly alone in this by the end of the century) was that they were 'Arminian' rather than 'Calvinist'. The differences between these theological traditions are complex but they can be boiled down to the extent of free will permitted by God and the existence (or otherwise) of an 'elect' core of Christians who had been chosen by God to believe and to be saved. Although as Protestants they did not believe that good works could earn God's favour, the Methodists gave more space than Presbyterians to free will and less to divine foreordination or pre-destination.[21] They also shared Brethren concerns about the dangers of a professional ministry and found a compromise in having a minister, who was moved every three years or so, superintending a number of lay-led chapels. By the 1950s Scotland had also acquired a small number of Pentecostal churches: the Church of the Nazarene, the Apostolic Church and the Elim Pentecostalists being the main bodies. As will be explained further in Chapter 8, these bodies were distinguished by their claim that certain 'charismatic gifts' – speaking in the tongues of men and angels, prophesying and healing – which most Christians think were a privilege of the disciples who literally, rather than metaphorically, knew Christ – were still available to the true believer.

Bishop Hay's census of 1780 says there were only about 6,600 Roman Catholics below the highland line.[22] In 1795 there were only fifty Catholics in Glasgow. By 1829 there were 25,000 and in 1843 almost twice that number. Edinburgh in 1829 had some 14,000 Catholics where thirty years earlier there had been no more than a thousand.[23] As we will see in Chapter 3, this and subsequent growth was largely a result of migration from Ireland. In the 2001 census just over 800,000 Scots said they had been raised as Catholics.

The New Scots

Having introduced the main Christian churches, we can now turn to the other Scots. The oldest non-Christian community is that of the Jews. The earliest clear references to Jews in Scotland come in the seventeenth century but most Scottish Jews today are descended from the central European migrants who settled in Glasgow (and to a lesser extent Edinburgh, Dundee and Aberdeen) in the late nineteenth century. The community was increased by refugees from Nazism and reached 80,000 in the mid-twentieth century.[24] In 2001 there were only some 6,400 Jews in Scotland, with almost 80 per cent of them in Glasgow.

Scotland's Muslims, Hindus and Sikhs are almost all recent immigrants, a potent reminder of the spread of the British Empire. In 2001 there were 42,577 Muslims in Scotland, just under 1.0 per cent of the Scottish population. Almost half of them were born outside the UK and two-thirds described their ethnicity as Pakistani; the rest were Bangladeshi, 'other South Asian' and African. Scots Muslims are highly concentrated: almost half live in Glasgow and 16 per cent live in Edinburgh.[25]

Scotland's small Hindu community (some 5,600 strong in 2001) is largely of Indian origin although many came in a roundabout route that involves a second part of our imperial history: African anti-colonialism. Many Indians worked for the British in other parts of the empire. In the 1890s, for example, over 30,000 Indians were sent to East Africa under indentured labour contracts to build the railways and about 7,000 remained once the project was completed. By the 1960s, when Britain granted independence to most of its African possessions, Asians had established themselves as a successful commercial class, which made them ready targets for nationalist scape-goating. In 1969 Kenya expelled its Asian population and in 1972 Uganda followed suit. The Sikh history of migration, both direct and via East Africa, is very similar. In 2001 there were 6,600 Sikhs in Scotland, most of them in Glasgow: of the six gurdwaras in Scotland, there are four in Glasgow and one each in Dundee and Edinburgh.

Muslims, Hindus and Sikhs have added new elements to Scotland's religious constitution. They have also made it a slightly more religious country than it would otherwise have been because they are typically more religious than the average Scot. But beyond that they have had little impact on the natives. Conversion is rare. In the 2001 census, the proportions of those three traditions who said they were raised in that faith were respectively 95, 94 and 91 per cent. Only the Buddhists, with 54 per cent having been raised as something else, have grown much by conversion and their numbers are small. In 2001 there were just over a thousand Scots who had been raised in the Church of Scotland but become Buddhists and 538 Catholics who had made the same journey. The Buddhists also differ in constituting a religious category but not a community. They come from a very wide variety of ethnic backgrounds: in

2001 just over half were White British and the next largest group was Chinese. They are more widely dispersed than any other non-Christian category and the areas of concentration are interesting. Of Scotland's thirty-two council areas, the Buddhist top five consists of Edinburgh and Glasgow (the two largest cities), Aberdeen (the oil industry and the third-largest city), the Shetland Islands (the oil industry and some back-to-nature hippies) and Dumfries and Galloway (the home of Scotland's Tibetan monastery). The obvious sign that they do not form an ethnic community is that their inter-marriage rate is much the same as that for 'Another Religion', which is a very mixed bag of things that did not fit any of the main census headings. While 80 per cent of Muslims, 76 per cent of Sikhs and 55 per cent of Jews are married to people of the same faith, for Buddhists the figure is only 30 per cent. Buddhists are more likely to be married to people who said they had no religion than to Buddhists.

We should also briefly mention the new religious movements of the nineteenth century. It is a mark of Scotland's general resistance to religious innovation (to which I will return in Chapter 8) that the Mormons and Jehovah's Witnesses barely register in Scotland. In 2001 there were 361 Witnesses and 177 Mormons.

Finally, in this brief review, we come to the new religious movements of the 1960s. Despite attracting a great deal of academic and press attention because they were exotic, their lasting impact on Scotland has been so slight as to be barely discernible. In 2001 there were 58 members of the Church of Scientology and 25 members of the International Society for Krishna Consciousness (or 'Hare Krishnas'). There were no recorded members of the Unification Church (or 'Moonies'). There were also 1,930 Pagans and Wiccans, 421 Baha'is, 47 Rastafarians and 53 Satanists.

Conclusion

In concluding this brief introduction to the main players in Scotland's religious drama, I want to extract from these introductions the key to understanding its plot. The key is not decline, though it is hard to write about religion in modern Scotland without repeating that word. It is choice. In the seventeenth century it was thought perfectly reasonable to use the militia to coerce people to conform to the state's chosen church. Increasing civility saw violence replaced by discrimination. The 1829 Catholic Emancipation Act removed the last serious disabilities imposed on dissenters but positive privileging of the national Church was still accepted until the end of state funding in 1925. With a few exceptions – such as the state funding of Catholic schools or the honorific status accorded the Kirk – Scotland now has a free market in religion which offers the spiritual seeker a vast cafeteria of options. We now have all the major world religions and every variety of Christianity. We also have a wide variety of new religious movements. And this range is not just available in the practical sense that we can find out about and participate in almost every conceivable kind of religion; it is also available in the social sense that minority religions are no longer stigmatised. The Royal Navy now accepts 'Pagan' as a valid religious preference.

Many Scots still stay with the churches into which they were born: the most popular options remain the Church of Scotland and the Catholic Church. But there are two other choices which are important for understanding religion in modern Scotland. First, there is the choice to ignore religion. By far the most significant change over the twentieth century has been the rise of religious indifference. The arguments that excited the Victorians and Edwardians now fall on deaf ears and, as we will see in Chapter 8, even many churchgoers are indifferent to once-pressing theological differences.

Second, there is the choice to prefer choice itself. A sample of people who had moved from the Brethren to the Baptists were asked why they had shifted.[26] The main reason was narrowness: the Brethren were too narrow in discouraging contact with other churches, in rejecting new ideas and in pre-scribing conservative ways of behaving. Moving to the Baptists gave greater freedom. We can understand much of what is happening across Scottish religion if we just generalise that preference. Liberty has trumped rectitude and personal autonomy has trumped obedience. We see it in the movement between generations from conservative to mainstream churches. We also see it in the way that those who have stayed attached to the churches in which they were raised have become more selective and assertive. As we will see, the same complaint can be heard from a Catholic cardinal, a Buddhist abbot and a Presbyterian minister: even Scots who adhere to some religious tradition claim the right to decide which of its teachings they will accept. People are no longer willing to accept authority.

Notes

1. This was still the case in 1939: see D. F. Clark, *One Boy's War* (Aberdeen: Aberdeenshire Council, 1997).
2. I. Henderson, *Scotland: Kirk and People* (London: Lutterworth Press, 1969), back cover.
3. This is notwithstanding the tendency for some capital cities to be more religious than their surrounding counties, in good part because they attract migrants from more traditionally religious cultures.
4. P. Brierley, *UK Religious Trends Vol. 1* (London: Christian Research Association, 1999). Figure 2.7.1 and Tables 2.12.1, 2.12.2 and 2.12.2. These data are based on clergy counts of attenders. Surveys of claimed attendance normally show higher figures but they follow the same pattern.
5. As with all such surveys, the data are available for re-analysis from the UK Data Archive.

6. C. Field, 'Scottish Social Attitudes Survey 2011', *British Religion in Numbers*, May 2013; http://www.brin.ac.uk/news/2013/05/.

7. The 2001 Scottish Social Attitudes Survey figure for attending church 'once a month or more often' was 24 per cent. For 2011 it was 19 per cent. See Field, 'Scottish Social Attitudes'.

8. P. Brierley and F. Macdonald, *Prospects for Scotland 2000* (London: Christian Research, 1995).

9. This figure has to be given as a range because the 1851 Census of Religious Worship counted attendances at all services. To turn that into an estimate of attenders we need to make guesses about what proportion of churchgoers attended more than one service.

10. Baptism figures for 1930 and 1970 are from R. Currie, A. Gilbert and L. Horsley, *Churches and Churchgoers: Patterns of Church Growth in the British Isles Since 1700* (Oxford: Oxford University Press, 1977), table B.2. That for 2010 is from the *British Religion in Numbers* website.

11. Registrar-General for Scotland, *Vital Events Reference Tables 2011*, table 7.7; http://www.gro-scotland.gov.uk/statistics/theme/vital-events/general/ref-tables/2011/section-7-marriages-and-civil-partnerships.html. The table misleads by classifying humanist ceremonies as religious. If these are added to civil marriages as 'secular', the secular/religious ratio is 60.33/39.67.

12. The first is from the Church of England's *Book of Common Prayer*; the second is Psalm 46:1.

13. For the 1960s, see P. Sissons, *The Social Significance of Church Membership in the Burgh of* Falkirk (Edinburgh: Church of Scotland, 1973), pp. 56–7 and J. N. Wolfe and M. Pickford, *The Church of Scotland: an Economic Survey* (London: Geoffrey Chapman, 1980), p. 73. Further data and a sociological explanation can be found in M. K. Trzebiatowska and S. Bruce, *Why Are Women More Religious Than Men?* (Oxford: Oxford University Press, 2012).

14. This phrase is the sub-title of G. R. C. Davie, *Religion in Britain Since 1945* (Oxford: Blackwell, 1994). For an empirical refutation of Davie's thesis, see D. Voas and A. Crockett, 'Religion in Britain: neither believing nor belonging', *Sociology* 39 (2005), pp. 11–28.

15. C. Field, '"The haemorrhage of faith?" Opinion polls as sources for religious practices, beliefs and attitudes in Scotland since the 1970s', *Journal of Contemporary Religion* 16 (2001), pp. 157–75.

16. Opinion Leader Research, *Glasgow Citizens' Jury: the Future of Public Service Broadcasting* (London: Opinion Leader Research, 2000).

17. The name came from their commitment to the National Covenant of 1638 which bound the civil magistrate (what we now call the state) and the true church in mutual support.

18. This should not be confused with the country Armenia: the title derives from the teachings of the late sixteenth-century Dutch theologian Joseph Arminius.

19. The Anti-Burgher Auld Lichts became part of the United Original Secession Church

in 1822, which split in 1852, one party joining the Free Church of Scotland, the others finally reuniting with the Church of Scotland in 1956.

20. In the nineteenth and early twentieth centuries it was common for the senior clergy, especially the bishops, to be recruited from England. This was more snobbery than racism: an Oxbridge education was expected. G. White, *The Scottish Episcopal Church: a New History*; http://www.episcopalhistory.org.uk/.

21. As is often the case, the Wikipedia entry on Calvinism is concise but clear; http://en.wikipedia.org/wiki/Calvinism#Five_points_of_Calvinism.

22. C. A. Pigott, *A Geography of Religion in Scotland* (Edinburgh: University of Edinburgh PhD thesis, 1979), p. 63.

23. These figures come from J. E. Handley, *The Irish in Scotland* (Glasgow: Burns, 1964), a collation of his *The Irish in Scotland* and *The Irish in Modern Scotland* published by Cork University Press in 1945 and 1947 respectively.

24. http://en.wikipedia.org/wiki/History_of_the_Jews_in_Scotland. For a detailed account of Edinburgh's Jewish community between the two World Wars by the son of the rabbi, see D. Daiches, *Two Worlds: an Edinburgh Jewish Childhood* (Edinburgh: Canongate, 1997). For a very different Jewish childhood of the same period, see R. Glaser, *Growing Up in the Gorbals* (London: Chatto & Windus, 1986).

25. Office of the Chief Statistician, *Analysis of Religion in the 2001 Census: Summary Report* (Edinburgh: Scottish Executive, 2005), Table 1.17.

26. N. Dickson, 'Brethren and Baptists in Scotland', *The Baptist Quarterly* 33 (1990), pp. 372–87.

2

THREE ISLANDS COMPARED

An account of religion in modern Scotland could start anywhere but this will begin with Scotland's maritime fringes for three reasons. The first is trivial: in their very different ways Lewis, Orkney and Shetland are breathtakingly beautiful. The second is relevant: too often Scotland is reduced to Glasgow and its religious culture is reduced to sectarian conflict. The third is important: it is easier to see social processes at work in small and clearly defined areas. In 1900 the peoples of Lewis, Orkney and Shetland were similarly likely to be churchgoing. By 2000, the people of Lewis were almost three times as likely as those of the Northern Isles to attend church. And, as we will see, that divergence came before the oil industry changed Orkney and Shetland. So we have something to explain.

We also have a good chance of explaining it. The value of Lewis, Orkney and Shetland for systematic comparison is that in 1900 the three islands were similar in many respects. They were part of the same state, had the same national church and were subject to the same system of law and public administration. They were economically similar: their peoples eked out mostly thin livings in combinations of subsistence farming and fishing that were protected by the Crofters Act of 1886. There were differences in weighting – the people of Lewis and of Orkney were crofters with boats while the typical Shetlander was a fisherman with a croft – but they were more like each other than any was like the people of the lowlands.[1]

The religious history of each island will be described before the differences are explained by social features to which we will return a number of times in later chapters.[2]

Lewis

In his 1833 entry for the *New Statistical Account of Scotland*, the minister of Lochs described the poverty of his parish through its buildings. There was only one house of stone and lime and there were three houses built of stone and mud, only one of which had a tiled roof. 'The other habitations are wretched. They are built of stones and moss; but mostly of moss'.[3] With poorly thatched roofs and no chimneys, the hovels let in the rain but failed to let out the peat fire smoke. The single-room dwellings were barely fit for the cattle that occupied one end, let alone the people who lived at the other. And the infra-structure was as primitive as the agriculture and the buildings. As the minister bluntly noted: 'There is no road of any description in the parish of Lochs'.[4]

The rubric that guided the essayists of the *New Statistical Account* asked about the relative strength of the Kirk and dissenting alternatives. Perhaps because they had no dissenters to report and hence no need to estimate their relative popularity, the parish ministers of Lewis provide little statistical data on membership or attendance. However, the narratives suggest that in good weather – a key qualifier to any observation about life in the islands – a majority of people who could attend church did so and the major constraint was lack of provision. The 250 people who lived at Tolsta, for example, were twelve miles from the Stornoway parish church and, as that seated less than a third of the parish's adult population, they would not have found space had they made the journey. Lochs, with a new church seating 700 and a population of over 3,000, was little better provided. The few figures that are given show that churchgoing was popular among those within reach of the few churches. The Barvas min-ister, for example, claimed 400 to 500 attending 'when the weather permits'.

Some data is provided on membership but this needs careful interpretation. Uig, with a parish church that seated 1,000 and was often full, claimed only 60 communicant members.[5] This was not, as it might have been in the low-lands, a sign of irreligion. It was the result of caution combining with piety. In the highlands and western islands, communion was a matter of immense solemnity. The usually twice-annual communion season lasted three days and attracted considerable crowds. An important prelude to the act of communion was known as 'fencing the tables'. Ministers dissuaded those who were not saved from taking communion by preaching at length on the characteristics of the true Christian, which even the casual listener would have to conclude were rare.[6] In the 1820s one minister caustically noted of another's fencing the tables speech that 'he debarred everyone in the congregation; he debarred me; and in my opinion he debarred himself'.[7] Very many highlanders attended church frequently their entire lives and yet never took communion because they could never be certain that they were saved and it was a damnable sin to presume. Hence the pattern of very high church attendance rates but low rates of membership.

In 1833 the minister of Lochs confidently asserted: 'There is not a single dissenter from the established Church in any part of the Lewis islands'.[8] The Seceders set up a mission station in Stornoway in 1841 but made little headway and closed it five years later. Dissent required independence of mind and financial independence and the people of Lewis had little of either. Levels of education were low: almost half of Lewis families had no one who could read.[9] Even if any of the dissenting religions available in the lowlands had appealed, outside of Stornoway there was almost no money economy and scarce resources to replace the heritor-funded Kirk.

The internal unity of the religious culture was preserved by its distance from the Scottish mainland and by a significant language barrier. The outer Hebrides were Gaelic-speaking. An 1825 survey asked clergy to divide families between those that best understood English or Gaelic. Of 1,675 families for which we have data (the minister of Lochs did not report), only 51 understood English better than Gaelic and they were all in the Stornoway parish: the small cadre of professional people and incomers who dealt with the wider world.

The important point about the people of Lewis in the nineteenth century is that, having only recently embraced evangelical Protestantism, they were reluctant to give it up. While Scottish Presbyterianism changed around them they stood still and stood united. When the Kirk split in 1843, Lewis was firmly on the side of the evangelicals: over 90 per cent of the people joined the Free Church.[10] As described in Chapter 1, the Free Church in the lowlands gradually became more liberal and united first with the United Presbyterians in 1900 and then returned to the national Church in 1929. In anticipation of the Free Church's merger a section of supporters in the highlands and islands split off in 1892. Local peculiarities explain why the majority of people in Harris joined the breakaway Free Presbyterian Church while in Lewis they confined themselves to grumbling. But there was no hesitation when it came to rejecting the merger that came eight years later. All but one of the Lewis ministers accepted the change but few of their congregants followed them. The vast majority joined the re-formed Free Church.[11] The Kirk retained its buildings but it was a long time before it filled them and it did so only by appointing clergy who were almost as theologically conservative as those of the Free Church.

Lewis had a single shared religious culture to which almost everyone paid lip service and which very many enthusiastically endorsed. That consensus allowed the formal religious culture of the church to become deeply embedded in the everyday lives of the people. The social gap between the clergy and the people was filled by a cadre of lay catechists, schoolteachers and elders. Most families prayed together daily. In addition to giving thanks before and after meals, lengthy prayer sessions with Bible readings were common. The Sabbath was so rigorously observed that the chastisement of any children bold enough to defy the norms was delayed until Monday. So that Sunday labour was confined to the necessary care for the animals, food would be prepared on the

Saturday, and such time as was not spent in church was filled with family devotions or private reading of suitably religious texts such as *Pilgrim's Progress*.
The Sabbath even trumped Hogmanay: when New Year's Day fell on a Sunday
festivities were postponed until the Monday.[12] We now say 'Goodbye' care-
lessly, with no thought to the 'God be with you' of which goodbye is a contrac-
tion but originally such commonplace utterances were a reflection of the social
power of religious precepts. A woman who grew up in the highlands recalls
that as late as the 1930s: 'We were never permitted to say "We'll do that in
May" or even "I'll see you next Monday". Those who could not quite bring
themselves to say "God willing" could at least be expected to manage "If all's
well"'.[13] One inadvertent sign of the power of religion was that it managed
to incorporate even those who defied it. Binge drinking (which was common
in Lewis) was seen not so much as an alternative to the Christian life but as a
stage on the way to conversion and salvation.[14]

While the power of religion visibly declined across most of Scotland in the
twentieth century, Lewis remained sabbatarian and churchgoing. The parish
entry for Kinloch in the *Third Statistical Account of Scotland* written in 1953
notes that 'the Sabbath is strictly observed in the parish' and that 'Family
worship . . . in Gaelic is daily observed in most houses'.[15] As late as the 1970s
over 70 per cent of the adult population were church members; most of them
members of the Free Church. The following figures were presented by their
author as evidence of decline but given the norm elsewhere in Scotland they
are better read as evidence of enduring piety: in the late 1990s one-third of the
people of Barvas attended church every week and 40 per cent attended once a
month. For the village of Point the numbers were one-quarter and one-third.[16]
That such high figures are entirely plausible is clear from a census of church
attendance conducted in 1994. We cannot extract Lewis from the figure for the
'Western Highlands' but that showed 39 per cent of adults attending weekly
and we can be sure that Lewis would have had more churchgoers than most
other parts of the western highlands. As we see from Table 2.1 below, church
membership declined rapidly in the last quarter of the twentieth century and
that coincided with two other major changes: the decline of Gaelic-speaking
among the young and the encroachment, partly through mass communication and partly through the reverse migration discussed in Chapter 7, of
mainstream Western culture.

Orkney

As in Lewis, church provision in Orkney at the start of the nineteenth century
was poor. In 1825 there were twenty-nine Church of Scotland ministers, each
serving on average 900 people, who were often spread across very large areas
and, in some cases, across a number of islands.[17] But unlike Lewis, Orkney
had a considerable body of dissenters. The largest was the Antiburgher Seceder

Church. The main Seceder growth was among the professional and commercial classes of the lowlands but in 1793 a group in Kirkwall began to raise money for the church that opened three years later and became extremely popular, recruiting some 500 members. Its original Kirkwall core was made up of tradesmen – a shopkeeper, two shoemakers, a blacksmith and three master tailors – but it attracted farmers and fishermen and congregations were formed across the islands.[18]

The itinerant evangelist James Haldane had toured in the islands in 1797 and his legacy was Independent congregations in Kirkwall, Harray and Rendall. He funded the training of a young North Ronaldsay man, James Tulloch, who on his return to Orkney founded an Independent congregation in Westray. This changed allegiance to the Baptists and other Baptist congregations were founded in Burray and Eday.

At the time the accounts were being written for the 1830s *New Statistical Account*, all eighteen parishes had a Church of Scotland church; some had more than one. There were twenty-one dissenting chapels in total. Only Kirkwall, the island's main town, had three alternatives to the Kirk. Six parishes had two dissenting chapels, six had only one, and five parishes had none. Fifteen of these alternatives were Seceder churches. There were four Independent chapels and two Baptist chapels; all of them small. Of Sandwick's population of 1,088 in 1835, for example, 430 were communicant members of the Kirk, 47 were members of the Seceder chapel and there were only eight Independents.[19]

Of the eighteen parish reports in the *New Statistical Account*, six give no data on church numbers. Three ministers suppose their entire population had some church attachment and give the proportions of families they know to be church or dissent. Two give attendance figures only. The Kirkwall report suggests some 43 per cent of adults attended church while the reported Westray attendance figure was larger than the adult population. This may have been a printing error or the minister may have included children but it may not be a large error: we know from congregational histories that churchgoing was popular in Westray and that some dissenters periodically attended the parish church and may thus have been counted twice. Five parishes report membership; these range from a low of 31 per cent in the case of Holme and Paplay to highs of 79 per cent for Evie and Rendall and 86 per cent for Sandwick. Only two allow us to compare membership and attendance and the ratios are similar. St Andrews had no dissenting chapels in the parish but an unspecified number of people attended chapels elsewhere. Its parish church claimed a membership of 200 (or 37 per cent) and an attendance of 275 (or 51 per cent of adults). In Harray and Birsay, a third of the people were church members and over half attended the two parish churches. Birsay also had a Seceder congregation and Harray had an Independent chapel. Both were small but a reasonable estimate for their popularity would take total church membership to over 40 per cent and attendance to around 60 per cent: both just slightly higher than the St Andrews figures. If we pool the membership data for seven parishes and make due allowance for missing dissenting data, it seems likely that at least half of Orkney adults were church members and that over 70 per cent attended church when the weather allowed.

The growth of the Secession in Orkney is interesting because it did not touch Lewis and was hardly a force in Shetland. That it did so well in Orkney owes much to James Anderson, the founder of *The Orcadian* newspaper, who retired early so he could travel the islands promoting the Secession cause. The original 1796 congregation in Kirkwall, which grew so quickly it demolished its first church after just three years and replaced it with one seating 1,000, was followed by Sanday and Stronsay, both in 1800, and Birsay and Stromness in 1803. Another seven followed before 1843. This growth was significantly helped by support from the Secession Church in Edinburgh.

People did not join the Secession because they preferred its creeds or rituals to those of the Kirk: in those the two bodies were remarkably similar. The attraction was political.[20] Conflict over land was never as severe in Orkney as in the highlands but what their promoters called agricultural 'improvements' did hurt the interests of crofters. 'The well-to-do tried to block peat-cutting rights, and to prevent communal pasturing by enclosing fields. Ministers of the Established Church, who owed their livings to the patrons and obtained their stipends from the tithes paid by these larger farmers, must have seemed unsympathetic'.[21] Class resentment could be long-lasting, as the second Seceder minister in Stronsay discovered when he became engaged to the daughter of an improving laird. His congregation refused to pay him and he had no option but to leave.[22]

That Orkney already had a strong dissenting presence explains why the Disruption had little immediate impact. Few people left the Kirk in 1843 and the Free Church had to build slowly a presence from scratch. By 1885 there were 63 churches in Orkney: 15 Free Church congregations, 13 United Presbyterian (that is, Seceder) churches, two Congregational churches, one Evangelical Union chapel, three Baptist churches, a small number of Catholics who met in private houses, and one Episcopal chapel. The Kirk, with twenty-eight churches, remained the dominant presence.[23] In terms of membership the three Presbyterian alternatives were similar: the Kirk claimed 4,512, the UPC 4,375 and the Free Church 3,812. With an estimated 500 members in the alternatives, just over 60 per cent of Orkney's adults were church members. We may suppose that the considerable increase in worship outlets had improved regular church attendance but overall the degree of church attachment in the Orkney islands was much the same in 1885 as it had been in 1841. Sixteen years later, considerable decline was apparent. There was net decline caused by a fall in population, especially in the islands, with people moving to Kirkwall and its surrounds, but decline in church membership was greater than in the adult population as a whole, so that the proportion fell to 54.3 per cent.

The first half of the twentieth century was characterised by relative stability. The main changes were the consolidation of the national Church that followed the Presbyterian re-unions, a slight decline among the old alternatives, and the addition of some new options. While the Kirk had at least 31 places of worship in 1951, Presbyterian dissent was represented by three small UFC congregations and the lone 'Kirk Abune the Hill'. In terms of congregations, the Open Brethren were next with five meetings. Then came the Baptists and Scottish Episcopalians, each with three. The former Independents, now the Congregational Union, had only two congregations and there was one each for Roman Catholics, Exclusive Brethren and Salvation Army. But outside of the parish churches only two congregations, both in the town of Kirkwall – the Congregational Union and the Episcopalian Church – had more than 50 members. There was now a greater range of types of Christianity on offer and more people could get to them. Both World Wars brought thousands of military personnel and their families to Orkney and that broadened the cultural horizons of many Orcadians. Reflecting on his schooldays on Flotta during the Second World War, one man said:

> Talking personally – having gone to school with people from south – and listening to, and seeing the attitudes of people from the cities and the towns, growing up with them, it gave me a different outlook on life in Orkney to guys that just probably lived on like a farm or croft all their lives, and you sort of looked at things from a different point of view.[24]

Both wars also improved the roads. To prevent German incursions into the safe haven of Scapa Flow the channels between the small islands south of Kirkwall were filled with a concrete causeway. That, plus rapidly growing car ownership, meant that Kirkwall's seven varieties of Christianity were readily accessible to almost half the population of the islands. But fewer people were interested in attending any of them.

In 1951, 57.1 per cent of Orcadians were church members.[25] While this suggests little or no change since 1885, reports of attendance suggest a different picture: life was quietly draining out of the churches. On Eday only half the members regularly attended; for Orphir, and for Hoy and Graemsay, it was around a third; and in the large parish of Sanday, Cross and Burness, only 15 per cent of members attended regularly. Although he gives no figures, the author of the *Third Statistical Account* entry for Kirkwall bluntly notes that attendances are 'usually a mere fraction of' membership.[26]

The extent of the decline can be illustrated with the example of North Ronaldsay. By the 1960s a single congregation used the island's two nineteenth-century churches. In summer, when weather-resistance was less important than distance, services alternated between the two chapels. In winter only the newer and more watertight building was used. In 1967, when Robin

Ditchburn was the island's general practitioner, the population stood at 140. Typical church attendance was around twenty to twenty-five people but photographs of church events show they included few men of working age. When the charge became vacant the Church of Scotland could not find a replacement and, despite being a Quaker whose knowledge of the Kirk was confined to the few services he had attended on North Ronaldsay, Ditchburn was asked to lead the worship and preach.[27] Simply because they were the island's only professional couple, his wife ended up running the Sunday School and he became the de facto minister. Another sign of just how marginal religion had become to the island's life is the fact that the North Ronaldsay resident who wrote a weekly column for *The Scotsman* on island life between 1976 and 1986 mentions neither church nor religion.[28] She offers many tales of quaint customs and superstitions – for example, a marriage should be celebrated on a waxing moon and a flowing tide – but Christian festivals are noted with no mention of religious significance or celebration: Christmas is a time of family togetherness and the harvest festival is just a dinner and ceilidh in the village hall.

Shetland

In 1798 James Haldane reported that, while the people were generally Christian and were all baptised, with only twelve ministers for the whole archipelago's population of 26,000, preaching and teaching were rare.[29] As he was in the business of alerting pious lowlanders to the parlous spiritual state of Scotland's fringes, we might expect that he exaggerated the lack of provision, but many other sources support his account. Matters were little improved by 1826 when there were seventeen clergy. The minister of Dunrossness was expected to provide services for Fair Isle which, as he told the Kirk's committee on church extension, 'lies at a distance of 30 miles from the nearest point in Shetland' with 'a very rough and dangerous sea intervening'.[30] Scalloway, Shetland's second town, had a population of 600 and no church. The Yell minister lived on Fetlar and had preached on Yell only three times in the previous five months. There were almost no roads on the islands and people walked great distances over difficult terrain. Provision was improved by the work of the Baptists. Sinclair Thomson, a Dunrossness crofter and fisherman, left the Kirk in 1815 and over the next 48 years he travelled over 6,000 miles to promote the Baptist cause throughout the islands. He founded six congregations.

In much of Scotland the Protestant alternatives competed bitterly and demanded the exclusive attention of their members. A member of an Anti-Burgher congregation who went to hear his Burger minister son preach was disciplined by his Kirk session for the sin of 'promiscuous hearing'.[31] The geological obstacles to providing religious offices in Shetland go a long way to explaining a spirit of cooperation that was at odds with the sectarian bitterness common elsewhere. In 1837 the Commissioners of Religious Instruction visited and noted that Baptists and Congregationalists attended each other's services and: 'The Independents at Sandness attended the parish church, or the Methodist chapel there, when there was no service in their own chapel'.[32] On his farewell tour after a long Independent ministry, Peter Peterson repeatedly found that his audiences were too large for the Independent chapels: he was loaned the Free Churches in Burrastow and Uyeasound, and the Methodist chapels of Tresta, Sandwick and Unst.[33]

Even the state church cooperated with the dissenters. In 1823 Congregational minister Alexander Kerr reported that he was allowed to preach in the school house at Tingwall and was afterwards 'treated . . . with the utmost civility' by the parish minister.[34] He toured by preaching in parish churches on the Sundays when ministers were holding services in their out-stations. In the 1830s the minister of Hillswick lent his church to visiting Quakers and announced their other meetings at his services.[35] Thirty years later his successor allowed Methodists to use the parish church on the first Sunday of every month, when he was preaching in Ollaberry.[36] Even more remarkable is the 1860s testimony of the Methodist minister in Walls. The laird of Melby, a ship's surgeon who was often absent from home, had instructed his housekeeper that any clergyman visiting the neighbourhood should be given hospitality. While enjoying their host's table on a Saturday evening, the Methodist and Free Church ministers and the lay agent of the Church of Scotland decided who would preach where and when the next day so as to offer the widely scattered population of that remote part of Shetland the best chance to attend a service.[37] When the new Lerwick Baptist church was opened in 1894, the congregation was addressed by the Free Church, Church of Scotland and Methodist ministers.[38] The man appointed Baptist pastor in 1903 had previously worked in the north isles as a Methodist lay agent. That degree of cooperation remained common to the present day. Between 1945 and 1958 the Church of Scotland minister of Mid-Yell preached 124 times in the East Yell Methodist chapel.[39]

The three guests of the laird of Melby would have explained their willingness to coordinate by the particular difficulties of the Shetland landscape. However, Orkney had similar difficulties but did not generate the same cooperative spirit to overcome them. The identity of the competition to the parish church may explain the difference. In Orkney, as in the rest of Scotland, the Kirk was opposed by large competing Presbyterian bodies (first the Seceders and then the Free Church) which had ambitions to replace it. In Shetland, the alternative to the parish church was provided by three small bodies – Independents, Baptists and Methodists – which posed no threat to the status of the Kirk. Hence their agents could be seen as missionaries aiding the general work rather than as competition.

The diaries of preachers who worked in Shetland and denominational histories suggest a curious paradox. On the one hand, considerable interest in the Christian gospel was displayed whenever a proficient preacher visited.

Itinerant evangelists often found that their arrival would draw the entire free population of the area, even when it was unexpected, as, for example, when sea conditions forced them to land somewhere other than where they were headed. The chapel in Sullom had average Sunday attendances of only twenty-five when a layman led the service but the visit of a professional cleric would bring out two hundred.[40] On the other hand, dissenters found it hard to establish new congregations and many fellowships lasted only a generation or less. This disjuncture between keenness to hear sermons and reluctance to invest effort in sustaining an enduring presence is odd because, of course, the defining characteristic of Protestantism is the equality of believers. In rural England the Methodists had no difficulty building congregations on the labours of members and lay preachers. Writing in 1867, William Grigg, the superintendent Methodist minister, noted that most of his seven chapels did not have viable weekly meetings and that 'the chapels were not opened unless on the occasion of the minister's visit – say, once in six weeks, and so people were left to wander where they would, attending the ministry of other churches or none'.[41] In nineteenth-century Shetland, the large and appreciative audiences for visiting preachers suggests strong interest in consuming religion but little interest in producing their own religious activities.

The parish essays of the *New Statistical Account of Scotland* allow us to make the following observations. In 1840 the Church of Scotland had twenty-four churches in twelve parishes. There was one Seceder chapel in Lerwick but otherwise there were three forms of dissent: from least to most popular, Baptists, Independents and Methodists. They were unevenly distributed. In four of the ten parishes for which we have data, dissenters were less than 10 per cent of church members. In a further four parishes, dissenters were 10 to 19 per cent. In only two parishes were dissenters more than 20 per cent of church members. Unsurprisingly the principal town, Lerwick, was one. The parish of Walls, where a third of church members were Methodists or Independents, was the other. That may be explained by geography. Walls was in effect four quite distinct districts, each with its own church building. The minister rotated services between Walls and Sandness – parts of the mainland divided by a large hill – and the two islands of Papa Stour and Foula. That created ample gaps for dissenters to fill. Additionally, both Independents and Methodists had a minister resident in the parish. Although, like the Kirk man, they had other responsibilities, their congregations were more regularly serviced than most and hence were larger than most. Of the nine parishes for which statistics are given, church membership varied from a high of 73 per cent in Fetlar and North Yell to a low of 45 per cent in Sandsting and Aithsting, with an average of 60 per cent of the adult population.

Even more so than in Lewis and Orkney, attendance was curtailed by the environment. Of Sandsting, the minister wrote: 'The parish church is very inconveniently situated . . . and a considerable proportion of the population is distant from it about seven miles of marshy road and many of them impeded by arms of the sea'.[42] The minister of Mid and South Yell said: 'In a parish . . . the surface of which is, in winter, one continued mossy swamp, and over which there is neither road nor bridge, it is only in fine weather, that anything like good attendance can be either given by or expected from, those at more than two miles distance from church'.[43] The ministers of Fetlar and Unst claimed: 'In good weather, the Established Church is generally thronged: on sacramental occasions, crowded almost to suffocation' and 'The people generally attend well. When the weather is favourable the church is full'.[44] As evidence that demand for services exceeded their supply we may note the minister of Bressay saying of dissenters: 'Many of them, when their hours of meeting differ, attend the parish church'.[45] The minister of Sandsting and Aithsting noted the same principle in reverse: dissenting 'meetings are pretty well attended in the evenings, or when there happens to be no sermon at the parish kirk'.[46] Where attendance was not constrained by environment, it was generally considerably higher than membership. The Lerwick Independents, for example, had 109 communicant members but attendances averaging between 250 and 300.[47] The 1851 Census data for the Methodists shows 2,528 attendances at twelve chapels. If the attendance was similar at the six that did not complete the census forms, 'a generous guess is that about 3,800 attended worship'.[48] As the membership was then 1,265, this suggests that the core of members was accompanied by a penumbra of non-member attenders twice the size.

To summarise the position at the end of the nineteenth century, the three Presbyterian churches had 9,902 communicant members between them and the other bodies (of whom the Methodists and Congregationalists were the largest) together had 2,742 members. Together this suggests 63.5 per cent of adults were church members; a higher figure than for Orkney or Lewis.

The main change over the first half of the twentieth century was the decline of the alternatives to the Church of Scotland. As in Orkney, the strands of Presbyterianism reunited with almost no dissension. Baptist membership peaked in 1905 at 481 and then fell, with Scalloway closing in 1924 and Sandsting and Lunnasting losing their pastor in 1937.[49] Congregationalists declined severely: many of their congregations lasted only one long generation. All but one of thirteen were formed between 1808 and 1840 and by 1880 six had ceased to meet. By 1918 there were only five.[50] The fate of the Methodists is interesting. They peaked six years earlier than the Baptists in 1899 and then experienced continuous decline over the twentieth century that is so regular that had the figures been constructed post hoc one would suspect cheating.

The decline in dissent did not strengthen the national church. It too declined. As we can see from Table 2.1, by 1951 the churches in Shetland – with under 50 per cent of adults in membership – were markedly less popular than they were in Lewis and Orkney, and by 1971 only a third of adult Shetlanders were church members. Although we have no Shetland-wide data for church attendance, we can be sure that it declined faster. There were considerable variations. Out Skerries in the 1970s still had half its population of eighty-eight people regularly attending services in the old schoolhouse, which had been renovated as a small church.[51] But only some 10 per cent of the adult population of Whalsay attended its one church.[52]

The arrival of the oil industry in the mid-1970s changed Shetland's religious culture in two ways that rather cancelled out each other. That some of the migrant workers and immigrants were churchgoers increased the variety of religion on offer: incomers added a charismatic fellowship and reinforced the Baptists and the two small Pentecostal fellowships that had been founded in the 1950s. That most of them were not churchgoers increased the proportion of the population that had no interest in any variety of Christianity. As Shetland prospered, its people travelled more and became better integrated in mainstream Western culture, and that culture was largely secular.

The Three Islands Summarised

The change in the religious constitution of our three islands can now be summarised. At the start of the nineteenth century Christian (in the loosest sense) beliefs were universal and everyone had some church connection. Rites of passage were universally celebrated in the Kirk, even if, as in the case of Fair Isle parents who took their infants on the long sea crossing to the mainland for baptism, considerable effort was required. Most people attended church when they could and popular interest in preaching outstripped its supply.[53] The second half of the nineteenth century saw supply improve and, although we cannot fix a single date, it seems likely that church involvement peaked in the last two decades of the nineteenth century. Although nominal membership remained relatively stable until the Second World War, church attendance declined. In 1851 more people attended church than were members; in 1951 only half the nominal members regularly attended, even though roads, cars and a degree of prosperity had removed the practical obstacles to attendance. In the second half of the twentieth century church attendance declined steadily but membership fell more rapidly as each new age cohort felt less obliged to profess loyalty to religious beliefs they no longer shared.

With the qualifications that the date at which decline began, and its speed, vary slightly, the above story could be told of most of Scotland. Orkney and Shetland are unusual only in that the physical obstacles to worship in the early nineteenth century meant that churchgoing was then probably below the national rate and that the geographical (and hence cultural) isolation of the islands meant that the secularisation of the local culture began later and was slower than in the lowlands. However, there remains our main problem. Between 1885 and 1951 levels of church affiliation were much the same in all three islands. But then they diverged. Church membership declined first in

Table 2.1 Church Membership in Lewis, Orkney and Shetland as % of Adult Population, 1885–2011

	Lewis	Orkney	Shetland
1885	59.8	61.3	63.3
1901	61.3	55.5	59.4
1931	58.6	57.0	62.4
1951	61.8	57.8	49.0
1971	71.4	55.0	34.4
1991	N.A.	35.6	22.9
2011	34.6	21.9	14.2

Shetland and it did so long before the oil industry arrived. It remained high in Lewis and even grew before dropping dramatically at the end of the twentieth century.

Explaining the Differences

A surprisingly common explanation for the current irreligion of Orkney and Shetland is the supposed influence of Norse paganism. Northern Islanders now make considerable play of the Norse history and culture and some evangelical Christians cite it as an obstacle to mission work.[54] However, as the same Northern Islands sustained an evangelical religious culture in the nineteenth century, it hardly seems likely that sublimated paganism explains current religious indifference. As a perceptive resident of Ollaberry put it: 'Norse place-names do not a Scandinavian influence make'.[55] The point is less that Norse paganism survived to subvert Protestant Christianity and more that modern people prefer Norse religion because it is a pliable substance into which they can read what they wish and Neolithic religion even more so. Standing stones can prompt spiritual reflection but, because we know so little about their purpose or the people who erected them, they do not prevent us seeing in them what we wish. Calvinist Presbyterianism is too recent and too obdurate a presence for selective reinterpretation into New Age spirituality.

More generally the claim is made that Northern Islanders never really took to evangelical religion. The author of one entry in the *Third Statistical Account of Scotland* explained the secularisation of Orkney by its culture and the personalities of its people: 'In view of the fact that Sanday was subjected to a wave of fervent evangelicalism during the latter part of the nineteenth century, surprise is often expressed that the descendants of such pious Church people should be so casual in the outward observance of religion'. His explanation is that evangelical religion was too austere and too fervent: 'By nature, the Orcadian abhors a strong display of emotional fervour and, as far as religion is concerned, he prefers an orderly Service in which reason is more

in evidence than deep emotion'.[56] The problem with that logic is that it is cir-
cular. Evangelicalism declined because Northern Islanders were too rational
for it. How do we know they were too rational? Because enthusiastic religion
declined, which is less an explanation and more a restatement of the problem.

A popular explanation of the late conversion of the highlands and western
islands to evangelical Protestantism is that it was a reaction to the social stress
caused by rapid change in the agricultural economy. This can come in two
forms – one stressing the psychology of religion; the other pointing to political
allegiances – or in a combination of the two.[57] The clearance of the people from
their ancestral lands to make way for sheep walks caused economic hardship,
disrupted customary social relationships and undermined much of the shared
culture. This in turn made people receptive to an enthusiastic 'religion of the
oppressed' that could both explain their problems – sin on their part and even
more sin on the part of their landlords – and promise rewards for their suffering in the next life. A contemporary commentator noted: 'It is well-known that
no itinerant preacher ever gained a footing among the Highlanders, till recent
changes in their situations and circumstances made way for fanaticism'.[58] The
political component had two elements. Part of the attraction of evangelical
religion was that it was presented by 'the Men'. So-called not because they
were not women but because they were not clergy, this group of lay catechists,
Gaelic schoolteachers and church elders shared the class position of the people
they addressed. The Men were openly critical of the Moderate clergy of the
national church who (with a few brave exceptions) supported the landlords:
'Some of these reformers of religion, as they wish to be considered, intermix
their spiritual instruction with reflections on the incapacity and negligence
of the clergymen of the established church, and on the conduct of landlords,
whom they compare to the taskmasters of Egypt'.[59] For some details regional
differences are important but generally speaking this account of the religious
revival of the highlands and islands is entirely plausible. But it does not radically distinguish Lewis from Orkney or Shetland. Lewis was less affected by
clearance than many parts of the highlands and islands, and in Orkney and
Shetland religious dissent also benefited from class conflict. Matthew Armour,
the Free Church minister of Sanday from 1848 to 1903, was a popular evangelical preacher and a political progressive who was briefly jailed for disrupt-
ing a Tory political meeting, and many of the Orkney Seceder congregations
had their origins in local tensions over land use. The same could be said for
Methodist congregations in Shetland.

Cohesion: Causes and Consequences

What is most striking about Lewis, as compared with Orkney and Shetland,
is its religious cohesion. Social scientists have long argued about the effects of
diversity on religious conviction. One side argues that religious beliefs are most

persuasive when everyone sees the world in the same way and when the shared religion is reinforced by important social institutions (such as the schools) and by everyday social interaction. That is, religion benefits from being 'taken-for-granted'. The other side argues that competition between religious providers forces them all to try harder to win followers and that a range of faiths, like Heinz's famous '57 varieties', allows more people to find some religious body which best suits their interests.[60] There is some merit in the competition case. Orkney and Shetland provide many examples of dissenters either making up for the Kirk's poor provision or scaring it into remedying its neglect. But overall the contrast between Lewis and the Northern Isles strongly favours the case that religious consensus and cohesion offer a better defence against secularisation than does diversity.

Lewis had a single shared religious culture which incorporated almost everyone and which spread from the church down into private life, with its sabbatarianism and family devotions, and up into social norms. Orkney and Shetland had a wide range of churches, none of which achieved the same degree of social penetration. Why did Lewis maintain a uniform religious culture? Geology is certainly important. Lewis is a single island with few internal obstacles to travel. Orkney and Shetland consist of a large number of small islands surrounding a large 'mainland'. Easier internal movement made it easier for Lewis than for Orkney and Shetland to develop and maintain a single culture.

There are also subtle but important economic differences. Although all three areas were crofting regions in the definition of the 1886 Act, their economies differed in ways which arguably had social consequences. Lewis was unusual in having a very large number of small crofts, none of which were owned by the crofters, and which were grouped together in townships. The typical smallholding in Orkney was 21 acres; in Lewis it was under 10 (and in the northern part of the island, under 5) acres.[61] In Orkney two-thirds of smallholdings were owner-occupied; in Lewis none were. In Orkney and Shetland less than 10 per cent of grazing was common land; in Lewis more than 50 per cent of rough grazing was common pasture. The differences in land use were reflected in the settlement patterns. In most crofting counties, crofts were scattered thinly across the countryside. In Lewis they were grouped in clusters of twenty or more crofts. In brief, Orkney and Shetland had a far greater variety of smallholding type and size.[62] That people work in similar ways and enjoy a similar standard of living does not guarantee that they will think alike but it much increases the odds. That the crofters of Lewis were similarly situated explains how they could sustain a common view of this world, which in turn explains how they could be persuaded of a similar vision of the next life. Likewise, physical proximity does not guarantee that neighbours will monitor each other's behaviour and press each other to conform to the community's standards but it is a precondition for such mutual encouragement and it was more often absent in Orkney and Shetland.

Lewis's cultural cohesion may be further explained by age profile. People's attitudes are much affected by inertia. The elderly are rarely the carriers of social and cultural innovation; it is the young who are receptive to new thought and new ways of behaving. Hence it is worth considering if the three islands differ in age profile. Here we have to guess because in the official population statistics Lewis is often subsumed within the Western Isles or within largely mainland counties and Shetland is sometimes grouped with Orkney, but it is likely that the elegiac stories that Lewis people told of townships bereft of young people were correct. Over 1,000 young Lewis men died in the First World War and a further 174 died when the ship bringing them home from the war, the SS *Iolaire*, foundered at the mouth of Stornoway harbour. In response to the inability of the Hebridean economy to provide sufficient opportunities in the early 1920s, a large number of young people were persuaded by assisted passages and the offer of work to emigrate to Canada. In 1923 300 sailed on the SS *Metagama* and small groups left in the following years.[63] When added to the steady constant trickle of youth to the mainland, this amounted to the removal of a very large proportion of those people who, had they stayed in Lewis, might have been the agents of social and cultural change. In 1851 only 6.4 per cent of the population of the Western Isles was 65 and over; by 1931 this had risen to 13 per cent. In 1951 it was 14 per cent. In 1971 it was 19.2 per cent.[64] The editor of the *Stornoway Gazette*, writing of the late 1930s, said: 'Lewis had become a hollow shell. An island of the old. A surprising number of them unmarried. Dry spinsters and crusty bachelors . . . Black had become the prevailing colour'.[65]

The Northern Isles also lost population. From around 1860 the population of Orkney and Shetland declined, largely from emigration. In the period 1861 to 1901 Orkney lost more than 10 per cent of its people every decade.[66] In the same period 18,420 people emigrated from Shetland to other parts of Scotland; we do not know how many went further afield. But it seems likely that Orkney and Shetland had more immigration than Lewis. Between 1861 and 1901 there were over 5,000 migrants to Shetland. Whether Shetlanders returning after a period away or incomers, they represent a considerable source of cultural innovation. For Orkney it was the two world wars – when the deep harbour of Scapa Flow served as a base for a large part of the British fleet – which provided the external encouragement to social change.

But the most significant difference between Lewis and the Northern Isles, as both symptom and cause of cohesion, was the persistence of Gaelic, which united its people and separated them from the lowlands of Scotland. One reason the Seceders and the Methodists made no inroads in Lewis is that they could not provide Gaelic-speaking missionaries and itinerant preachers. So long as most Lewis people spoke Gaelic, outsiders found it hard to make their alternative beliefs intelligible, let alone attractive.

It is important to add one qualification to the point I made that the defection of Lewis en masse to the Free Church in 1843 and again in 1900 should be seen as persistence rather than change. Though the religious culture was unchanged, the shift in status, from being in the establishment to being dissenters, was significant. It represented and reinforced the popular nature of Lewis's Presbyterianism. In twice standing against the prevailing institutional climate, the people of Lewis took charge of their own religious culture: acts which symbolised how well evangelical religion had penetrated the everyday lives of the people and which reinforced popular responsibility for the faith. In brief, evangelical religion in Lewis acquired the rare but sociologically strong position of being both the dominant faith and a popularly embraced creed of opposition to the social and religious establishment.

That Lewis's enduring religiosity owes much to its isolation and insulation seems confirmed by the recent history of decline. Changes in the nature of communication have gradually incorporated Lewis in mainstream Scottish (and Western European) culture. Improved transport links have allowed residents to move back and forth more easily and thus more often. Electronic mass media (in particular satellite TV and the internet) have allowed the youth of Lewis to consume mainstream cultural products. There has been an attendant decline in the proportion of the population speaking Gaelic. In 1881 over 98 per cent of the people of Lochs were Gaelic speakers. In 1951 the proportion was still over 90 per cent and in 1981 it was 86.4 per cent.[67] By the end of the century it had fallen to 60.5 per cent, an average which disguises the gulf between young and old.[68] In the last decade of the twentieth century the number of Gaelic speakers in the 15–24 age group halved. The churches had to accommodate that shift. By the 1950s most church youth work was being done in English because even those young people who could speak Gaelic were not comfortable with the Gaelic used in preaching and in the singing of metrical psalms.[69] By 2012 all churches were conducting their most popularly attended service in English. As Lewis has become less socially and culturally distinctive, it has also become less religious.

Conclusion

Even Christians who wish to see the hand of God in every significant event in their biographies and in the histories of their cultures often recognise that religious change can have social causes. Evangelical preachers who supposed they were doing the Lord's work were happy to see economic changes such as the highland clearances as preparing the people for the gospel by bringing them 'under conviction of sin'. One of the purposes of this chapter has been to establish that social science can help our understanding of religious beliefs and behaviour in two ways. The social structure of a society can explain why certain types of people are attracted to certain types of religion and social interaction can explain how religious cultures are maintained.[70]

The decline of interest in religion is characteristic of all modern liberal industrial democracies. The societies of Western Europe and their settler off-shoots in North America, Australia and New Zealand differ only in the date at which the decline begins; once started it follows a remarkably similar trajectory. What is valuable about our three islands comparison is that it allows us to see how circumstances can aid resistance to the prevailing secular winds. The key to that resistance is community cohesion and insulation. Because the people of Lewis in the nineteenth century were economically and socially more similar than those of Orkney and Shetland, they found it easier to be subjectively similar: that is, to see the world in similar ways. This in turn allowed them to be 'inter-subjectively' similar: that is, to create and sustain a shared culture. The enthusiastic evangelical Calvinist religion of the Men spoke to the hardship of their daily lives and the strength of the community allowed that common religion to become deeply embedded in a widely shared way of life. A number of characteristics, present in Lewis and absent from Orkney and Shetland, insulated the outer Hebridean island from the social and cultural changes that were weakening the power of religion in the rest of Scotland. Because it was more remote, because it was Gaelic-speaking and because it exported a larger proportion of the young people who would have been the carriers of change, Lewis was able for longer to resist the liberalising trends that elsewhere produced first religious toleration and later religious indifference.

Although Orkney and Shetland were apparently similar to Lewis in economy, there was a greater variety of individual circumstances and the dispersed nature of their populations inhibited the development of strong community cohesion. Although their religious culture was superficially similar to that of Lewis, there was never the same concerted and popular commitment to Calvinist Presbyterianism. In Lewis the Men and ministers were largely of one mind. In Orkney there was competition between churches that eased only as people lost interest in the substance of the arguments. In Shetland the peculiarities of geography encouraged cooperation on the basis of the lowest common denominator. Some Shetlanders shared the common fondness of fishing communities for enthusiastic religion but the Church of Scotland always remained the dominant force and its ministers were more likely to be moderate in their faith. That the Kirk in Shetland was less challenged by the Secession and by the Disruption than Orkney (and the contrast with Lewis is greater) both showed and reinforced the greater passivity of Shetlanders. In contrast to Lewis and to a lesser extent Orkney, Shetlanders missed the opportunity to make their religion a popular, rather than an institutional, culture. There were pockets of popular evangelical religion but there was not, as there was in Lewis, a shared community faith, and religious precepts and practices did not become as deeply embedded in the popular culture or in the social norms.

Notes

1. Livingstone, *Shetland and the Shetlanders* (Edinburgh: Thomas Nelson, 1947).

2. This formulation may pose a problem for some Christians because, even though social science may see itself as professionally agnostic rather than atheistic, it implies that a social science explanation is complete and there is thus no space for God. It is not a problem for those Christians who are happy to believe that God works in society and culture in the same way he works through nature: through regularities which can be analysed without reference to God but also without denying his creation. In defence of social science it is worth noting that even many of those Christians who wish to attribute their faith to God alone often use lay versions of social science principles to explain the behaviour and nature of other people.

3. R. Finlayson, 'Parish of Lochs', *New Statistical Account of Scotland: County of Ross and Cromarty* (Glasgow: William Blackwood and Sons, 1845), p. 159. The complete texts of this and the original *Statistical Account of Scotland* are available online at http://edina.ac.uk/stat-acc-scot/.

4. Finlayson, 'Lochs', p. 166.

5. Donald Macleod has pointed out that Uig was extreme in this respect. When Alexander Macleod went to Uig around 1823 he judged the majority of parishioners to be little better than pagan and he temporarily suspended the sacrament. When after a period of intense preaching he restored it, few came forward for membership.

6. They also reassured those who should be taking communion. Over the twentieth century that emphasis became more important than the stress on exclusion.

7. M. Macauley, *Aspects of the Religious History of Lewis up to the Disruption of 1843* (Back, Lewis: the author, 1985), p. 186.

8. Finlayson, 'Lochs', p. 169.

9. Anon., *Moral Statistics of the Highlands and Islands Compiled from Returns Received by the Inverness Society for the Education of the Poor in the Highlands* (Inverness: Society for Educating the Poor in the Highlands and Islands of Scotland, 1826), pp. 49–50.

10. J. MacLeod, *Banner in the West: A Spiritual History of Lewis and Harris* (Edinburgh: Birlinn, 2008), p. 170.

11. D. B. A. Ansdell, 'The disruptive union, 1890–1900, in a Hebridean presbytery', *Records of the Scottish Church Historical Society* 26 (1996), p. 88.

12. K. Macdonald, *Peat Fire Memories: Life in Lewis in the Early Twentieth Century* (East Linton: Tuckwell Press, 2003), pp. 46–8.

13. M. Steven, *The Heart is Highland: Memories of a Childhood in a Scottish Glen* (Derby: Breedon Books, 2001), p. 16.

14. S. Parman, 'Orduighean: A Dominant Symbol in the Free Church of the Scottish Highlands', *American Anthropologist* 92 (1990), pp. 295–305.

15. A. McKillop, 'Parish of Kinloch', in A. S. Mather (ed.), *Third Statistical Account*

of Scotland: County of Ross and Cromarty (Edinburgh: Scottish Academic Press, 1987), p. 412.

16. MacLeod, *Banner*, p. 327.

17. Anon., *Moral Statistics*, p. 72.

18. D. P. Thomson, *Orkney Through the Centuries: Lights and Shadows of the Church's Life in the Northern Isles* (Barnoak, Crieff: the author, 1956), p. 19.

19. *Specimens of the Ecclesiastical Destitution of Scotland in Various Parts of the Country* (Edinburgh: Church Extension Committee of the General Assembly of the Church of Scotland, 1835).

20. C. G. Brown, *The People in the Pews: Religion and Society in Scotland since 1780* (Edinburgh: Economic and Social History Society of Scotland, 1993), p. 29.

21. F. Bardgett, *Two Millennia of Church and Community in Orkney* (Edinburgh: Pentland Press, 2000), p. 106.

22. C. M. M. Dabbs, *The Kirk Abune the Hill: a History of the old Secession Church in Birsay* (Birsay: Birsay Publications, 2004), p. 21.

23. F. Groome (ed.), *Ordnance Gazetteer of Scotland: A Survey of Scottish Topography, Statistical, Biographical and Historical* (Edinburgh: Thomas Jack, 1885).

24. Remembering Scotland at War, 'Fortress Orkney', Oral History; http://www.rememberingscotlandatwar.org.uk/Accessible/Exhibition/198/The-lasting-impact-of-WW2-on-Orkney.

25. North Ronaldsay has been omitted because it appears to have 138 per cent of adults in membership; Walls and Flotta has been omitted because there is no separable population data.

26. W. S. Hewison, 'The parish of Kirkwall and St Ola', in R. Miller (ed.), *The Third Statistical Account of Scotland: County of Orkney* (Edinburgh: Scottish Academic Press, 1985), p. 87.

27. R. Ditchburn, *North Ronaldsay Doctor: The Life Of An Island GP* (Kirkwall: Orcadian Press, 2010), pp. 35–6.

28. C. Muir, *Orkney Days* (Edinburgh: Scotsman, 1986).

29. W. D. MacNaughton, *Early Congregational Independency in Shetland* (Lerwick: Shetland Times, 2005), p. 2.

30. Anon., *Specimens of the Ecclesiastical Destitution*, p. 51.

31. D. Scott, *Annals And Statistics Of The Original Secession Church* (Edinburgh: Andrew Elliot, 1886), p. 28.

32. MacNaughton, *Early Congregational Independence*, p. 45.

33. MacNaughton, *Early Congregational Independency*, pp. 77–80.

34. MacNaughton, *Early Congregational Independency*, p. 19.

35. R. Sandison, *Christopher Sandison of Eshaness (1781–1870): Diarist In An Age Of Social Change* (Lerwick: Shetland Times, 1997), p. 86.

36. Sandison, *Christopher Sandison*, p. 91.

37. H. R. Bowes, *Revival and Survival: Methodism's Ebb and Flow in Shetland and Orkney, 1822–1862* (Aberdeen: University of Aberdeen MTh thesis, 1988), p. 216H.

38. J. A. Leslie, *Lerwick Baptist Church: a History* (Lerwick: Lerwick Baptist Church, 1993).

39. L. Johnson, *Chapel in the Valley: the Story of East Yell Methodist Chapel 1892–1992* (Brae: Tanglewood, 1993).

40. MacNaughton, *Early Congregational Independency*, p. 44.

41. H. R. Bowes, *Quantum Sufficit; Know Your Heritage 9* (2010), p. 16.

42. J. Bryden, 'Sandsting and Aithsting', *New Statistical Account of Scotland: County of Shetland* (Glasgow: William Blackwood and Sons, 1845), p. 135.

43. J. Robertson, 'Mid and South Yell', *New Statistical Account of Scotland: County of Shetland* (Glasgow: William Blackwood and Sons, 1845), p. 90.

44. J. Ingram and J. Ingram, 'Unst', *New Statistical Account of Scotland: County of Shetland* (Glasgow: William Blackwood and Sons, 1845), p. 49.

45. T. Barclay, 'Bressay', *New Statistical Account of Scotland: County of Shetland* (Glasgow: William Blackwood and Sons, 1845), p. 17.

46. Bryden, 'Sandsting and Aithsting', p. 136.

47. MacNaughton, *Early Congregational Independency*, p. 51.

48. Bowes, *Revival and Survival*, p. 177.

49. G. Beyell, 'Shetland', in D. Bebbington (ed.), *The Baptists in Scotland: a History* (Glasgow: Baptist Union of Scotland, 1988), p. 333.

50. H. Escott, *A History of Scottish Congregationalism* (Glasgow: Congregational Union of Scotland, 1960), p. 266.

51. T. C. Bogle, 'Out Skerries', *The Third Statistical Account of Scotland: County of Shetland* (Edinburgh: Scottish Academic Press, 1984), p. 123.

52. A. Cohen, *Whalsay: Symbol, Segment and Boundary in a Shetland Island Community* (Manchester: Manchester University Press, 1987), pp. 33–4.

53. The geographical and meteorological obstacles have been discussed. The other great obstacle was poverty. One might have imagined that committed Christians would have attended church services in any clothes that kept them minimally decent but there is evidence in the letters and diaries of a number of clergy that some people were so poor that they felt inhibited by their lack of decent clothes and that such people did indeed attend when they were provided with second-hand clothes.

54. K. M. Gordon, J. W. Scott and M. A. Scott, 'Orkney', in D. Bebbington (ed.), *The Baptists in Scotland: a History* (Glasgow: Baptist Union of Scotland, 1988), pp. 317–25.

55. D. Ratter, 'Northmavine', *The Third Statistical Account of Scotland: County of Shetland* (Edinburgh: Scottish Academic Press, 1984), p. 135.

56. J. D. Mackay, 'Sanday', *The Third Statistical Account of Scotland: County of Orkney* (Edinburgh: Scottish Academic Press, 1985), pp. 117–18.

57. S. Bruce, 'Social change and collective behaviour: the revival in eighteenth-century Ross-shire', *British Journal of Sociology* 34 (1983), pp. 554–72; J. Hunter, 'The emergence of the crofting community: the religious contribution 1798–1843', *Scottish Studies* 18 (1974), pp. 95–116.

58. Sir David Stewart of Garth, *Sketches of the Character, Manners and Present State of the Highlanders of Scotland etc* (Edinburgh: Archibald Constable, 1822), p. 130.

59. Stewart of Garth, *Sketches*, p. 130.

60. The merits of the 'supply-side' approach to religious change are discussed at length in S. Bruce, *Choice and Religion* (Oxford: Oxford University Press, 1999).

61. Smallholding here means under 50 acres.

62. H. A. Moisley, 'The highlands and islands: a crofting region?', *Transactions and Papers (Institute of British Geographers)* 31 (1962), pp. 83–95.

63. J. Wilkie, *Metagama: a Journey from Lewis to the New World* (Edinburgh: Mainstream, 1987). For a detailed township-by-township account of mass migrations to North America, see B. Lawson, *Lewis – the West Coast – in History and Legend* (Edinburgh: Birlinn, 2008).

64. Livingstone, *Shetland*, p. 191.

65. J. S. Grant, *Stornoway and the Lews* (Edinburgh: James Thin, 1985), p. 183. Arguably James Grant was partisan. Although he followed his father as editor of the *Stornoway Gazette*, he reputedly had little knowledge of inland Lewis and even less sympathy for the island's religious culture but others, including the authors of the parish entries for the *Third Statistical Account of Scotland*, have made a similar point in more prosaic language.

66. J. Shearer, W. Groundwater and J. D. Mackay, *The New Orkney Book* (London: Nelson, 1966), p. 51; R. H. Osborne, 'The movements of people in Scotland 1901–1951', *Scottish Studies* 2 (1958), pp. 1–10.

67. K. C. Duwe, 'Eilean Leòdhais: Na Lochan', *Gàdhlig Local Studies* 7 (2006), p. 9.

68. Registrar General for Scotland, *Census 2001 Report: Gaelic Report* (Edinburgh: General Register Office for Scotland, 2006), p. 6.

69. C. MacIver, 'Parish of Barvas', in A. S. Mather (ed.), *The Third Statistical Account of Scotland: County of Ross and Cromarty* (Edinburgh: Scottish Academic Press, 1987), pp. 390–2.

70. Nothing in this proposition implies that the causal links between social structure and religious culture run only one way. Much of my research has been concerned with the social influence of religion. See, for example, S. Bruce, *Politics and Religion* (Cambridge: Polity, 2003).

3

SCOTS CATHOLIC GROWTH

In 1982 John Paul II became the first Pope to visit Scotland. On an unusually pleasant first day of June some 300,000 people, supposedly the biggest crowd ever assembled in Scotland, gathered at Glasgow's Bellahouston Park to attend Mass. During the event, John Paul was offered several symbolic gifts including a pipe banner with the Pope's coat of arms, a piece of Caithness glass and a firkin of whisky. He was also given a Scotland football shirt and a football: presumably in recognition of the former goalkeeping Pope's interest, rather than Scotland's achievements, in the sport. As we will see in Chapter 5, not all Scots welcomed the papal visit but for the Church that organised it, it was a triumphal seal on a century of growth and integration.

Migration often produces a subtle but important shift in the migrant's relationship to his or her faith. In societies with a single shared religion, the faith is carried as much by social institutions and habitual patterns of behaviour as by any individual, with conscious thought, choosing every time to make this or that act of affirmation. Like the rain, it is just there. The migrant can no longer be accidentally or passively religious but must make a positive effort and, because it is rarely a comfortable experience, migration offers good reasons to make that effort. Apart from the hardship which drives them to leave their native lands in search of a better future, migrants often feel adrift and at a loss in an alien environment. Hence they may be disposed to stay close to what is familiar. Churches (or mosques, gurdwaras and temples) acquire new value as places where one can meet fellow countrymen and women, temporarily slip into old identities, speak the mother language and inhabit again a character that is not reduced to 'alien'. Such religious centres also often provide practical assistance in adapting to the new world.

There is a second clutch of reasons why immigrants might be unusually religious: their religious identity might be one of the few shared characteristics that separates them from the natives of the new world that can be maintained without jeopardising the future. Continuing to speak Irish (or Urdu or Bengali) at the expense of learning English would hinder trade or work prospects; staying loyal to one's religious heritage church is usually quite compatible with accommodating to the new environment. And to the extent that the natives are of a different faith, being religiously observant can serve as a badge of pride and honour: a way of reversing the objective status hierarchy. When a people who share a common religion that distinguishes them from their neighbours feel their identity under threat, they may become increasingly attached to that faith as the cement that binds them together. The popularity of the Catholic Church in Poland during the period of communist domination from 1945 to 1991 is a well-known example. Catholicism distinguished the Poles from their Lutheran German neighbours to the west and from their Orthodox (and later communist) Russian neighbours to the east. The Catholic Church was one of the few national institutions that could not be suborned by the intrusion of communist Russian sympathisers. Its beliefs provided Poles with an ideological justification for feeling superior to their enemies and its supernatural power gave Poles hope that they would eventually triumph. As demonstrated by the Gdansk shipyard workers starting each day of their occupation with Mass and the Solidarity trade union's use of images of the Black Madonna of Częstochowa, Catholic rituals provided Poles with relatively safe opportunities for showing their hostility to the communist state. Poles did not pretend to be religious in order to oppose Soviet Communism. They already were Catholics. The point is that under the particular social circumstances of the Soviet era, Poles had an additional reason – communal solidarity – to overlook such doubts as they may have entertained about the value of their shared religion.

In the position of the Catholic Church in Scotland we can see elements of both cultural defence and cultural transition. The long history of conflict between the Protestant English and Scots settlers and Catholic natives in Ireland had established a set of political polarities: with few exceptions Protestant meant British and Unionist and Catholic meant Irish and Nationalist. We can easily recognise the role the Church played in giving meaning to the lives of a poor and dispossessed immigrant population, harassed by some in an unwelcoming environment. The Irish who settled in Scotland had little capital, were relatively ill-educated and lacked the industrial manufacturing skills which allowed entry to the better-paid work. They also aroused hostility because their presence as a reserve army of cheap labour weakened the bargaining power of working-class Scots and added to the competition for resources such as housing. Not surprisingly, because this was the attraction, the arrival of the Irish in Scotland coincided with the great wave of urban expansion and industrialisation. In the long run industrial growth brought increased prosperity but the early stages were often unpleasant. Rural life may not have been the bucolic paradise imagined by romantic critics of industrial life but it was familiar and secure. The life of the industrial worker was often harsh and cruel. Those native Scots who found their conditions uncongenial could observe that the Irish and the problems of industrialisation arrived at the same time and some blamed the former for the latter. A small part of this association was accurate: some mine owners used Irish labourers as 'scabs' to break the emerging power of organised labour.[1] But most of it was scapegoating. Distressed people like to find a simple cause of their problems. For some Scots, that was the Irish.

The Catholic Irish also faced considerable hostility and suspicion because of their religion and not just from the majority Protestant Scots. Centuries of being surrounded by a strongly reformed Protestant culture had shaped the faith of the Scots Catholics of Aberdeenshire and the highlands and islands so that the Catholicism of the Irish seemed garishly alien. Native Scots Catholics were as likely as their Presbyterian neighbours to share the invidious stereotypes of the Irish: that they were slothful, intemperate, drunken, illiterate, lacking in self-discipline and prone to having families larger than their efforts could support.[2] Initially the Scottish church did not welcome Irish priests because it feared being colonised by its much larger Irish sister.[3] Although quickly overwhelmed by the Irish influx, the Scottish church officials were reluctant to recruit Irish clergy and few attained senior posts before the late nineteenth century.[4] But Irish priests came to dominate in the industrial areas out of necessity, leaving only the northern dioceses traditionally Scottish in character. The reception the native Catholic laity gave the immigrants was at best lukewarm: 'native Roman Catholics did little to welcome their pauperized co-religionists – the division of class, culture and nationality proved greater than the bonds of shared religion'.[5]

Initially the Catholic Church's main contribution was to reinforce the walls surrounding the Irish in Scotland. Driven by the double imperative of providing for their own people and ensuring that the Irish remained their own people, the Church provided community leadership that has been neatly described as encouraging the Irish in 'communal self-help under close religious supervision'.[6]

SCOTLAND AND ULSTER

Because the violence in Northern Ireland has loomed so large in British life, there is a tendency to see Protestant–Catholic conflict in Scotland through the Ulster lens and hence to exaggerate its severity. The composer James MacMillan once referred to Scotland as being like Northern Ireland but without the bombs and bullets, as though this was a trivial difference.[7] A better comparison is with Australia or the United States, where initial hostility to the immigrants proved no lasting obstacle to their upward social mobility and their eventual integration.

One important difference between Scotland and Northern Ireland is that in Ulster all the lines of social division – class conflict, religious conflict, competing political aspirations – matched up and reinforced each other. In Scotland they did not. More will be said about this but here I note one happy geographical accident. By the time the Irish settled lowland Scotland in large numbers, a large proportion of lowland Scots were only nominally Protestant. Those Scots who had the strongest religious objections to Popery were in the highlands and islands: their theoretical anti-Popery was hardly troubled by interaction with actual Papists. There were occasional disputes. For a short period in the 1870s the elected school board for South Uist had a Protestant majority despite the population being overwhelmingly Catholic and the Board refused to appoint Catholic teachers. A subsequent election saw the imbalance rectified. Father Allan MacDonald was elected chairman of the Board and the first Catholic head was appointed to the local primary school. Overall, 'Relations were often cordial enough between Highland Catholic priests and Protestant ministers, despite the conviction of one that the other was going to hell and taking his congregation with him'.[8]

Another great difference is that those Scottish elites that had the power to deepen division did not while their counterparts in Ulster most obviously did. The dismal view of sectarianism in Scotland makes much of florid expressions of anti-Catholic sentiment but overlooks the more important fact that such expressions were the reactions of losers, not winners. Those who lamented the growth of Catholicism were powerless to prevent it. When in the 1840s Glasgow town council decided that sufficient time had passed since Guy Fawkes attempted to blow up the Houses of Parliament that it was no longer appropriate to commemorate his failure by ringing the town's bells, the small-circulation, anti-Catholic *Scottish Guardian* complained bitterly but the policy change was not reversed.[9] For fifty years the British government had been sporadically giving financial assistance to the Catholic college at Maynooth in Ireland. In 1845 it decided to make the grant regular and thus prevent it occasioning opposition every time it was debated. Many complained about this subsidy for Popery but it went ahead anyway. In 1878, when the Catholic Church in Scotland was permitted by the Pope to create the full hierarchical structure of a mature church, *The Glasgow Herald*, the house journal of the Glasgow business class, judged that it would give the Pope pleasure and do Scotland no harm.[10] The preeminent historian of the Irish in Scotland, James Handley, notes: 'By the last quarter or so of the nineteenth century newspapers had for the most part dropped their hostile attitude towards the religion of the majority of the immigrants' and that when the Catholic hierarchy was restored, what excited the bigots 'evoked only moderate response' from the mainstream of Scottish opinion.[11] More detail will be added in Chapter 5 but it is enough here to note:

Though much has been written of the development of popular anti-Catholicism in the 1920s and 1930s, with the growth of Protestant Action, the Scottish Unionist Party's varied efforts to play the Orange card, and the Church of Scotland's declaration to reverse Irish immigration to Scotland, these political activities had little impact on actual public policy in Scotland.[12]

Getting On

In 1901 the Irish Catholics formed a distinct and distinctly lower-class community. By the time of the 2001 census the socio-economic status of Catholics was little different to that of non-Catholics and such differences as can be discerned were found largely in the oldest age groups.

There were two main routes to prosperity and power. The first was providing goods and services to a relatively enclosed community which preferred to buy from its own at a slightly higher price than buy from outsiders. By his own account John Wheatley, the Independent Labour MP for Shettleston from 1922 to his death in 1930, was a man who prospered by providing some of the more respectable services; by rumour he also benefited from some less reputable ways of making money. Born to a poor immigrant family, Wheatley began work down the mines aged twelve. Educated at night schools, he joined his brother's grocery business and then sold advertising space for small-circulation, local Catholic newspapers. Still in his twenties he started the printing business which made him rich. One of the men he defeated in his many elections – W. Reid Miller – did not believe that Wheatley had prospered legitimately and accused him of illegal betting and loan-sharking and, his professed teetotalism notwithstanding, investing in pubs and bars. Wheatley resigned his place in the Labour opposition front bench to pursue a libel case against Reid Miller but his rebuttal of the slurs was not entirely convincing and many on the left (including the saintly if sometimes sanctimonious Beatrice Webb) hinted at racketeering.[13]

More honourable careers, heavily promoted by the Church, were to be had providing the community with professional services. Sean Damer recalls:

> My father was in the very first generation of working-class Edinburgh Catholics for whom it was feasible, if still not common, to go to the University of Edinburgh . . . the purpose of a university education in the 1930s was to enter a very restricted number of professions – school-teaching, medicine and criminal law – and go back and serve your own people, meaning the next generation of working-class Catholics.[14]

Wheatley can also stand as an exemplar of a channel of social mobility that not only benefited the individuals who pursued it but also aided the peaceful integration of the Catholic community as a whole: Labour politics. Irish

Catholics could have followed the Dutch or Belgian examples and formed Catholic trade unions and parties but instead they became active in the existing secular organisations and thus prevented religion becoming a centre focus of party politics. Secondly, Labour's success in local government elections ensured that as the local state expanded its role as an employer, it did not (as it did in Northern Ireland) become a 'pork barrel' for rewarding and thus encouraging sectarian identities.

As there were far more Irish Catholics than Ulster Protestants in Scotland, it is no surprise that at the time of the Home Rule crisis support for Sinn Fein was considerably greater than support for the Ulster Volunteer Force: 'By 1921 almost every Scottish town with a sizeable Irish presence had its own IRA company'.[15] The aftermath of the 1916 rising brought an increase in Irish political activity, with a large number of Sinn Fein branches being founded on the west coast of Scotland and a lot of money being raised for the nationalist cause. But the partition of Ireland and the consolidation of the Free State and Northern Ireland governments allowed the Irish question to slide from the front pages.

It was the genius of John Wheatley to combine the class and Irish impulses within Catholic politics and to direct them toward the emerging labour movement. A committed Catholic, despite the Church's initial hostility to his politics, Wheatley formed the Catholic Socialist Society in 1906, which aimed to show that socialism and Catholicism could be honestly combined. He was elected to Lanarkshire County Council in 1909 and the Glasgow town council in 1912. His position was initially uncomfortable; he was denounced by many Glasgow priests and once memorably found himself burnt in effigy outside his front door by an angry Catholic mob.[16] He became a leading figure in the Independent Labour Party, was elected to parliament in the famous 'Red Clydeside' election triumph of 1922, and served in Ramsay MacDonald's 1924 government.

Patrick Dollan was another son of a poor immigrant family who began life in the pits and educated himself sufficiently to become a journalist.[17] He became a key organiser for the Catholic Union, the principal lay Catholic organisation in Glasgow, which among many other tasks organised the Catholic vote for the elected school boards. He also used his skills as a community organiser to produce the Red Clydeside victory. He stood once for parliament but on failing devoted himself to local government. He had been elected to the Glasgow town council in 1913 and he remained there for thirty-three years, sixteen of them as leader of the Labour group and three as Lord Provost. Knighted in 1941, he retired in 1946 but continued until his death in 1963 to act as a figurehead for Glasgow's civic interests.

Given the popularity of the dismal sectarian story of Glasgow, it is worth stressing just how successful were Wheatley, Dollan and their less well-known colleagues. Of seventy-six Labour councillors elected between 1922 and 1931, a fifth were Catholic: well in proportion to Catholic support for Labour.[18] By the mid-1980s over half of elected Labour members in Glasgow District Council were Catholic.[19] With the exception of Geoff Shaw, a popular Church of Scotland cleric who gave up his ministry for social work and community politics and who was the first leader of Strathclyde Regional Council, every leader of the Labour party in the regional council's twenty-year history – it was created in 1975 and disbanded in 1995 – was Catholic. A study of Labour councillors in Glasgow in the late 1980s showed that, out of fifty-four surveyed, half described their current religion as Catholic, with several more having been brought up as Catholics.[20]

The political integration of Scotland's Catholics is clearly demonstrated in two major surveys from 1999. We know the religious identifications of some 800 council candidates from across Scotland and over 1,000 candidates for the first elections to the Scottish Parliament. Catholics are slightly under-represented among Labour councillors for Scotland as a whole but the beneficiaries are not Protestants; it is those of no religion, which suggests the explanation is unlikely to be discrimination. More likely the small difference is a consequence of Catholic voters being concentrated on the urban west coast. As councillors are chosen locally and the survey is national, the data reflect party selections for the whole of the country but Catholics can only effectively compete for selection in the places where they live. Hence geographical concentration leads to them being slightly under-represented. The picture for candidates selected to contest the first elections to the Scottish Parliament is much the same as for local council candidates.[21] There is a slight under-representation of Catholics in the Labour lists but Protestants are about par; it is non-Christians and those with no religion who are over-represented.

Finally we can consider Westminster MPs. We have no comprehensive survey data but my own estimate is that in the early 1990s sixteen out of twenty-two Labour MPs in the industrial heartlands of west and central Scotland were Catholic. That is, 73 per cent of these MPs were Catholic. Set against the 24 per cent of Labour voters who were Catholic this is a considerable over-representation.

Catholic Schooling

It is worth dwelling on the history of Catholic schooling in Scotland because it shows the political influence of the Church and the deep commitment of its adherents. It is also important because it stands as a firm riposte to those who exaggerate the importance of anti-Catholicism.

Most Scots schools were originally provided by the churches. John Knox's seventeenth-century blueprint for a Presbyterian kingdom included compulsory national education. It took some time to achieve but by the 1750s most Church of Scotland parishes had a school of some sort attached to the church, which was fine so long as the population all belonged to the national church and were distributed in the same way as its churches. The growth of the Secession Church was one blow to the Kirk's ability to provide education; the 1843 Free Church split was another. Like these Presbyterian dissenters, Irish Catholic immigrants provided their own schools. Although some who opposed Popery also objected to Popish schooling, many Protestants were sympathetic to the struggle of Catholic communities to educate their children. The Catholic Schools Society was founded in 1817 with the support of Protestant manufacturers and Thomas Chalmers, the leading Presbyterian of his day, preached to raise money for Catholic schools.[22]

Through the nineteenth century the government increasingly became involved in shaping and funding what was becoming a national system of education. The 1872 Education Act required a popularly elected school board to be established in every parish and burgh with the power to manage those schools transferred to it by the churches. It would also be able to create new schools, to levy rates to pay for the erection and maintenance of those schools and to enforce attendance of all children aged between five and thirteen. Religious education was not compulsory but was left to the new boards to arrange as 'wont and usage' required. To protect religious minorities, it was clearly specified that parents could withdraw their children from any religious education of which they disapproved and to make that easy, such religious education as took place should occur at the start or the end of the day. With hindsight we can see this as the start of a secular system but the Presbyterian churches handed over their schools willingly because they took it for granted that the popularity of Presbyterianism would be reflected in the composition of local school boards, which in turn would preserve the ethos of the schools. They never anticipated that local 'wont and usage' would become thoroughly secular.

Despite the best efforts of civil servants to persuade them otherwise, Catholic Church leaders declined to join the 1872 structure because they objected to the separation of religious instruction from secular teaching: 'board schools were seen as either an instrument for advancing the interests of the Church of Scotland or, at worst, as a force promoting apathy and leading ultimately to the possibility of secularism dominating National Education'.[23]

A consequence of rejecting the 1872 settlement was that Catholic schools improved less quickly than state schools. In 1886 almost three-quarters of the female staff employed by the boards had been educated in a training college but the comparable figure for Catholic schools was less than half.[24] By the end of the First World War the gap between Catholic and non-denominational schooling was widening; less than 3 per cent of the Catholic school-aged population received secondary education and there was a shortage of well-qualified teachers.[25] The financial burden was so heavy that the Catholic school system could no longer survive without participating in the public sphere.

Catholic schools were transferred to the state system under the 1918 Education (Scotland) Act, which gave the Church the right to appoint teachers and to control curriculum content. The burden for financing the schools was removed: 'in no other predominantly Protestant country did Catholics enjoy such latitude in the educational sphere'.[26] In fact, the Catholic Church secured a much better deal than did the Free Church of Scotland, which had also built its schools through voluntary contributions but received no safeguards when it handed over control in 1872. Catholic schools have enjoyed both financial security and autonomy ever since.

The new structure soon produced advances. In Lanarkshire, for example, the staff/student ratio in 1919 had been 1:41 for non-denominational schools and 1:61 for their Catholic counterparts. In just over a decade the difference was reduced to 1:34 and 1:40.[27] But even with improved funding, the Catholic system still had two weaknesses which constrained the social mobility of its pupils. Because they had little acquaintance with industrial engineering in Ireland, because they valued highly the scholarship and studiousness of the priest and because they were often taught by the clergy and by members of teaching orders, the Irish Catholic model of the benefits of education stressed bookishness and academic learning. There was no Catholic equivalent of Allan Glen's, established in 1853 by Glasgow businessmen to promote scientific, technical and craft education. Those Catholic teachers who were not members of religious orders were recruited from secondary schools where the curriculum had been essentially scholastic. Neither St Mungo's Academy nor St Aloysius College had departments of technical or commercial education and there was thus no great flow of people qualified to teach in these areas. Furthermore, there was not a large pool of experienced skilled Catholic engineers from which a teaching force may have been drawn.[28] Thus the legacy of Catholic absence from technical occupations from the 1860s kept future generations of Catholics at an educational disadvantage.

The second problem was universal: schools generally reproduce the class position of their pupils' parents. Because Catholics were generally poorer than non-Catholics, they were concentrated in the junior secondary schools that did not offer instruction up to the level required for university entrance. In 1964 there were only three Catholic schools in Lanarkshire that taught to the level required for university access: one in each of Motherwell, Bothwell and Coatbridge. The introduction of comprehensive reform radically changed that: 'within 15 years that number had risen to 13'.[29] The effects of those changes can be seen very clearly in the number of Catholics at Glasgow University. In 1930 Catholic students were 9 per cent of the student body.[30] By 1956 they were 12 per cent and in 1972 there were some 2,000 Catholics at the University, which at 22 per cent was a slight over-representation.

The advance of Catholic education can be clearly seen in the 2001 census, which shows no significant differences between Catholics and Church of

Scotland identifiers in educational qualifications. At the bottom end, 38 per cent of one and 39 per cent of the other had no qualifications; at the top end 16 per cent of both groups had degrees or higher qualifications.[31]

As one would expect from the evenness of educational qualifications and from the political power of Scots Catholics, the socio-economic disadvantages we can identify in the older age groups are absent from the young, and overall the 2001 census shows no evidence that Scots Catholics are worse off than Church of Scotland identifiers. It is worth stressing that I am not describing the results of a sample survey, which might well be unrepresentative. The following figures are for the entire working-age Scottish population: a 'sample' of 1.5 million. Catholic and Church of Scotland identifiers had the same proportion in the higher managerial class (4 per cent) and in routine occupations (9 per cent) and the differences in the middling categories are only 1 or 2 per cent. Of course we cannot directly infer discrimination from disadvantage: it may be that a community has some accidental or even self-chosen characteristic that explains its disadvantage. Scots Muslims, for example, have the highest rate of people who have never been employed but this is explained by the choice of Muslim women not to seek work outside the home. However, the logic does work the other way round. Unless we suppose that Catholics are naturally more talented than the rest of the population, that they have much the same socio-economic profile as Church of Scotland identifiers shows that there is no effective labour market discrimination.

In summary, over the course of the twentieth century the Catholic community in Scotland increased in size, in wealth, in status and in political power to match the people of the host society.

Contemporary Hostility

Yet for all the social changes discussed above, sectarianism remains the distorting lens through which the Scots Catholic experience is often viewed. Despite the census data, discrimination is still widely assumed, as is sectarian violence. A major Glasgow survey concluded 'two-thirds of respondents perceived sectarian violence to be very or quite common in Glasgow'. But it went on: 'However, less than one percent of all respondents said that in the last five years, their religion had been the cause of a physical attack against them'.[32] To be more precise, of 1,000 respondents, 147 claimed to have been physically attacked in the previous five years. Of the reasons given by victims that were not personal or domestic, the most common was 'area where you live', which was cited by eighteen people. Only seven people, less than 1 per cent, cited 'religion'. Glaswegians were more likely to have been attacked because of their country of origin, gender or sexuality.

There are many reasons why sectarian violence is exaggerated. One is that the press routinely bundles stories that have little sectarian connotation under that heading.[33] A more subtle cause is the relish that Scots white-collar workers have for out-dated labourist images of Scotland as a land of tough no-nonsense people. A small but revealing point is that middle-class Scots are much more likely than their English counterparts to classify themselves as 'working class'.[34] People who work in what their grandparents wore for Sunday best, two generations away from the docks, the mines, the shipyards and the tenements, avidly consume a popular culture that celebrates that lost world. Since it first appeared in 1983, the series *Taggart*, featuring a hard-bitten Glasgow cop and a large cast of corpses, has been STV's most successful programme. Greenock-born Peter McDougall was one of Scotland's most successful playwrights in the 1980s and such works as *Just a Boy's Game* (starring the gritty-voiced rock singer Frankie Miller) have at their heart working-class violence and crime. Jimmy Boyle, convicted killer-turned-sculptor and author, was a prominent figure in Scotland's arts world in the 1980s and 1990s. Two of Scotland's most successful contemporary painters – Ken Currie and Peter Howson – specialise in depicting working-class heroes and scenes of violence. Until his drying out and return to the Catholic faith of his childhood, Howson was a hard-drinking, often violent, body-building drug-abuser.[35] We might add the novels of William McIlvanney, Ian Rankin, Christopher Brookmyre or James Kelman. Ron Mackay's *Mean City* was a deliberate homage to Alexander McArthur and Kingsley Long's *No Mean City*, a crime thriller based on the life of John Ross, the man who succeeded Billy Fullerton as leader of the Bridgeton Billy Boys. In bringing the McArthur and Long fiction up to date, Mackay seems to have modelled the characters and events closely on the life of the real-life gangster Arthur Thompson and his family. Even Scots comedy fuelled the stereotypes. Scotland's most popular comedian, Billy Connolly, in an act which used to feature episodes from his life as a working-class Glaswegian, shipyards and all, was one of the first stand-ups to use what was euphemistically called 'industrial language'. The much-loved character Rab C. Nesbitt was an alcoholic down-and-out from Govan's 'Wine Alley' who happily described himself as 'scum'. If this analysis seems exaggerated, consider the following. In 2002 the Glasgow *Herald* advertised *Glasgow's Hard Men* with the enticing text: 'For more than 100 years Glasgow was known worldwide for its gangsters, villains and violence. From the slums and the deprived areas of the city came the hard men, the gangs and the godfathers ... packed full of images from the archives of Scotland's leading newspapers ... to receive your copy by Christmas please ensure that your order ...'.

Ironically, a third reason for the exaggeration of sectarian violence is the wish to diminish it. To justify measures to tackle the problem, well-meaning people frighten themselves with its extent. Though the details may seem unnecessary, it is worth spelling out how a perfectly legitimate wish to control a problem can give a false impression of its prevalence.

In October 1995 Mark Scott, a young Celtic fan, was attacked and fatally wounded as he walked from Celtic's ground through Bridgeton. His murderer was Jason Campbell. Campbell's father and uncle had twenty years earlier been leading members in the small and ineffective Bridgeton cell of the Ulster Volunteer Force: they had been responsible for the fortunately injury-free bombing of two Glasgow pubs.[36] Although few commentators appreciated the significance of this family connection, it shows just how little impact Northern Ireland's violence had on Scotland. The same one family was responsible for Scotland's only Troubles-related bombing and for its best-known recent sectarian murder. In 2000 Cara Henderson, a friend of Scott, and two others formed Nil By Mouth to campaign against sectarianism. One of Henderson's newspaper articles was headed 'Stop Glasgow's Killing Fields'. In it she asserted that there was violence after every Old Firm game and then – after describing the game she attended at which there was no violence – ruefully added 'nobody was murdered within hours of the final whistle, a state of affairs provoking surprise among the Glasgow constabulary, which has grown wearily accustomed to weeding out killers from both communities – but especially the Protestant sector'.[37] 'Weeding out killers' is strong stuff. And if most of the four or five Old Firm matches every year were followed by a sectarian murder that would add up to an impressive total.

An article in a scholarly journal claimed that eleven Rangers and Celtic fans had been murdered between 1995 and 2009: a rate of 0.8 per annum.[38] The *Sunday Herald* unquestioningly reported Peter Maclean, a spokesman for Nil By Mouth, saying: 'Eight murders with a sectarian element in the last few years – mostly in and around the Glasgow area – is an issue that shouldn't be minimised'.[39] A few months earlier he had told a committee of the Scottish Parliament: 'in 1999–2000 no racially motivated murders were recorded. However, Nil By Mouth has researched sectarian-related offences and has found eight murders during that time that had a clear sectarian element'. Six months earlier he had given the same figure to the *Daily Record*: 'Our statistics for 1999–2000 show no racist murders but at least eight sectarian murders in Scotland'.[40]

The source for these dramatic but different claims was the same: a report written by an academic and a journalist that identified eleven Old Firm-related murders between 1984 and 2001, a span of seventeen or eighteen years.[41] In that period there were 2,099 homicides at an average of 116 a year.[42] Hence, if the researchers had not missed any cases, the proportion of Scottish homicides that were sectarian was 0.5 per cent. Nil By Mouth, reading the same research, reduced the number of murders to eight but shortened the timescale to just two years so that 3.4 per cent of murders were now sectarian.

Arguably the original report's figure, which identified 0.5 per cent of Scottish homicides as sectarian, is an exaggeration. When I and my colleagues worked through each case we concluded that the Old Firm football element was often tangential to the crime at best.[43] For example, the original report summarises a murder which occurred in May 1999 thus: 'John Ormiston . . . Rangers fan died after being beaten up in West Lothian after an Old Firm game'. The details given in court suggest something rather different. Ormiston had been involved in a serious road accident which left him with a damaged spleen. He drank heavily and had a reputation for pestering women at his regular haunt, the Fa'side Inn in Wallyford, East Lothian. Justin Smith, 23, was in the pub on 2 May 1999 when his girlfriend went to the bar to order drinks. Ormiston grabbed hold of her. She stuck her elbow into him and shouted to her boyfriend, 'Get rid of this idiot'. Smith and Ormiston went outside, where Smith punched Ormiston on the body, knocked him to the ground, then punched and kicked him again. The victim apparently offered no resistance. Afterwards, the two men shook hands and Ormiston went back to the bar for another drink before making his way home. The next morning he told his uncle he was not going to work. The uncle left under the impression that Ormiston had a hangover. Later that day he returned to find his nephew dead. Although the fight occurred the same day as an Old Firm game, nothing in the evidence suggested that football or religion had anything to do with the incident.

From our reading of the press reports and court details we concluded that, of the eleven homicides at issue, only six were sectarian. In most of the others such football links as can be found were simply background noise, there because most fatal attacks involve young working-class men, a high proportion of whom are football fans. To put the data in its proper context, less than one-third of 1 per cent of Scotland's homicides in the period 1984 to 2001 were sectarian. And it is vital to note that 'sectarian' here means related to Celtic–Rangers football rivalry. We found no cases of being people murdered in that time period for their religious beliefs and identity, and I know of none since.

That the rate of sectarian murder was inadvertently multiplied almost tenfold is bad enough but what is worse is that, with the honourable exception of the chair of the Justice 2 committee of the Scottish Parliament, no one questioned the accuracy of the data, and hence no one noticed the casual multiplication. None of the many journalists who repeated the implausible figures felt any need to repeat and thus check the research on which they were based. Some Protestants see this credulity as proof of an anti-Protestant animus in public life. More likely the mistakes occur simply because sectarianism is so obviously a bad thing that few people wish to appear mean-spirited by challenging the evidence for its occurrence.

A similarly uncritical attitude is found in reaction to the other source of recent reports of sectarianism: data from the Crown Office and Procurator-Fiscal's Service (COPFS) on 'religious aggravation'. Since June 2003 it has been possible for a criminal offence to be aggravated by religious prejudice. A mugger who shouts obscenities at his victim can now be hit with a second charge if those obscenities include expressions of religious hatred. When the first data on the new law's operation was issued, the press mostly led their reports with a comparison of victims, as when the *Daily Telegraph* opened with: 'Catholics are twice as likely as Protestants to be the targets of sectarian abuse'.[44] Or they reported the Catholic Church's condemnation of the data: 'Church leaders yesterday condemned the scourge of sectarianism'.[45]

A detailed reading of the COPFS report showed firstly that almost all of the original offences (92 per cent) were breaches of the peace and the aggravation was verbal. Almost half the accused were drunk. And one-third of those abused were police officers. The typical case was not a bigot searching for members of the public to assault: it was a drunk shouting at the police and others trying to discipline his uncivil behaviour.

Most important and entirely missed in the reports: the religion of the victims was not actually known. The police recorded the content of the verbal abuse, which was often directed at no one in particular. We cannot infer the identity of victims from the reports. If this point is not obvious, consider the case of former Hibernian football star Derek Riordan, who in November 2012 was fined £800 for shouting homophobic abuse at bouncers who ejected him from an Edinburgh nightclub.[46] Riordan did not know that the bouncers who annoyed him were 'fucking poofs' and it is pretty certain that they were not. The insult tells us that Riordan does not like homosexuals; it does not tell us that his victims *were* homosexuals. As the perpetrators of sectarian abuse in almost every case could not know the religion of the people they were insulting, we must assume that the insults were produced ritualistically and hence tell us about the identity of the abuser, not the abused. The original COPFS report was wrong to say that two-thirds of the victims were Catholics. It should have said that two-thirds of the perpetrators expressed anti-Catholic sentiments and hence were probably Protestant and one-third expressed anti-Protestant sentiments and were probably Catholic. If the drunken hooligans of Glasgow and the western lowlands divide two-thirds Protestant and one-third Catholic that is about par for the area. Incivility is pretty evenly distributed, which should be no surprise: only the most partisan observer would expect a systematic difference in manners and self-control of working-class Catholics and Protestants.[47]

The problem with a lot of contemporary writing and thinking about relations between Catholics and Protestants is that it is distorted by the prominence of the Old Firm. It is probably no accident that two of the scholars who argue that sectarianism remains an important force in Scottish life are primarily experts on football, while the political scientists who start at the other end by trying to identify what shapes political attitudes and choices consistently find no support for the sectarian trope.[48] Two football academics have written: 'For the Catholic/Irish community, Celtic are the greatest single ethno-cultural focus because they provide the social setting and process through which the community's sense of its own identity and difference from the indigenous community is sustained, in and through a set of symbolic processes and representations'.[49] A perspective that sees Celtic as more important than the Catholic Church is strange indeed. As a corrective it is worth reminding ourselves that only some Scots are football fans, that only some fans support one or other side of the Old Firm, that only some Old Firm fans are bigots, and that only a very few of those continue their bigotry outside the ritual confines of the match and the stadium.

We may also note that the obsession with the Old Firm coincides with an almost complete disregard for the lives of women. A memoir by sociologist Angela McRobbie, who grew up in a second-generation middle-class Irish Catholic family in Glasgow in the late 1950s, includes a remark which puts sectarianism in its place. She notes: 'Protestant working class culture only surfaced occasionally in Orange Walks or in football matches between Celtic and Rangers. But in a family of girls with a father who was not at all interested in football this meant very little'.[50]

Conclusion

What we see is often coloured by what we expect. If we approach the subject of the Irish in Scotland expecting discrimination, we can read James Handley's descriptions of the hardships endured by poor people in the nineteenth century as accounts particularly of the lives of Irish Catholic migrants and miss two key points: such hardship marked the lives of the poor irrespective of religion and that the majority of the poor people were native Protestant Scots. If we take Northern Ireland as our model for interpreting Scotland, we miss the more pertinent parallels of the migrant Catholic experience in the USA and Australia. Short of capital and industrial skills, Irish Catholic migrants entered the Scottish labour market at the bottom but they quickly prospered. Those who resented the economic competition or the threat to the cultural dominance of Presbyterianism huffed and puffed but, as we will see in Chapter 6, they lacked the numbers or the power to exacerbate seriously the conflict, and the Scots with the economic and political power to encourage conflict did not do so.

It is important to appreciate, as Angela McRobbie put it, that the politics surrounding the growth of Catholicism in Scotland 'meant very little' to most Catholics who got on with the tasks of building their lives and building up the Catholic Church in a new country. Father Thomas Taylor, the parish priest of the small mining village of Carfin just east of Motherwell, was a devotee of the shrine of Our Lady of Lourdes for whom building was not just a metaphor. To allow Scots who could not travel to France to share his experience of the Marian shrine, he built a replica in a damp field opposite the chapel. Begun in 1920 the project was given an unexpected boost by the general strike of

1921: local miners who found themselves unexpectedly idle joined Taylor as volunteers. When the shrine opened in 1922 it attracted thousands of pilgrims.

Notes

1. A. B. Campbell, *The Lanarkshire Miners: a Social History of their Trade Unions 1775–1874* (John Donald: Edinburgh, 1980); M. Mitchell, *The Irish in the West of Scotland 1797–1848: Trade Unions, Strikes and Political Movements* (Edinburgh: John Donald, 1998).
2. A. L. Drummond and J. Bulloch, *The Church in Victorian Scotland, 1843–1874* (Edinburgh: Saint Andrew Press, 1975), pp. 70-4.
3. T. Gallagher, *Glasgow: the Uneasy Peace* (Manchester: Manchester University Press, 1987), p. 12.
4. C. G. Brown, *The Social History of Religion in Scotland Since 1730* (London: Methuen, 1997), p. 33.
5. E. H. Hunt, *British Labour History 1815–1914* (London: Weidenfeld and Nicolson, 1981), p. 162.
6. T. Gallagher, 'Bearing of the green', *Observer Scotland*, 9 April 1989.
7. Joyce Macmillan, 'Scotland's shame', *Guardian Weekly*, 18 August 1999; http://www.guardian.co.uk/theguardian/1999/aug/18/guardianweekly.guardian-weekly11. He was similarly reported by *The Times*, 20 September 1997.
8. R. Hutchinson, *Father Allan: the Life and Legacy of a Hebridean Priest* (Edinburgh: Birlinn, 2010), p. 76.
9. J. Handley, *The Irish in Scotland* (Cork: Cork University Press, 1945), p. 242.
10. J. Cooney, *Scotland and the Papacy: Pope John Paul II's Visit in Perspective* (Edinburgh: Paul Harris, 1982), p. 36.
11. Handley, *The Irish*, p. 260. It is worth adding that the restoration of the hierarchy in Scotland caused little public clamour. The greatest opposition came from the Scottish Episcopal Church, which insisted that it was already the rightful occupant of the ancient sees of the Christian Church in Scotland.
12. P. Lynch, 'The Catholic Church and political action in Scotland', in R. Boyle and P. Lynch (eds), *Out of the Ghetto? The Catholic Community in Modern Scotland* (Edinburgh: John Donald, 1998), p. 49.
13. R. Ronsson, 'A secret history', *New Statesman*, 31 August–6 September 2012, p. 43.
14. S. Damer, 'Memoirs of a Catholic boyhood: a map of Catholic Edinburgh', *History Workshop Journal* 44 (1997), p. 192.
15. Gallagher, *Glasgow*, p. 91.
16. I. S. Wood, 'Hope deferred: Labour in Scotland in the 1920s', in I. Donnachie, C. Harvie and I. S. Wood (eds), *Forward! Labour Politics in Scotland 1888–1988* (Edinburgh: Polygon, 1989), p. 30.
17. There are excellent biographies of Wheatley and Dollan in W. W. Knox, *Scottish Labour Leaders 1918–1939* (Edinburgh: John Donald, 1984).

18. W. W. Knox, 'Religion and the Scottish labour movement c. 1900–39', *Journal of Contemporary History* 23 (1988), pp. 609–30.
19. Gallagher, *Glasgow*, p. 272.
20. M. Keating, R. Levy, J. Geekie and J. Brand, 'Labour Elites in Glasgow', *Strathclyde Papers on Government and Politics* 61 (1989), p. 19.
21. S. Bruce, T. Glendinning, I. Paterson and M. Rosie, *Sectarianism in Scotland* (Edinburgh: Edinburgh University Press, 2004), p. 70.
22. A. L. Drummond and J. Bulloch, *The Scottish Church 1688–1843* (Edinburgh: Saint Andrew Press, 1973), p. 141.
23. J. H. Treble, 'The development of Roman Catholic education in Scotland 1878–1978', in D. McRoberts (ed.), *Modern Scottish Catholicism* (Glasgow: Burns, 1979), p. 111. It is simply wrong to say, as Williamson does, that the 1872 Act 'forced Catholics to fund and support their own school'; despite rejecting the 1872 Act's scheme, the Church continued to receive state grant aid until 1918; C. Williamson, '"An antidote to Communism": Catholic Social Action in Glasgow 1931–1939', in R. Boyle and P. Lynch (eds), *Out of the Ghetto? The Catholic Community in Modern Scotland* (Edinburgh: John Donald, 1998), p. 17.
24. L. Paterson, *Scottish Education in the Twentieth Century* (Edinburgh: Edinburgh University Press, 2003), p. 40.
25. T. A. Fitzpatrick, *Catholic Secondary Education in South-West Scotland before 1872* (Aberdeen: Aberdeen University Press, 1986), p. 34.
26. Gallagher, *Glasgow*, p. 103. In his 1982 visit to Scotland, Pope John Paul II fulsomely praised the 1918 Act; http://www.thepapalvisit.org.uk/Visit-Background/A-Retrospective-of-the-1982-Visit/Scotland/Address-of-John-Paul-II-to-the-staff-and-the-students-of-Saint-Andrew-s-College-of-Education-BEA.
27. Paterson, *Scottish Education*, p. 59.
28. Fitzpatrick, *Catholic Secondary Education*, p. 80.
29. J. Devine, 'A Lanarkshire perspective on bigotry in Scottish society', in T. Devine (ed.), *Scotland's Shame? Bigotry and Sectarianism in Modern Scotland* (Edinburgh: Mainstream, 2000), pp. 102–3.
30. Gallagher, *Glasgow*, p. 115.
31. Office of the Chief Statistician, *Analysis of Religion in the 2001 Census* (Edinburgh: Scottish Executive, 2005), Table 3.1.
32. NFO Social Research, *Sectarianism in Glasgow – Final Report* (Edinburgh: NFO Social Research, 2003), p. 59.
33. For examples, see Bruce et al., *Sectarianism*, pp. 144–5.
34. D. McCrone, *Understanding Scotland* (London: Routledge, 2001), pp. 89–90.
35. *Sunday Herald Magazine*, 6 April 2003.
36. S. Bruce, *No Pope of Rome: militant Protestantism in Scotland* (Edinburgh: Mainstream, 1985), pp. 170–90.
37. *Scotland on Sunday*, 4 February 2001, p. 6.
38. J. Conroy, '"Yet I live here": A reply to Bruce on Catholic education in Scotland', *Oxford Review of Education* 29 (2003), p. 410.

39. *Sunday Herald*, 2 March 2003.

40. *Daily Record*, 7 May 2002.

41. Gregory Graham has pointed out that the report he co-authored with Eleanor Kelly did not claim to be exhaustive and hence it may be an under-estimate. Given the prominence of any case which has even the most tenuous links to football or religion, this seems very unlikely.

42. I am grateful to the Justice Statistics branch of the Scottish Executive for supplying these details.

43. For details, see Bruce et al., *Sectarianism*, pp. 135–40.

44. *Daily Telegraph*, 22 November 2004.

45. *Daily Express*, 22 November 2004.

46. *The Scotsman*, 23 November 2012.

47. One such was Cardinal Keith O'Brien; R. Dinwoodie, 'Anti-Catholic bigotry is deep and pervasive says Cardinal', *The Herald*, 28 November 2006.

48. Gerry Finn and Joseph Bradley, who have written extensively about football, are on the James MacMillan side of the argument. Among the Scots political scientists who are not are James Mitchell, David McCrone and Lindsay Paterson.

49. D. Burdsey and R. Chappell, '"And if you know your history": An examination of the formation of football clubs in Scotland and their role in the construction of social identity', *The Sports Historian* 21 (2001); http://www2.umist.ac.uk/sport/SPORTS%HISTORY/sh211.html.

50. A. McRobbie, 'Catholic Glasgow: a map of the city', *History Workshop Journal* 42 (1995), p. 180.

CHAPTER

4

THE IRONY OF CATHOLIC SUCCESS

Father Taylor of Carfin did not let up when his grotto opened in 1922. Over the next forty years the shrine was regularly expanded to include what Wikipedia describes as:

> many life-size depictions of Christ, Our Blessed Lady and many saints. It also contains a life-size representation of Jesus' life with Mary and Joseph in their Loretto house and carpentry shop, which is depicted in an underground cave; a Reliquary; as well as a sunken garden.

Taylor added many 'holy statues and artifacts' to the core imitation of Lourdes. He was a devotee of St Thérèse of Lisieux, a young French Carmelite nun who died of TB at the age of twenty-four and whose spiritual autobiography attracted a vast readership. She was beatified in 1923, canonised two years later and now has her own saint's day.[1] Correctly anticipating her later popularity, Taylor had a statue of St Thérèse erected directly opposite that of the Virgin Mary and appointed her secondary patron of the grotto after Our Lady. If the expansion of the Carfin site can stand as a metaphor for the growth in Catholic numbers and confidence in the first half of the twentieth century, the Church's subsequent change of fortune can be symbolised by the fate of two extraordinary building projects: St Andrew's College, Bearsden and St Peter's Seminary, Cardross.

St Andrew's was opened in 1969 to train teachers for Catholic schools.[2] Designed by the Glasgow firm of Gillespie, Kidd and Coia, it was a marvellous example of modern concrete work in the style of Le Corbusier and its status was recognised with a Category A listing for architectural merit. Its detractors called it 'Stalinist' and 'East German' but it was an impressive statement of the Church's confidence in its place in Scotland: the teachers who would ensure the successful transmission of the faith to every new generation would be trained in the most up-to-date facilities in an ultra-modern style on a large site in the most expensive suburb of Glasgow. During his 1982 visit to Scotland, Pope John Paul II visited the college and praised its fine buildings; perhaps being Polish made him sympathetic to poured-concrete structures. Thirty years after its opening the college joined Glasgow University and in 2002 the site was declared redundant. Parts of it found a curious after-life as film location sites. In 2010 the student residence blocks were demolished to make way for a new secondary school.

The same firm also designed Cardross Seminary: 'one of the most important modernist buildings in Scotland'.[3] Like St Andrew's, St Peter's was Category A listed by Historic Scotland in 1992. In October 2005 it was named Scotland's greatest post-Second World War building by the architecture magazine *Prospect*. Unfortunately this did not change the fact that it was built too late. It was planned in the 1950s but not completed until 1966 and it never reached its planned intake of 100 students. The seminary closed in 1980. The buildings suffered from a number of structural problems which discouraged potential purchasers and were finally abandoned in the late 1980s. Scots film-maker Murray Grigor captured the beauty of St Peter's when it was still in use in his 1972 film *Space and Light*. As part of the campaign to save the buildings, he repeated such of the original sequences as the dilapidated and dangerous conditions of parts of the buildings would allow for a 2009 follow-up, *Space and Light Revisited*. Praise from professional architects did nothing to find a new use for what was very much a Catholic seminary and it is now crumbling and overgrown.

Communal Identity

The previous chapter showed the gradual rise of the descendants of the Irish immigrants. Here we consider various elements of a distinct Catholic identity and show how the decline in community cohesion interacted with a decline in church involvement.

While it is common to describe parts of Glasgow as Green or Orange, the city was never segregated. Protestant strongholds such as Bridgeton were partly mixed, as were such Irish Catholic enclaves as Garngad. In 1914 Glasgow was one of Europe's most congested cities, with over 700,000 people living in its central three square miles, and lack of space was an obvious constraint on the creation of the rival ethnic ghettos.[4] Glasgow Corporation assumed control of working-class housing during the 1920s and over the next four decades cleared the slums, rebuilt the inner city and constructed large peripheral housing schemes. In Northern Ireland, control over housing allocation was a key pillar of Unionist power because careful allocation could ensure advantageous electoral outcomes.[5] Such residential mixing as did occur was reversed with the outbreak of the Troubles in the late 1960s: Catholic and Protestant families were forced to move back into their respective traditional strongholds. In Scotland, Labour-dominated councils had no reason to separate Catholics and Protestants in the shift of population.[6]

The 2001 census allowed us to compare, for the first time, segregation in Glasgow and Belfast. Catholics made up 29 per cent of the population of Glasgow. In no council ward did they form a majority, although they came close in Toryglen (45 per cent) and Hutchesontown (43 per cent). The common view that Garngad remained a very Catholic part of Glasgow was revealed to be a myth: for every Catholic living in the Royston ward (which approximates to the old Garngad district) there were two non-Catholics. The supposedly Protestant strongholds of Bridgeton and Govan were both 30 per cent Catholic. The area with the smallest proportion of Catholics (12 per cent) was Pollokshields East, where four out of ten residents were Muslim. In Belfast, 42 per cent of the population was Catholic and we can clearly see the effect of serious social conflict in their distribution. Eleven council wards contained at least twice this figure, with five being at least 90 per cent Catholic. At the other extreme, Catholics formed less than 3 per cent of the population in thirteen wards. If Catholics were to have been equally spread across Belfast, then 40 per cent of the Catholic population would have needed to relocated. The corresponding figure for Glasgow was only 11 per cent. In brief, Belfast was segregated; Glasgow was not.

The extent to which two populations inter-marry is important both as a symptom and as a cause of integration. It is a symptom because we can only marry those we meet; hence inter-marriage shows the extent to which people mix as equals. Furthermore the willingness to marry someone of another race, nation, ethnic group or religion shows the importance of those characteristics as against personal emotional attachment. Inter-marriage hastens integration because for bigots to maintain a climate of discrimination they must be able to divide those they wish to advance from those they wish to deprive of opportunities. The more that 'we' marry 'them' and produce children who cannot easily be labelled, the harder it is to discriminate and the more likely it is that religious or ethnic preferences will be over-ridden by other considerations. As populations mix, being a good uncle or brother-in-law competes with being a loyal Catholic or Protestant, and in stable affluent societies that are not divided by competing political agendas, real family ties trump the mythic blood ties of the religio-ethnic group.[7]

The 2001 Scottish Social Attitudes Survey and a similar survey conducted by Glasgow City Council the same year offer ample evidence on inter-marriage. First, they show that the vast majority of Scots had no objection to a relative marrying someone of a different religion. Across Scotland, only 3 per cent minded a 'great deal'; a further 7 per cent minded 'slightly'. Over two-thirds did not mind at all. There were no significant differences between the expressed views of Protestants and Catholics, irrespective of age. The same pattern was found in Glasgow, where only 3 per cent minded a great deal and over 80 per cent did not mind at all. Around a third of the Glasgow sample who minded a great deal about mixed marriages were Muslim; a considerable over-representation. Catholics in Glasgow express, marginally, more tolerant views than Protestants. In turn, Protestants in Glasgow express more tolerant views than both Catholics and Protestants in Scotland as a whole.

The sentiment expressed in answers to the hypothetical survey question is matched by action. Put simply, it was once the rule for Catholics to marry other Catholics.[8] In the Scottish survey, almost all of the married Catholics aged 65–74 (94 per cent to be precise) were married to a Catholic. The corresponding figure in the Glasgow study was 80 per cent. For Scotland as a whole the figure for those aged 55–64 was 86 per cent (69 per cent in Glasgow), and it gradually goes down for each age cohort until, for those aged 25–34, more than half of the Catholics are married to non-Catholics. For Glasgow, over 40 per cent of married Catholics have non-Catholic spouses. To put these figures in context, we can note that in Northern Ireland in 1991 only 2 per cent of marriages were religiously mixed and in the USA in 1999 only 3 per cent of marriages were racially mixed.[9] The point is compelling and simple. Young Scots no longer regard religion (or more precisely religio-ethnic identity) as an important consideration in the biggest personal decision they make. This relative indifference to religion also shows up in socialising patterns. In the Glasgow survey only 6 per cent said that religion was a factor in whom they could have as a friend and that response was much more common from Muslim respondents than from Catholics or Protestants.[10]

It is a mark of the power of the dismal sectarian view of Scotland that as soon as one claim for sectarianism is refuted, another is substituted. Once it was clear that there were no significant socio-economic differences between the heirs to the Irish and other Scots, it was suggested that sectarianism could be found in a degree of 'cultural exclusion' which has caused Scots Catholics of Irish descent to discover a renewed or entirely new interest in 'Irishness' as a distinct cultural identity.[11] The claim can be tested with three sources: two major surveys and the 2001 census. The Glasgow survey showed little evidence that Scots Catholics think of themselves as Irish. It allowed respondents to choose as many national or ethnic identities that they felt best represented them, and while 81 per cent of Catholics chose Scottish and 23 per cent chose British, only 8 per cent chose an Irish identity (and they probably were just Irish people living in Glasgow).[12]

The political scientist Luis Moreno devised a simple way of assessing the balance between two competing identities. Table 4.1 shows the results of three applications of his question. In 1992 there was a visible difference between Catholics and Kirk identifiers, which gradually reduces in 1999 and 2001. But the difference was not that Scots Catholics thought themselves

Table 4.1 National Identity and Religion, 1992, 1999 and 2001

	1992			1999			2001		
	RC %	Kirk %	None %	RC %	Kirk %	None %	RC %	Kirk %	None %
Scottish, not British	26	17	23	34	31	37	40	35	38
More Scottish than British	37	41	45	41	40	31	34	31	30
Equally Scottish and British	30	37	28	17	24	19	19	27	20
More British than Scottish	1	2	2	1	2	4	1	3	3
British, not Scottish	1	2	15	2	1	5	1	2	4
Other or none	5	1	0	5	1	4	4	1	6
Total	100	100	100	100	100	100	100	100	100

Source: Scottish Social Attitudes Surveys

Irish: it is that they were more likely than Kirk identifiers to think of themselves as Scottish. The main change is that everyone became more Scottish and less British. The third point is the trivial number who chose 'Other or none'. It was open to those who felt Irish rather than Scottish or British to say that. They did not.[13]

In an effort to create their own evidence of Catholic distinctiveness, some scholars placed in periodicals such as the *Irish Post* (a London-based paper) and *Celtic View* adverts which encouraged people to record their ethnic identity in the 2001 census as 'Irish'. Despite this, the number of people resident in Scotland on census day who chose to describe themselves as Irish was actually smaller than the number of people who had been born in Ireland. That is, they were not Scots Catholics reacting to oppression by going Irish theme pub; they were Irish people living in Scotland.

Even before the census, a convenient explanation for the failure of reality to fit the theory was being composed. It was asserted that 'people born in Scotland with Irish parents or grandparents frequently hide their roots because they fear hostility' and hence 'the "Irish" box will not be fully used by those who feel they have an Irish cultural background'.[14] This seems implausible. When survey respondents are quite happy to declare their income, views about abortion, religious upbringing and attitudes to capital punishment, it is not likely that they become coy over ethnic identity.

Another place we might find evidence of Catholic alienation is in attitudes toward devolution. Although surveys provide little evidence for this, some commentators supposed that Catholics were reluctant to support devolution during the 1970s campaigns because they feared that an autonomous Scotland would be a more unpleasantly Protestant country than one run from London.[15] In the run-up to the referendum on the Scottish Parliament, Cardinal Thomas Winning announced very publicly that Catholics had nothing to fear from a Scottish Parliament.[16] Whether he led or merely represented a change is not clear but the voting suggests no Catholic hostility: 62 per cent were in favour. Of those who did vote, Catholics were as likely as Protestants to vote for a devolved parliament and less likely than Protestants to have voted against.

Scots Catholics and Protestants do differ in their party political preferences but the differences are declining. Not surprising given its role in their political rise, Catholics have a distinct preference for Labour. More importantly, they remain so even when we control for social class: in the 2001 Scottish survey 50 per cent of middle-class Catholic respondents said they voted for Labour. They were less likely than Protestants to support the Scottish Nationalists or, come to that, the Liberal Democrats and are even more distinctive in their hostility to the Conservatives: almost none voted Conservative. Looked at from the other end, although current levels of support are low, Scottish Protestants remain much more likely than others to vote Conservative.[17]

The rise of the SNP since the 1990s has seen the religious differences eroded. In 1970 4 per cent of Catholics compared with 11 per cent of the population at large voted SNP. In 1987 the figures were 9 and 14 per cent. Five years later, the Catholic and the general SNP vote were almost identical: 20 and 21 per cent; and in 2011 43 per cent of Scots Catholics voted SNP, which was only one percentage point less than the overall SNP vote.[18]

The partition of Ireland in 1921 removed Irish home rule from the British agenda for fifty years. Until then many Irish Catholics supported Sinn Fein. From then until the 1960s Scots Catholics were politically distinctive in their enthusiastic support for Labour. But even when religion was at its most salient, the political differences in Scotland were quite unlike those in Northern Ireland. In Northern Ireland the overwhelming majority of each population voted (and still votes) for religio-ethnic parties with incompatible constitutional ambitions. In Scotland, they differed only in the degree of their support for the most popular party. Scots Catholics were a bit more Scottish in their politics than were Scottish Protestants. With the rise of the SNP even that difference has gone.

The Self-image of the Church

Too often the cohesion of the Catholic community is treated as if it was entirely or largely a response to external hostility. That the vast majority of Catholics in the 1920s married other Catholics, for example, could have been a response to native Scots shunning the new migrants and their descendants. More likely it was a combination of two considerations that had little to do with Protestant reaction: socialising patterns and religious preference. Just as most Muslims now wish their children to marry other Muslims, Catholics who were committed to their faith naturally wished to find a life partner who shared that preference. That Protestants were not regarded as suitable partners owed a great deal to the monopolistic claims of the Catholic Church. Since the Reformation the Vatican has insisted that it and it alone possesses the true Christian faith and that all Protestant churches are false guides. In 1927 the leading English Catholic Ronald Knox said: 'a body of Catholic patriots, entrusted with the government of a Catholic state, will not shrink even from repressive measures, in order to perpetuate the secure domination of Catholic principles among their fellow-countrymen'. More telling, he made it clear that the Church's support for liberal democracy was opportunistic: 'For when we demand liberty in the modern state, we are appealing to its own principles, not to ours'.[19] As late as the 1950s the Catholic Church still maintained officially that it had a right to impose its will on non-believers; the American Jesuit theologian John Courtney Murray was disciplined for suggesting that this was unacceptable in a democracy.

The Second Vatican Council of the early 1960s represented a major shift in Church thinking. Barriers to mixed marriages were lowered in the 1980s and the requirement that the children of such unions be raised as Catholics was relaxed. However, some priests still insist that they will not accept for First Communion children who do not attend a Catholic school. And in Vatican eyes Protestants have moved from 'heretics' only as far as 'our separated brethren'. A good illustration of the Catholic Church's official attitude to other churches can be found in its attitude to sharing communion. Since 1971 members of all the major Scottish churches have collaborated in a pilgrimage to St Mary's, Haddington. The Protestants share communion at a single altar and the Church of Scotland gave permission for the Catholics to conduct a Mass in the church. For many years the officiating priests turned a blind eye to the fact that many Protestants were stretching the limits of ecumenical cooperation by joining the queue for the Catholic Mass. In 1998 Archbishop Keith O'Brien wrote to the pilgrimage organisers telling them that this had to stop.[20]

The gradual improvement in relations with other Christian churches has not changed the Catholic Church's belief that it is fundamentally superior. At a dinner in Glasgow's City Halls to celebrate the fiftieth anniversary of his entry to the priesthood, Cardinal Winning said that Catholicism would be Scotland's sole faith in the twenty-first century. He said the papacy was willing to cede control of Scottish Catholicism in the cause of ecumenical unity but that such unity required that the Protestant churches admit they were wrong:

> The other churches will have to accept Bishops. There will be no movement on doctrine and no movement on the seven sacraments . . . When we speak to other churches, we have the right to say to them, 'Look right back to the beginning and ask yourselves, why did you abandon us?'[21]

The official position was given in 2001 by the Church's parliamentary officer in a letter to *The Herald*:

> The Catholic Church takes the position that Christ did entrust authority to the church, with one person given a special position of authority as described in Matthew's gospel ... Christ also gave authority to the church to teach and the promise that the church would maintain the faith.[22]

This disdain for other Christian organisations cannot be explained as a reaction to persecution. It is the posture historically maintained by the Vatican even in places where it has an unchallenged monopoly.

To summarise thus far, the Catholic Church in Scotland was revived by the migration of a large body of Catholics from Ireland in the late nineteenth and early twentieth centuries. As the community grew it prospered. During the first half of the twentieth century one could identify a distinct Catholic community but increased prosperity brought increased integration with the wider society and with it the decline of commitment to the Church, as we will now see.

Institutional Decline

For Catholics in Scotland, their faith is now a personal preference rather than an expression of an inherited ethnic identity reinforced by a strong and separate community. The consequence of that change has been rapid decline. The 2001 census allows us to compare current religion and religion of upbringing but its figures are not terribly informative because clearly much religious identification is purely nominal. If those who in 2001 said they were currently Church of Scotland or Roman Catholic actually attended church, both organisations would be growing, not contracting. The Scottish Social Attitudes questions seem to have produced more realistic responses. While the Catholic Church had done better than the Church of Scotland at retaining at least nominal allegiance, still 20 per cent of Scots who were raised as Catholics by 2001 regarded themselves as having no religion. A better indicator of commitment is church attendance. The decline in Catholic church attendance began later than that of the Church of Scotland but rapidly caught up. Mass attendance peaked in the 1950s at around 420,000. It then remained relatively stable until the early 1970s when it began to fall rapidly.[23] Between 1984 and 2002 Church of Scotland attendance fell from 361,340 to 228,500, a drop of over a third. In the same period the Catholic Church recorded a drop of 42 per cent, from 345,950 to 202,110.[24] That is, at a time when Scotland's adult population grew by 15 per cent, Catholic Mass attendance was halved. The Catholic celebration of rites of passage also declined markedly so that in 2012 there were more humanist weddings than Catholic ones.[25]

That decline was mirrored in recruitment to the clergy. The closure of

St Peter's has already been mentioned. From 1829 Blairs College, south of Aberdeen, served as a junior seminary for boys and young men studying for the priesthood. At one time more than half the priests ordained in Scotland had been to the college for all or part of their secondary education. 'For those who did not become priests, Blairs provided an excellent Catholic education, acting as a strong foundation and spiritual influence for their future life'.[26] It was closed in 1986; the main building is now a museum. Gillis College, opened in September 1986, was the replacement for St Andrew's College, Drygrange, Melrose (which had been opened in 1953) as the seminary for the Archdiocese of St Andrews and Edinburgh. It occupied what was formerly St Margaret's Convent, the first post-Reformation religious community in Scotland, established in 1834 by Revd James Gillis. Unfortunately it had only nineteen students and closed in 1995, with all training being concentrated on St Andrew's in Bearsden. From 1921 to 1961 St Vincent's College, Langbank was a holiday home for 'necessitous children' from the West of Scotland run by the Daughters of Charity. When local authorities assumed responsibility for much of the holiday home work, the Bishops took over Langbank as an extension to Blairs College. As its height it had some 120 pupils. The junior seminary closed in 1977.

In 2009 the Bishops' Conference of Scotland announced that it was closing the last training facility in Scotland: Scotus College in Glasgow. In future all candidates for the priesthood would be trained at the Pontifical College in Rome. That year there were just nine students at Scotus and eleven in Rome.

In two ways the closure of the junior seminaries and boarding schools reflects wider changes in attitudes to child-rearing and education: boarding schools are far less popular than they were and fewer people are happy with the idea that selection for the life of a celibate priest should begin in adolescence. But, as with the closure of the senior seminaries, it also reflects the decline in numbers of men coming forward to train for the priesthood. The peak years for seminary students were 1959 and 1960, when there were 184 men in training.[27] In 1990 there were just over 100 seminarians; in 2003 there were 37.[28] That in turn was a combination of two important changes. There were fewer religiously observant Catholics and fewer of them shared their grandparents' veneration of the priesthood or, for that matter, the teaching profession. The Church could no longer confine the ambitions of its more able members to reproducing the Catholic community. As Scots Catholics prospered far more opportunities became open to young men of talent and ever fewer were willing to sacrifice themselves for the faith.

The decline in numbers entering the priesthood further weakened the Church. The job became more demanding at the same time as men had less opportunity to prepare for it. In the 1950s an ordained man might serve as an assistant to a parish priest for many years before having to take full responsibility; by the end of the century, men with ever-less experience were being charged with managing ever-larger parishes. This probably explains the increase in drop-outs. Cardinal O'Brien estimated in 2002 that one in ten left within seven years of ordination.[29]

Although giving up the faith altogether is the most dramatic rejection of the Church's authority, a related change can be seen in the growing independence and selectivity of those who continue to support the Church. For example, few Catholics now avail themselves of Confession or the sacrament of reconciliation as it is now known.[30] Even fewer accept the Church's teachings on contraception. The 2001 Scottish survey asked if people agreed with church leaders speaking out on a variety of issues. The general pattern was clear: people were much more sympathetic to church leaders badgering the government about remote issues such as world poverty than they were to the churches telling them what to do in their private lives. Although regular churchgoers were overall more sympathetic than those Scots who did not attend church, their rank ordering of issues was the same, which rather suggests that the Catholic Church's strong interest in controlling sexuality may not be popular even with its core people. Almost all regular Mass-going Catholics (93 per cent) thought it is 'generally right' for church leaders to 'speak out about poverty'. For education the figure was 77 per cent; for abortion 73 per cent; and for the environment it was 68 per cent. But only 65 per cent of regular Catholic churchgoers thought it right for church leaders to speak out about personal sexuality. Or, to put it the other way round, almost 10 per cent declined to choose and just over a quarter of committed Catholic church adherents thought it 'generally wrong' for the hierarchy to pronounce on sexuality. A detailed summary of thirty years of opinion polls on religion in Scotland concludes: 'the statistics [show] a widening gulf between the leadership and teachings of the Catholic Church and people of all persuasions – Catholic and non-Catholic alike'.[31]

The Catholic Church's theological insistence on the sacramental power of the clergy constrains it considerably more than any Protestant church but the decline in the number of priests and the increasing need to persuade rather than command the laity combine to move it in a 'Protestant' direction. Increasingly roles are being found for lay people, and offices which were once confined to the clergy are being devolved to the laity.

The Changing Catholic Family

Behind these obvious signs of 'fortress Catholicism' crumbling are two social changes: the decline in family size and the growth of women's employment outside the home.

Between 1914 and 1939 the Catholic Church created thirteen new parishes. In a similar time period after the Second World War over 100 new parishes were added: the 'vast majority in housing schemes and new towns of the

Glasgow conurbation'. Often new schools were built besides new churches, church halls and clergy accommodation: 'creating vital community centres which combined devotional, educational and leisure facilities'.[32] Most discussion of Catholic Church control over schooling concentrates on the Church's ability or right to indoctrinate children. But schooling also provides an important secondary link between adult adherents and the Church. Having children brings Catholic adults into regular contact with the Church's officials and rituals and gives them a good reason to maintain ties that they might drop if they only had themselves to consider. Even parents of little faith may hesitate to deny their children a heritage which they can reject, if they wish, when they are adults. And having children in the same school brings adults together. If the school is a faith school, that provides an additional tie between adults of the same religion and thus reinforces the faith.

But schools only influence the social networks of adults who have school-age children, and the number of such children has fallen markedly. One way of producing a standard measure that can be used for comparisons across time, irrespective of marriage patterns, is to express the number of children women do have as a percentage of those they theoretically *could* have had, if they were typically fertile and had fertile male partners: in 1911 Scots women were typically achieving, if that is the right word, 26 per cent of their theoretical maximum fertility. By 1931 this had fallen to 19.2 per cent and in 1988 it was just 14.4 per cent. In 1911 'women married between the ages of 22 and 26 and living with their husbands for at least fifteen years had on average almost six children. More than one fifth had nine or more'.[33] This figure fell dramatically: by 1971 women who had married between the ages of 22 and 24 in the mid-1940s had a completed mean family size of around 2.5 children. Just over half had no more than two children.

Although the links between age of marriage, prevalence of marriage, number of children and life-span are complex, the basic point can be expressed like this. At the start of the twentieth century, many Scottish women would have spent at least a third of their lives producing and raising children. By the end of the century, fall in family size and increase in life-expectancy had reduced this to about 10 per cent.[34] And with fewer children, Catholic women spent fewer years involved with the parochial school and fewer years socialising with other Catholic parents.

The weakening of the home–school link was accompanied by a change in the frequency and nature of women's work. Between 1901 and 1931 the proportion of women in work changed little and was about 35 per cent. After the Second World War it rose rapidly so that by 1991 over two-thirds of women worked outside the home. Thinking about middle-class career women can cause us to forget that many women have always had to seek paid employment but in the 1930s or 1940s that work was often part-time and close by the home or in other people's homes; that is, in the sorts of workplaces most likely to hire by religion and most likely to involve mixing only with people of the same faith.

Of course this is a gross simplification but we can divide social relationships into two spheres: those of the home and those of the world of work. The private world of the home, the extended family and the neighbourhood reflects and reinforces personal preferences. The world of public work – in big factories, city centre department stores, local government and the professions – is governed by universalism. It involves mixing with large numbers of strangers and dealing with them all as equals. You may marry who you wish and socialise only with those who share your faith but if you work in a large office or city centre shop you cannot choose your workmates or your customers by religion. The decline in fertility rates and the expansion of women's horizons caused a subtle but in the long-run hugely important change in way people lived. In the 1940s the parish priest could walk from house to house and tenement flat to tenement flat visiting his women parishioners to remind them of their church and family obligations. By the 1980s such pastoral contact was limited to the committed core of active members and to the elderly.

At the same time as these social changes were reducing the importance of schools in the Catholic community web, the decline of religion was compromising the ability of those schools to provide a distinctly Catholic education. Catholic religious orders failed to attract recruits and had to give up their role in schools. For example, St Mungo's Academy used to be a boys' school run by the Marist Brothers but by 1988, when the first girls arrived in a merger with Our Lady and St Francis Secondary School, the Brothers had passed control of the school to lay staff and the school became a comprehensive, co-educational Roman Catholic state school. Although the Church retains the right to appoint only acceptably Catholic teachers, they are increasingly hard to find and many Catholic schools have had to confine the religious requirement to just teachers of religion and to senior staff.

If we put together the data on Catholic church attendance and the fact of the Church maintaining its own school system, and bear in mind the contrast between Northern Ireland and Scotland, we come to an important conclusion about the power of secularisation. What is often missed in heated arguments about the divisiveness or otherwise of a separate Catholic school system is the fact that it has failed in its primary purpose of reproducing the faith. Its schools gave the Catholic Church a powerful opportunity to socialise its children into the faith but in the absence of other good reasons to hold together (such as a distinctive political agenda or widespread anti-Catholic hostility) and in a climate where fewer and fewer people take any religious beliefs seriously, separate schooling has not been enough to maintain a vibrant religious culture. Young Catholics and Protestants now mix as equals and inter-marry. As it does everywhere, inter-marriage made it difficult to pass on the faith with the certainty and dogmatism with which it was received because, even if the children are raised in only one church, they cannot believe that the adherents of other churches are all bad when they have a parent from the other side. In such circumstances it is always likely that the children will conclude that there is good and bad in all faiths and that conclusion takes us a long way down the road to religious indifference.

Two Things Happened

In the sixth century the Bishop of Tours began his magisterial history with the famously non-committal: 'A great many things keep happening, some of them good, some of them bad'. Two things happened to the Scots Catholic Church at the end of the twentieth century; one of them good and one of them very bad.

The good thing was the unexpected boost to the Church from the collapse of communism and the subsequent expansion eastwards of the European Union. A large number of Poles had arrived in Scotland during the Second World War and many chose to remain. The French teacher at my Perthshire army school was an émigré Pole; he could not get a job teaching Polish but, like all upper-class Poles of that era, he was fluent in French. In 2004 Poland's accession to the European Union created a second wave of immigration estimated at between 40,000, according to the General Register Office for Scotland, and 85,000 as per the Polish Council.[35]

Since 2007 Polish masses have been celebrated in Aberdeen every Sunday at two sites, and as of 2012 two Polish priests served a community of whom over 500 attended Mass on a typical Sunday. Food blessing at Easter in 2009 attracted 1,200 Polish people and the Saturday Polish school accommodates between 60 and 80 children every week.[36] Some 2,000 Poles attend Mass in the Cathedral in Edinburgh every weekend, 'with about a third of that number in Motherwell Cathedral, with similar numbers attending Mass in Glasgow, Aberdeen and Dundee to say nothing of those attending Mass in West Lothian parishes'.[37] To serve that demand the Scottish Church recruited eighteen Polish priests, which is more than the number of Scots in training for the priesthood in 2012.

The bad thing that happened was sex scandal. It has long been a staple of anti-Catholic propaganda that the Church of Rome inadvertently encourages immorality by requiring its priests to remain celibate. Such lurid accounts as the 1836 *Awful Disclosures of Maria Monk and the Hotel Dieu Monastery of Montreal* were, and still are, dismissed as fantasies. But sixty years after self-styled Protestant controversialist Alexander Ratcliffe promised 'sensational revelations' when he advertised a talk by an ex-nun at the Caird Hall in Dundee, the truth turned out to be worse.[38] Although the vices of the Scottish clergy seem pallid, both in severity and in the extent of cover-up, when compared with those of sister churches in Ireland and the USA, the Church has been weakened by their exposure.

The following is a sample of the cases. In 1994 Father John Archibald of Milton of Campsie admitted abusing three children of parishioners.[39] A year later, Father Gerry Fitzsimmons of Livingston was suspended by the Church after claims he had inappropriately touched two boys.[40] In April 2000 Father Eugene Greene was jailed for forty sample offences of sexual assault, buggery and indecent assault. Father Desmond Lynagh admitted abusing boys in his care at Blairs College. The *Sunday Herald* reported that Cardinal Gray had been informed by other priests of Lynagh's record but allowed him to continue in post and to move to other offices.[41]

More common than child abuse was adultery. In September 1996 Roddy Wright, the Bishop of Argyll and the Isles, resigned his office to live with a married woman. He later admitted that he had earlier fathered a child with another parishioner.[42] In December 2005 Roddy MacNeil left his parish in Barra, supposedly to reflect on his vocation but actually because he had impregnated his cousin. She denounced him when she found he was also having an affair with a young student.[43] In the 1990s three north-east priests left the priesthood to pursue sexual relationships, two with married mothers who had been parishioners.

Father Joseph Creggan had an eighteen-year affair with a married woman.[44] She turned against him when he abandoned her to buy a home with another woman. When the spurned mistress showed Bishop Logan of Dunkeld the proof, Creggan was suspended. Father Eugene O'Sullivan left his parish in 2006, apparently retiring on grounds of ill-health. His concerned parishioners thought he had retired to Ireland to die. Actually he had bought a pub in Spain and was living with a young woman at whose marriage he had officiated twenty years earlier.[45]

Rather stranger was the case of Father James Lawlor who resigned from the parish of Penilee in Glasgow after being found lying half-naked in his chapel surrounded by sex toys. An elder had let himself in with his own keys. 'The man had only just got inside when he spotted a half-naked body lying on the floor. Naturally he panicked and called the police straight away, as anyone would'.[46] Indeed, as anyone would.

Angelika Kluk was a Polish student studying in Glasgow in 2006. She was murdered by a convicted sex offender who, under a false name, was employed as a church handyman in St Patrick's Roman Catholic Church, Anderston. Kluk had been staying in the parochial house. She was stabbed, tied up, raped and beaten to death with a table leg, before being concealed in a void beneath the church floor. During the trial, parish priest Father Gerry Nugent, a self-confessed alcoholic, repeatedly changed his story about his relationship with Kluk and how he had come to know the location of her body. He eventually admitted to having had sex with her three or four times. He was found guilty of contempt of court by prevarication.

In addition to the cases of child abuse and the incidences of vows of celibacy

being broken, often by taking advantage of emotionally disturbed parishioners, the Catholic Church was damaged by stories of brutality at church-run
homes. A case against Nazareth House in Australia prompted stories in the
British press that encouraged former inmates of homes run by the Poor Sisters
of Nazareth in Scotland to come forward. A general defence of being old-
fashioned can be entered. The priest who ran the Scots College in Valladolid
in the late nineteenth century was not unusual in believing that 'teenagers at
least were in regular need of what he called "skelps and cane-ology"'.[47] But
even allowing that the treatment of children fifty years ago was harsher than
we would now accept, that the Church was always behind the times and that
many of the children in its charge were in every sense difficult, the details of
the routinely cruel treatment of young inmates showed a travesty of the idea of
care. In the 1960s I was being educated in an army boarding school. We were
routinely yelled at on the parade square by regimental sergeant majors recently
retired from the regular army. We were sometimes belted and occasionally
caned (though cross-country running in the snow was a more common punishment). A boy who had a friend in a Catholic-run home was adamant that our
life with the military was cushy compared to the regime his friend described.
We didn't believe him then. I believe him now.

One inmate of the Aberdeen Nazareth House said: 'the nuns regularly beat
him and made him witness the violent degradation of other children. Sleep was
routinely interrupted by their constant checks for children wetting their beds
and the beating that followed. One bed-wetter was held out of the window by
her ankles as punishment.'[48] One woman recalled the fear of bedtime:

> They'd come round the beds and make sure you were in the right position: flat on
> your back with arms crossed out of the covers (otherwise you'd be touching your-
> self). If you were lying on your side, you'd be yanked back. They'd lift the covers to
> see if your bed was wet. If it was, then you'd be yanked out, called all filthy names
> . . . Wetting the bed was a nightmare – they'd strip the covers off and the child would
> be made to stand with the wet sheets for hours, to set an example. They stood there
> like ghosts, covered in the wet sheets. My sister didn't wet the bed at home, but one
> night she was crying and came to us and said she'd wet the bed. So we swapped our
> sheets for her, rinsed the wet one out and went to dry it on the radiator . . . My sister
> got caned on the hands and the back for that. The nun would roll her sleeves up, so
> she got a real good whack. I felt she took relish out of that.

Punishment for crimes real or imagined was an ever-present danger: 'You
never knew when or what. There is still never a day when my sister does not
fear being punished for something'. At meal-times children were often force-
fed: a nun would be 'pulling your head back, then she'd hold your nose so
you couldn't breathe, until your mouth opened, and she'd shove food in. Then
you'd choke and the food would end up on your plate again and she would

force-feed you your own vomit'. One inmate recalled an incident when a nun grabbed her as she was playing on swings: 'She took me off by the hair, twisted me round and threw me against the church wall. She broke all my front teeth, my face was a mashed mess, the other kids were all screaming.'

In September 2000 Sister Marie Theresa Docherty, 58, was convicted of four of seven charges. Her crimes were dragging children along corridors, punching them and force-feeding them. The nun responsible for the swing attack, known in her childcare career as Sister Alphonso, was convicted of cruel and unnatural treatment. Forty nuns belonging to the Poor Sisters of Nazareth and the Daughters of Charity of St Vincent de Paul were named in a civil action brought by more than 500 people, mostly middle-aged or elderly, who are claiming compensation from the religious orders. The action was dismissed on the grounds that too much time had elapsed since the alleged incidents, which gave a technical victory to the orders (or more precisely to their insurers, who would have stood the bill), but the Catholic Church was the loser because the charges were so well-substantiated that only the most partisan observer found them implausible. Unfortunately for its reputation, the Catholic Church was that partisan. Archbishop Mario Conti accused former Nazareth House inmates of being seekers not of justice but of 'pots of gold'.[49] Many of the claims were denied. Others were excused either by 'the standards of the day' or by the children's psychological problems. One apologist, signally failing to appreciate how craven this defence would sound, pointed out that the Church's homes cared for children who were too difficult for council-run facilities to take.

It is too early to quantify the damage that such disclosures have done to the Church, though we can be sure that the average Scots Catholic teenager will be less impressed by the clergy than were his or her parents or grandparents. Like the US evangelical Protestants who in the 1980s discovered that some of their star television evangelists had feet of clay, committed Catholics can deal with the abuse and sex scandals by arguing that they just show how much we need the discipline of the Church. That such pious people can also sin proves just how much the rest of us need the faith. But there are two crucial intertwined differences. Although Protestant ministers can sometimes seem as obsessed with sex as their Catholic counterparts, celibacy is not a central plank of their claims to authority and Protestants do not claim a sanctified status for their clergy. Hence personal failings among Protestant clergy are more likely to be seen as reflections of general human weakness than as a threat to the authority of the clergy as an institution. The Catholic Church's particular problem is that its claims to be the one true church incorporate the assertion that only its clergy are properly ordained and properly hierarchical, so that those at the top are closer to God than the laity. That is the context which we need if we are to appreciate just how great a blow to the status of the Church in Scotland was the disgrace of its most senior official.

In February 2013 Cardinal Keith O'Brien was sacked after four priests and one former priest complained to the Vatican that thirty years earlier O'Brien had sexually molested them or made inappropriate sexual advances. Initially O'Brien said that he contested the claims. Then he admitted that his sexual conduct had failed to meet the 'standards expected of a priest'. In short he was admitting that he had engaged in gay sex acts, that he had abused his authority over young men as head of the seminary and as bishop, and that his vocal condemnation of homosexuals was personally hypocritical. In describing this scandal as the greatest crisis to face the Catholic Church in Scotland since the Reformation, historian Tom Devine was exaggerating but possibly not much.[50]

There is a natural tendency to follow the Gregory of Tours method of concentrating on the things that keep happening. It is the dramatic events that catch the eye and events do not come more dramatic than O'Brien's resignation. Social scientists generally prefer to explain cultural changes by changes in social structure that are often so subtle that their effects can only be seen in retrospect. In the case of religion in Scotland the evidence shows that the decline in church involvement is sufficiently regular that it fits a model of regular generational change better than a model of adults reacting to crises. We will have to wait twenty or so years to see how the exposure of the country's leading Catholic official as a hypocrite who abused his positions of authority changes the graph of declining Catholic membership and attendance but it is hardly risky to predict that O'Brien's disgrace will not have been good for the Church.[51]

Conclusion

For most of the twentieth century the unusual social circumstances of Scotland's Catholics gave them good reason to be unusually loyal to the Church. By the last quarter of the century those circumstances were largely gone. As the descendants of the Irish rose in economic, social and political status they became less distinctive. The reduction of difference allowed the rapid growth of inter-marriage, which further eroded the divisions. That in turn produced a marked decline in Catholicism.

In the early 1990s I presented a version of the above argument to a meeting of the Catholic Historical Society that was attended by Cardinal Thomas Winning and a number of senior clergy. At the end of my talk I was button-holed by the Cardinal and, expecting to be heavily criticised for an overly positive view of Protestant–Catholic relations, was surprised to find the Cardinal re-presenting my account from his perspective as the head of the organisation. He remarked that he had been saying similar things to his priests, particularly those recruited from Ireland, for decades. The Church could no longer suppose that Scots Catholics were passively 'our people' and that they 'would follow our lead' like their grandparents did. He said: 'We no longer have a people in that sense of being able to take their loyalty for granted'. Twenty years later the loyalty that could no longer be taken for granted was being severely tried.

Notes

1. Wikipedia, 'Carfin Grotto'; http://en.wikipedia.org/wiki/Carfin_Grotto.
2. This was initially Notre Dame College but changed its name when it was merged with Craiglockhart college.
3. Wikipedia, 'St Peter's Seminary Cardross'; http://en.wikipedia.org/wiki/St_Peter%27s_Seminary,_Cardross. Accessed September 2012.
4. S. G. Checkland and O. Checkland, *Industry and Ethos: Scotland 1832–1914* (London: Edward Arnold, 1984).
5. Details vary but the idea of 'gerrymandering' is simple. So that the votes of your opponents have less effect than the votes of your likely supporters, you group as many of 'them' as possible into a small area: they win that seat with 90 per cent of the vote but all of the votes above the winning total are wasted. You spread your own supporters carefully so that they form, say, 60 per cent of the voters of as many wards as possible. Your people thus win more seats with their due.
6. I. Paterson, 'Sectarianism and municipal housing allocation in Glasgow', *Scottish Affairs* 39 (2002), pp. 39–53.
7. Note that this assertion refers only to stable affluent societies. The atrocities that accompanied the break-up of the former Yugoslavia remind us that the replacement of large group loyalties by a combination of kinship bonds and universalism is not irreversible.
8. R. D. Lobban, 'The Irish community in Greenock in the nineteenth century', *Irish Geography* 6 (1971), p. 279, says that 20 per cent of Irish Catholics in Greenock in 1851 married out. The general pattern is this: when there were few Catholics in Scotland, Catholics married out because the alternative was to remain single. As the Catholic population grew, endogamy became possible and hence common. It declined towards the end of the twentieth century as religion declined in significance. That is, marriage patterns are explained by the interaction of two factors: the availability of partners of the same religion and the importance of religion.
9. V. Morgan, M. Smith, G. Robinson and G. Fraser, *Mixed Marriages in Northern Ireland* (Coleraine: Centre for the Study of Conflict, University of Ulster, 1996).
10. The figures were 20 per cent of Muslims but only 4 per cent of Protestants and 6 per cent of Catholics.
11. J. Bradley, *Ethnic and Religious Identity in Modern Scotland* (Aldershot: Avebury, 1985).
12. Even when we narrow the sample to just those Catholics who supported Celtic, we find the proportion claiming an Irish identity remained at 8 per cent, the same as for Catholics who didn't support a football team. A further investigation of those Catholics committed to Celtic by attending their matches 'nearly every week' shows that only two from twelve chose an Irish identity.

13. Major surveys in 1999, 2000 and 2001 contained a single-choice national identity question. Of the total 4,747 respondents, 0.6 per cent chose Irish and 0.4 per
cent chose Northern Irish, numbers so small that they almost certainly represent
actual Irish and Ulster people resident in Scotland rather than Scots with a grievance. I am grateful to David McCrone of Edinburgh University for supplying
these data.

14. E. Buie, 'Irish feel forced to hide roots', *The Herald*, 11 April 2001. The story
was based on quotations from Joseph Bradley. On the subject of hiding identity,
it is worth reporting that in at least one case the fact that a secondary school was
readily identifiable as Roman Catholic was the Church's choice. Because the state
secondary school in Motherwell in the 1930s did not have the word 'Motherwell'
in its name (it was Dalziel High School) the inspectors recorded the name of the
then Higher Grade Catholic school simply as 'Motherwell Higher Grade School'
on leaving certificates. The Director of Education asked for 'RC' to be included
and the reply was that RC was only used when there was a chance of confusion.
The Director consulted the Church authorities who suggested 'Our Lady's High
School' and thus turned down a chance to allow their pupils to disguise their religion. I am grateful to Lindsay Paterson of Edinburgh University for this historical
snippet.

15. On attitudes to Scots nationalism in the 1970s, see J. Kellas, *The Scottish Political
System* (Cambridge: Cambridge University Press, 1975), pp. 116–42. On the
1930s, see J. Brand, *The National Movement in Scotland* (London: Routledge and
Kegan Paul, 1978), p. 213.

16. For a detailed account of Cardinal Winning's shifting relations with the Labour
party and the SNP, see S. McGinty, *This Turbulent Priest: the Life of Cardinal
Winning* (London: HarperCollins, 2003), Ch. 17.

17. These calculations used nominal religious labels. The analysis was repeated for
only those who attended church regularly. Churchgoing Catholics were much
more likely to vote Labour (65 per cent) than nominal Catholics, nominal
Protestants and churchgoing Protestants (35, 36 and 37 per cent respectively). And
churchgoing Catholics were distinctive in their support for Labour irrespective of
their class background. On the other side of the divide, middle-class churchgoing
Protestants were most likely to support the Conservative party but this was still a
preference of only 23 per cent.

18. The 2011 figure comes from the Scottish Election Survey 2011 and was kindly
supplied by James Mitchell of the University of Strathclyde. The rest are from
D. McCrone, 'Catholics in Scotland: a sociological view', in G. Hand and
A. Morton (eds), *Catholicism and the Future of Scotland* (Edinburgh: Centre for
Theology and Public Issues, University of Edinburgh, 1997), pp. 12–29.

19. Quoted in E. Campion, *Rockchoppers: Growing Up Catholic in Australia*
(Harmondsworth: Penguin, 1982), p. 26.

20. J. Mclean, 'Church row places future of ecumenical pilgrimage at risk', *The
Herald*, 12 April 1998.

21. *The Scotsman*, 16 January 1999. It is possible to view Winning's speech as the Catholic equivalent of Donald Findlay QC singing *The Sash* to a private gathering of Rangers fans: an action intended to show membership of a community to other members of that community with the actual words spoken being merely 'form'. However, Winning repeated them for public consumption.

22. *The Herald*, 27 January 2001.

23. P. Brierley, *UK Religious Trends No. 2, 2000–2001* (London: Christian Research, 1999), Table 8.6.4.

24. P. Brierley, *Turning the Tide: The Challenge Ahead. Report of the 2002 Scottish Church Census* (London: Christian Research, 2003), pp. 16–17.

25. To be precise, 2,486 to 1,729; S. McNab, 'Figures reveal more humanist than Catholic weddings in Scotland', *The Scotsman*, 3 August 2012.

26. http://www.blairsaberdeen.co.uk/History.html. For the views of a seminarian who resented the cold discipline, see R. Hutchinson, *Father Allen: the Life and Legacy of a Hebridean Priest* (Edinburgh: Birlinn, 2010).

27. T. Gallagher, *Glasgow: the Uneasy Peace* (Manchester: Manchester University Press, 1987), p. 238.

28. M. Tierney, 'A tough career?', *Herald Magazine*, 14 June 2003, p. 10.

29. *Sunday Herald*, 10 June 2002.

30. For reflections on this change, see the speech of Bishop Phillip Tartaglia: http://rcdop.org.uk/index.php/index.php?option=com_content&view=article&id=307%3Aaddress-to-the-council-of-priests-of-the-diocese-of-dunkeld-&Itemid=55.

31. C. Field, '"The haemorrhage of faith?" Opinion polls as sources for religious practices, beliefs and attitudes in Scotland since the 1970s', *Journal of Contemporary Religion* 16 (2001), p. 166.

32. C. G. Brown, 'Religion and secularisation', in A. Dickson and J. H. Treble (eds), *People and Society in Scotland, Vol. 3* (Edinburgh: John Donald, 1992), p. 62.

33. M. Anderson, 'Population and family life', in A. Dickson and J. H. Treble (eds), *People and Society in Scotland, Vol. 3* (Edinburgh: John Donald, 1992), p. 36.

34. A. McIvor, 'Gender apartheid? Women in Scottish society', in T. M. Devine and Richard J. Finlay (eds), *Scotland in the 20th Century* (Edinburgh: Edinburgh University Press, 1996), p. 191.

35. http://www.guardian.co.uk/news/datablog/2011/may/26/foreign-born-uk-population#zoomed-picture.

36. I am grateful to my colleague Dr Marta Trzebiatowska for this information.

37. J. Devine, '2008 Gonzaga lecture'; http://www.catholicculture.org/culture/library/view.cfm?recnum=8079.

38. M. Monk, *Awful Disclosures of Maria Monk and the Hotel Dieu Monastery of Montreal* (New York: Arno Press: 1977).

39. *Daily Express*, 10 December 1994.

40. *The Herald*, 30 June 1995.

41. *Sunday Herald*, 23 July 2000.

42. R. Wright, *Feet of Clay* (London: HarperCollins, 1999), pp. 159–60. For the story

from Cardinal Winning's point of view, see McGinty, *This Turbulent Priest*, Ch. 16.
43. *Daily Record*, 6 March 2006.
44. *Sunday Mail*, 27 January 2008.
45. *Sunday Mail*, 24 February 2008.
46. *The Sun*, 18 July 2007.
47. Hutchinson, *Father Allen*, p. 57.
48. This and subsequent quotations are from B. Campbell, 'Sisters of no mercy', *Guardian*, 12 April 2003; http://www.guardian.co.uk/world/2003/apr/12/religion.childprotection.
49. Quoted by Campbell, 'Sisters of no mercy'. Winning took the same view of the mother of Bishop Wright's child; McGinty, *This Turbulent Priest*, p. 321.
50. *Daily Telegraph*, 19 June 2013; http://www.telegraph.co.uk/news/uknews/scotland/9887559/Cardinals-resignation-worst-crisis-since-Reformation.html.
51. One small opinion poll conducted in March 2013 for the *Sunday Times* asked if O'Brien's resignation made respondents more or less likely to attend church. Three-quarters said it would make no difference but 22 per cent said it made them less likely to attend; http://www.panelbase.com/news/Religionforpublication020313.pdf.

5

SCOTLAND ORANGE AND PROTESTANT

The Mound in Edinburgh is a busy thoroughfare: the middle of the three routes from the higher south side of the city to Princes Street and then down to the New Town, Leith and the Firth of Forth. Its most prominent building is the spired New College, the main theology hall of the Church of Scotland, and behind it, the General Assembly meeting hall. In 1982 the courtyard of New College was the setting for an historic meeting when leaders of the Church of Scotland, under the eyes of a statue of John Knox, greeted Pope John Paul II on the first papal visit to Scotland. Outside and behind a line of policemen, two famous Protestants protested. One was Ian Paisley, founder of the Free Presbyterian Church of Ulster and leader of the Ulster Democratic Unionist party. The other was the man habitually described as 'Scotland's Ian Paisley': Pastor Jack Glass. Paisley eventually led his party to victory in Northern Ireland and twenty-five years after his Mound protest took office as First Minister of a devolved assembly. Jack Glass continued to lead his tiny band of followers in street protests and remained a figure of fun for the Scottish press until his death in 2004.

I am not sure that he was playing at the Mound that day – his health had been poor – but had Alan Cameron been busking with his bagpipes at his usual spot, his presence would have perfected the symbolism of the Pope's visit to New College, for it encapsulated the main themes of this chapter's discussion of Protestantism in Scotland. Paisley's career was built on the enduring fusion of the political and the religious in Northern Ireland, while Jack Glass's unpopularity represented its demise in Scotland. The New College yard was selected because protestors could be easily excluded but, as it was originally the Free Church's college, the site was also a powerful symbol of ecumenical rapprochement. What Alan Cameron symbolised was the political impotence of the Orange Order, for he would have been better known to some elderly

Scots as Allan G. Hasson, one of the last Church of Scotland ministers to hold high office in the post-1945 Order.

This chapter will consider Scotland's Protestantism in its ethnic form: a fusion of the religious and the political. The next chapter will consider the fortunes of the Church of Scotland after that bond had dissolved.

Unionist Family Resemblances

From their late nineteenth-century opposition to Irish Home Rule (and especially after the creation of the Northern Ireland Parliament in 1921), the Protestants of Ulster formed a solid ethno-religious block. Community identity, religious affiliation and political programme were firmly welded together. The Presbyterian Church in Northern Ireland was solidly unionist in its politics. The episcopal Church of Ireland was in a more awkward position because it had congregations on both sides of the border but its Ulster congregations were firmly unionist. The Ulster Unionist party had the support of almost all Protestants in Northern Ireland and its leading figures were also prominent in the two churches. And the ecclesiastical and the political were linked through the Orange Order.

The Orange Order is a Protestant fraternal organisation based in Northern Ireland. Founded in 1796 near the village of Loughgall in County Armagh, it takes its name from William of Orange, the Dutch-born Protestant King of England, Ireland and Scotland, who defeated the army of Catholic James II at the Battle of the Boyne in 1690. It is committed to promoting evangelical Protestantism, which it claims to be the foundation of democracy. It has always had a large working-class membership and at times its capacity to mobilise popular violence (it would say 'to defend its people against Irish aggression') has made the establishment wary of it, but its influence was such that every leading Ulster unionist politician was a member. Its religious purpose is signified not only in its oaths and rituals (such as beginning lodge meetings with prayers and Bible readings) but also in the office of chaplain, which exists at every level of the structure, from the private lodges upwards. Until the Troubles in the late 1960s many Orange chaplains were Presbyterian or Church of Ireland clergy. Outside the main institutions of Ulster Protestantism were a number of populist 'ginger groups' dedicated to ensuring that the main bodies did not compromise their Protestant and unionist principles: it was from this fringe that Paisley built his successful church and party.

Scotland in the twentieth century resembled Northern Ireland in having a unionist party, a popular Protestant church, a large Orange Order and a number of fringe ginger groups ready to denounce any failure to promote the interests of Protestantism and Protestants but the similarity is only superficial. The Church of Scotland was far from uniformly unionist. The part that had been the Free Church until the 1929 merger had strong ties to the Liberal party which (especially in rural areas) continued after the Liberal party split over Ireland and its unionist wing joined the Tories to form the Scottish Conservative and Unionist party. The Orange Order was popular in the urban lowlands. It appealed because the Orange Lodges gave men who lived a hard and unrewarding life, often new to the impersonality of the town and the factory, a place in which they could develop their sense of self-worth and self-confidence. Those who were masters of very little found reward in becoming Worshipful Masters of their lodges. But its ties with the churches were much weaker than in Northern Ireland: its Scottish members were less likely to be churchgoers than their Ulster counterparts and far fewer chaplains were ministers of the Church of Scotland. It also had far less elite political support. Every Ulster prime minister until the election of Terence O'Neill in 1963 was an enthusiastic Orangeman and, though its rougher elements offended his Anglicised instincts, even he joined the Order when he decided on a career in politics. In Scotland the Order could claim a few Unionist grandees in the 1920s but influence on the Conservative and Unionist party was constrained by the Scots being only a small part of the national Conservative party. For example, Scots Tories could not consistently oppose the state funding of Catholic schools because English Conservatives were all in favour of church (that is, Church of England) schools.

Despite the apparent similarities between Ulster and Scotland, Scottish support for the Ulster unionist cause was always muted. When Sir Edward Carson, the leader of Irish opposition to Irish Home Rule, came to speak in Glasgow in October 1912, only 8,000 turned out to hear him. Liverpool, in contrast, managed to produce a crowd three times that size at 7.00 am on a Sunday morning.[1] The Glasgow Presbytery of the Church of Scotland passed a motion condemning Home Rule but it was left to an independent evangelical minister originally from Ulster, James McBurney Brisby, to give clerical legitimation to the Scottish branches of the Ulster Volunteer Force (UVF).[2] The Orange Order in Scotland could only raise seven UVF units, totalling no more than a thousand men.

The onset in 1914 of the Great War – people did not know then that it would be the 'First' world war – turned attention from Ireland but the Sinn Fein Easter Rising in Dublin in 1916 provoked a minor revival of anti-Irish sentiment, ably voiced by the character of Andrew Amos, the disillusioned Border radical in John Buchan's *Mr Standfast*, whose description of Ulster perfectly captures the grudging sense of Presbyterian common identity.

Glasgow's stinkin' nowadays with two things, money and Irish. I mind the day when I followed Mr Gladstone's Home Rule policy, and used to threep about the noble, generous, warmhearted sister nation held in a foreign bondage. My Goad! I'm not speakin' about Ulster, which is a dour, ill-natured den, but our own folk all the same.

But the men that will not do a hand's turn to help the war and take the chance of our necessities to set up a bawbee rebellion are hateful to Goad and man.[3]

As a Presbyterian Protestant church, the Kirk was theoretically opposed to Roman Catholicism but it is a mark of how popular racial thinking then was that its opposition to the Irish in the 1920s was framed in terms of race rather than religion. John White took great pains to dissociate his campaign against Irish immigration from 'petty' sectarianism. He told the 1927 General Assembly that:

They dealt with this very difficult, delicate, and important question entirely from the racial point of view. The religious factor did not enter the question at all ... Uncontrolled immigration was always a menace to a community, especially if it was to continue alongside the emigration of young and energetic native-born citizens.[4]

The Kirk's anti-Irish campaign began in 1922, against a background of rising unemployment, major advances by Labour in west central Scotland (aided by the urban Catholic vote) and the establishment of the Irish Free State. The spark for it came from Glasgow, where a small group of ministers had used anti-Catholic rhetoric to raise votes in elections to the education authority. Their leader, Duncan Cameron of Kilsyth, told the General Assembly that:

Roman Catholics of Irish origin ... were not only alien to Scots in religion; they were also alien in race. They had come to Scotland to take jobs from Scottish workers, to exploit Scotland's welfare resources and to stir labour unrest ... The presence of the Irish Catholic aliens, he prophesied, would soon bring racial and sectarian warfare to Scotland.[5]

Many Assembly members doubted the wisdom of such rhetoric and the matter was remitted for further consideration only on the deciding vote of the Moderator. The next year the Church and Nation Committee submitted its report, entitled *The Menace of the Irish Race to our Scottish Nationality*. Of Irish Catholic migrants and their descendants, it said:

They cannot be assimilated and absorbed into the Scottish race. They remain a people by themselves, segregated by reason of their race, their customs, their traditions and above all by their loyalty to their Church, and are gradually and inevitably dividing Scotland, racially, socially and ecclesiastically.[6]

The report listed a number of religious complaints (such as the state funding of Catholic schools, the Church's attitude to mixed marriages and the vague Vatican 'scheming') but its main point was that countries divided on racial lines could never prosper. Indeed, dire consequences were predicted:

Already there is a bitter feeling among the Scottish working classes against the Irish intruders. As the latter increases, and the Scottish people realise the seriousness of the menace to their own racial supremacy in their native land, this bitterness will develop into a race antagonism which will have disastrous consequences for Scotland.[7]

In 1928 the churchmen finally won an opportunity to present their case to the Conservative government: a delegation was granted less than an hour with Home Secretary William Joynson-Hicks and Scottish Secretary Sir John Gilmour, and was firmly rebuffed. To mollify them, they were promised 'the fullest inquiry' into the legal position of recent Irish migrants who became destitute but they were also handed government statistics that contradicted their case that the indigent Irish were a drain on the public purse. Despite being a Unionist MP and a member of the Orange Order's Grand Lodge, Gilmour told the petitioners that, even if it had been the problem they asserted, migration from the Irish Free State could not be prevented because it was not a foreign country: it was part of the British Empire![8]

With the government hostile, the campaigners changed tack. The 1930 General Assembly decided to appeal 'to the patriotism of their Scottish labour employers' to instigate an economic barrier against 'Irish' labour.[9] The new strategy quickly flopped. Edinburgh's *Scotsman* and the *Glasgow Herald* were cool towards the campaign. Specific assertions were shown to be false. For example, a senior churchman claimed that Irish foremen at Peterhead harbour works were discriminating in favour of their countrymen. Investigation found no Irish foremen and just two Irish-born workers in a labour force of nearly 400.[10] By the mid-1930s the campaign was without credibility, and a heated debate at the 1935 General Assembly effectively killed it off. One minister asked:

Was it worthy of the Church of Scotland, at a time when materialism was rampant and sheer paganism not only beyond the Rhine [a reference to the rise of the Nazis] but in their own midst, that they should engage in that agitation against a church which, however they deplored her errors, did stand for spiritual things, and on the side of Christ?[11]

The campaign against the Irish had little political purchase. The unionists who liked it lacked influence. Unionists with influence did not like it.[12] White's campaign found favour only on the unruly Protestant fringe and that association had the unintended but predictable consequence of discrediting the fusion of religion and politics.

Ratcliffe and the Scottish Protestant League

Alexander Ratcliffe (1888–1947) was a Leith railway clerk and lay preacher who founded the Scottish Protestant League (SPL) in 1920 as a 'new aggressive

Protestant movement' which intended to oppose 'spiritualism, Christian Science, and various other systems of anti-Scriptural teaching [and] Roman Catholic Sinn Fein'.[13] The SPL was actually concerned almost exclusively with classic No Popery themes: the evils of the confessional, convent horror stories, the power and secrecy of the Jesuits, and priestly immorality. In 1925 Ratcliffe manufactured a localised controversy over Catholic schools, on the back of which he was elected to the Edinburgh Education Authority. A lone ideologue on a body committed to the dull business of administering the city's schools, his time on the authority was unproductive. Even the elected representatives who were Kirk clergy and members of the Orange Order failed to support his attempts to make trouble.

In 1930 Ratcliffe moved the SPL to Glasgow where it quickly gained momentum. In the 1931 municipal election, Ratcliffe took Dennistoun from the Moderates (as the Conservatives were known in local government) and a former Communist SPL member took Dalmarnock from Labour. The SPL entered Glasgow politics at a time of ideological flux. With the right unpopular and the left divided three ways, the League benefited from a complex mix of grievance and anxiety in the Glasgow electorate, none of it connected to the League's primary purpose. After taking another seat in 1932, the SPL peaked in 1933, winning four more seats and 22 per cent of the poll. And then it disintegrated. As issues that could be given a sectarian slant were rare in the council's business, the seven SPL councillors often voted on different sides and few liked Ratcliffe's autocratic manner. All seven seats were lost at their first defence. That was the end of electoral Protestantism in Glasgow: the SPL stood no candidates in 1935 and in 1937 Ratcliffe polled weakly in Camphill ward. Far from advancing the Protestant cause, the League's flash-in-the-pan weakened the right's ability to resist an increasingly united Labour vote. Patrick Dollan took control of Glasgow in 1933 and for the rest of the century Glasgow was a one-party state.

Ratcliffe's defeat shows how unpopular extremism, by polarising choice, inadvertently encourages moderation. Knowing his party was in trouble, Ratcliffe agreed an electoral pact with the Moderates: a clear run against Labour in some wards (in particular Ratcliffe's Dennistoun) in return for not opposing Moderates elsewhere.[14] The Moderates got a bargain: Ratcliffe could produce only five candidates and three were in safe Labour wards where they had poor prospects. There was worse. Matthew Armstrong, a long-standing Moderate councillor with Orange connections, who had lost his seat in 1933 largely because of the SPL, refused to accept the pact and stood in Dennistoun as an independent. Labour, Independent Labour and Communist candidates withdrew and recommended that their supporters back Armstrong. The Orange Order finished off Ratcliffe. It could not alienate its base by denying his 'Protestant' credentials but it achieved the same end by proclaiming that both Armstrong and Ratcliffe were acceptably Orange, and that despite

Armstrong being quietly backed by the Catholic Union. Armstrong won handsomely and was accepted back into the Moderate fold with a haste which suggests that many Moderates had been embarrassed by their brief flirtation with extremism. Just three years after it began, Ratcliffe's political career ended. He continued with the Sunday services for a number of years before drifting into fascism and anti-Semitism, just as Britain went to war with Germany and Italy. He died virtually unknown in 1947.

John Cormack and Protestant Action

As one sun set in the west, another rose in the east. John Cormack (1894–1978) had been a League activist in the late 1920s, and had been a leading figure in the Edinburgh Protestant Society, the anti-Ratcliffe organisation which emerged after the League moved to Glasgow. Cormack had been raised as an independent Baptist and he became an accomplished outdoor speaker. In 1934 he was elected in North Leith, one of the poorest wards in the city, as a Protestant Action Society (PAS) candidate. Accused of having no policies on the issues affecting local people, Cormack responded bullishly:

> We have only one 'plank'. It is a comprehensive one. Wherever in the political life of our country, municipal or national, the Papist beast shows its head we must crush it or, at least, keep it in subjection. Our party is composed of Protestants of every political party who want Protestantism to have its rightful place in our country's jurisdiction, in other words, to defend our Protestant faith.[15]

That defence involved the abolition of Catholic state schools, expulsion of Catholic religious orders and the purging of Catholics from the armed services and judiciary.

In 1935 eight Protestant candidates won 23 per cent of the Edinburgh polls but only one seat: South Leith. The next year PAS pushed Labour into third place and won six more seats. However, like Ratcliffe, Cormack struggled to maintain party discipline. The absence from council business of issues on which people united only by a dislike for Popery could agree meant internal dissension. In 1937 PAS contested thirteen wards but the Moderates strategically withdrew from some and PAS, unable to beat Labour in straight fights, was confined to one win. In 1938 Cormack returned to the council for South Leith, but elsewhere the movement polled poorly and the political career of the PAS ended as rapidly as it had begun.

To some degree PAS occupied the same political space as the SPL in Glasgow. Both augmented anti-Catholicism with an economic populism designed to exploit discontent over the ruling Moderates and fear over an unproven labour movement. But in Glasgow the SPL faced a Moderate administration buckling under a Labour advance. In Edinburgh the Moderate

majority was strong and the left weak. In Glasgow the SPL did best in the affluent southern suburbs. In Edinburgh, nine of Protestant Action's ten victories
were in solidly working-class wards. That seven of them were in Leith suggests
that Cormack's rise owed more to local grievance over the effects of Leith's
recent incorporation into the city of Edinburgh than to his anti-Catholicism.[16]

What briefly brought Cormack to wider attention was a summer of public
disturbances. The Catholic Church planned to hold a Eucharistic Congress in
1935. Cormack promised a 'real smash up' if the city council granted an official
reception to the Catholic Young Men's Society (CYMS). PAS demonstrations
were large and rowdy: around 10,000 gathered for the CYMS protest and later
for the main anti-Congress demonstration. Many were drawn by curiosity and
some by a desire to see some trouble but it was still a formidable turnout.

Archbishop Joseph McDonald wrote to Prime Minister Stanley Baldwin
to protest that: 'Priests were savagely assailed, elderly women attacked and
kicked, bus-loads of children mercilessly stoned and inoffensive citizens abused
and assailed in a manner that is almost unbelievable in any civilised country
today'.[17] That depiction has been rather uncritically accepted.[18] One author
repeats the sentimental view when he says, 'John White's Kirk gave its blessing to the Protestant mob that stoned and bottled the buses carrying women
and children to the Eucharistic Congress in Canaan Lane'.[19] Contemporary
records suggest something less dramatic. The protests were noisy rather than
violent. For example, after a picket of the second day of the Congress, only
nine men were convicted and then only for minor public order offences. The
following day a very large crowd gathered outside St Andrew's Priory in
Morningside. Several Catholic buses were stoned but only four people were
arrested.

The violence of the PAS protests was exaggerated because Edinburgh was
less used than Glasgow to sectarian controversy. In McDonald's view, the
offence of the protests was magnified by an inadequately sympathetic response
from the authorities.[20] These concerns were echoed in a modern biography of
Cormack: 'The fact that no major Edinburgh institution such as the Kirk, the
police, or the press took a major stand against Cormack or consistently sought
to deflect public opinion away from him . . . causes apprehension even at a
distance of fifty years'.[21] Actually all those institutions were consistent in their
hostility to the PAS. Mainstream Protestants initially dismissed the militants as
unchurched and hence unworthy of attention, but after the Canaan Lane demonstrations they were quick to express their disdain. The Kirk's most senior
official denounced the PAS in *Life & Work* in September 1935. The Edinburgh
Presbytery condemned 'all methods of violence, all interference with personal
freedom, and every word and action which expressed the spirit of hatred' as
'fundamentally unchristian'.[22] Local newspapers consistently editorialised
against Cormack. The courts punished PAS demonstrators harshly while
treating leniently Catholics provoked into retaliation.[23] And, as the absence of

serious violence shows, the police handled the militants skilfully. Edinburgh may have been slow to mobilise against the PAS but once roused it effectively isolated militant Protestantism and ensured that, although John Cormack retained his Leith council seat for many years, he did so as a local 'character' rather than as the leader of a political force.

The First and Last No-Popery MP

Precisely because his political career was insignificant, it is worth mentioning Hugh Ferguson. An auctioneer and scrap metal merchant, Ferguson was an Orangeman and an active member of the Plymouth Brethren: another militant who belonged to a small sect rather than to the Kirk. He sat on Lanarkshire council as an independent but enjoyed a moment in the spotlight because of a temporary rift between the Orange Order and the Unionist party hierarchy.

The Scots Orange Order wanted the Unionist party to accord it the influence enjoyed by its Ulster counterpart (which had seats on the Ulster Unionist party's ruling council). Instead it got two representatives on the Western Divisional Council. How little that was worth became clear in 1921 when the Scottish Unionists endorsed the creation of the Irish Free State. The Order quit its seats and announced the formation of an Orange and Protestant Party (OPP), although little came of it. The OPP's only election was in Motherwell in 1922 when its two candidates were the only ones not elected to the Lanarkshire Education Authority. In Westminster elections the same year, the Unionists withdrew their candidate from Motherwell to give a free run to the National Liberal (that is, a Liberal who was in favour of continuing Lloyd George's wartime alliance with the Conservatives).[24] Ferguson, standing with OPP support, came a good second to Labour, which won the seat largely because the Liberal vote split between a National and a 'Free' Liberal. The next year, being able to present himself as the most conservative candidate not in favour of a national coalition, Ferguson gained the seat with a 1,000 vote majority over the Labour incumbent.

The Orange Order now had Westminster representation but little good it did. Although he took the Unionist whip, Ferguson was isolated. He was treated as a figure of fun and denounced from his own benches as a 'common informer ... despised by everyone'.[25] His single parliamentary achievement was to persuade Lanarkshire's Chief Constable that a Catholic procession to the Carfin Grotto was in contravention of the 1829 Catholic Emancipation Act. Like every other Protestant triumph, this one back-fired because it led directly to the removal of most of the remaining Catholic disabilities through the virtually unopposed 1926 Catholic Relief Act.

By then Ferguson was no longer an MP, and the manner of his defeat is telling. Like Ratcliffe, he was ambushed. The Liberals and Unionists agreed to stand aside, leaving the 1924 election field as a straight fight between Ferguson and Labour. Labour's choice of candidate was inspired and it is a powerful reminder that not all Presbyterians were right-wing. James Barr was a well-known UFC minister whose occupation meant that, without obviously playing the religion card, he cut away much of Ferguson's appeal. Barr did so well that Motherwell bucked the trend: it was the only Scottish seat that Labour took from the Unionists in 1924. Ferguson's defeat spelled the end of the half-hearted OPP project. Both he and it slid into obscurity.

Assessing Militant Protestantism

The sudden rise and fall of militant Protestant parties tells us a great deal about anti-Irish and anti-Catholic sentiment in modern Scotland. The rise shows us that antipathy towards Irish Catholics was widespread in certain circles. The fall shows that the circles were small and the antipathy shallow. The shifting fortunes of the main parties created small gaps which the PAS and SPL could exploit, but local council business gave little opportunity to pursue a consistent sectarian line and so the Protestant councillors could not use their positions to build political capital or create enduring obligations among their electors. Those who voted PAS or SPL as a protest quickly returned to parties which represented rational economic interests.

Comparison with Northern Ireland is telling. The churches in Ulster could be consistently 'Protestant' in religion and in politics because the religious and political competition was 'Catholic'. For a brief period, resentment over Ireland's break with Britain and fears of the rising power of the labour movement created a climate in which a faction in the Kirk could create a similar combination of ethnic and religious identity. But the success of John White's cabal was short-lived. Labour continued to grow in popularity, and few in the establishment or the wider public were moved by lurid warnings of the Irish menace.

It is easy to imagine the sort of support which would have helped and which was common in Ulster. Sir John Cargill, grandson of the founder of Burmah Oil, was a senior figure in the Unionist Association who sat on the board of Glasgow Rangers and sponsored the right-wing Economic League, but he gave Ratcliffe a wide berth. Sir Charles Cleland was a leading Unionist and Presbyterian. We may safely suppose he was privately hostile to Roman Catholicism and to Irish nationalist politics but as convenor of the Glasgow Education Authority he worked hard to improve Catholic schooling and ensured the smooth transition when Catholic schools were brought into the system under the terms of the 1918 Education Act.

We have already seen the failure of Sir John Gilmour to back the Kirk's anti-Irish campaign. Other leading Orangemen were also signally absent. Colonel Douglas MacInnes-Shaw, Grand Master of the Order in Scotland from 1924 to 1946, was born to local politics. His father was a Lord Provost of Glasgow and he served on Glasgow and Ayrshire councils. He was a successful business-man and proud soldier. He was awarded a Distinguished Service Order for bravery during the First World War, remained involved in the Territorial Army and returned to command a regiment in the Second World War. He stood for parliament as a Unionist candidate a number of times and was instrumental in bringing disaffected Liberals into the Unionist party. In the 1950s he was the convenor of Ayrshire County Council. MacInnes-Shaw was precisely the sort of person who would have added respectability to the militant Protestants. He conspicuously declined to be involved. Typical of Scottish Unionist grandees was Colonel Sir Thomas Moore, the MP for Ayr in the late 1920s: on the same day he opened a Catholic fund-raising bazaar in the town hall and addressed an Orange rally in Maybole.[26]

Anti-Catholicism in Scotland is often exaggerated because commentators note the prominence of short-lived anti-Catholic parties and the Church of Scotland's anti-Irish campaign and suppose the two were twin peaks of a submerged iceberg of ethno-religious Protestantism. In Ulster they would have been; in Scotland they were not. The difference can be seen in the relative size of the Orange Order. In the 1920s about a third of adult men in Fermanagh, Tyrone and Monaghan were Orangemen. In Scotland membership has rarely been above 1 per cent of adult males; in its Clydeside heartlands at its highest it was barely 2 per cent.[27] As well as being less popular than its Ulster sister, the Orange Order in Scotland was confined to a narrow class fragment that was left behind by changes in the economy. In the nineteenth century the typical Orangeman was socially very similar to the typical Scot. By 1991 Orangemen were unusual in having failed to benefit from the general change in class structure which had seen white-collar work displace manual labour.

As well as losing social status, the Order lost religious legitimation.[28] In the early 1950s Allan G. Hasson was the popular minister of the Church of Scotland parish of Bonhill, in the strongly Orange Vale of Leven. He helped found *The Vigilant* as a vocally anti-Catholic magazine and became its editor in 1955. Within the Church he was active in opposing the 'Bishops in Presbytery' scheme discussed in detail in the next chapter. A dynamic public speaker and attractive personality, he rose rapidly through the ranks of the Order and in 1958 was elected Grand Master. His short rule was not a success. He fell out with the Ulster leadership over what he later presented as principled opposition to anti-Catholic discrimination but which was actually just rudeness to Ulster Orange grandees who viewed him as a bumptious upstart. Suspecting that Hasson had been playing fast and loose with the Order's finances, his Scottish colleagues froze the Order's accounts. Hasson had himself admitted to the Royal Crichton mental hospital in Dumfries for three months and then fled to Canada.[29] A decade later he returned to Scotland to face fraud charges. He was initially convicted but the verdict was overturned on appeal. He was employed for a while as a social worker by the Church of Scotland but was again charged with embezzlement. This time charges were dropped. He was again charged with fraud in 1982, this time while selling double glazing for Paddy Meehan, one of Scotland's most celebrated minor criminals. He ended his career as a busker, playing the pipes for tourists in Edinburgh's city centre.

We can only guess what effect Hasson's rise and fall had on the attitudes of Kirk clergy to the Orange Order but we know that few followed him. In the 1970s 'little more than a dozen clergymen remained Orangemen compared to several hundred in Northern Ireland'.[30] The minister of Blackburn in West Lothian, J. Arnold Fletcher, was editor of *The Vigilant* in the late 1960s and Senior Grand Lodge Chaplain until his death in 2000. Ian Meredith, who was active in the Order at the end of the twentieth century, was a Kirk minister but defected to the Episcopalians. Gordon McCracken, a Kirk minister who was himself Grand Chaplain until 1998, when he resigned over the Order's involvement in violence at Drumcree in Northern Ireland, recalls four or five other ministers who were Orangemen in his time, but after Hasson most of the few clergy who supported the Order were Baptist, Congregational, United Free or Salvation Army.[31]

Another sign of the Order's alienation from the Kirk is the establishment of its own church: the Glasgow Evangelical Church in Cathedral Square. In the first half of the twentieth century, when a sufficient number of Orangemen were still churchgoers, every lodge had an annual church parade to their local parish church. By the 1970s many parish ministers were declining to provide this office; hence the purchase of its own facility and the employment of a salaried minister to officiate there. So what little religion remains in the Order no longer links it to the main body of Scottish Protestants.

When a movement's people and the supposed enemy are both defined by religion, the endorsement of the major churches is vital and it was freely given in Ulster. The very few clergymen who had any association with Cormack or Ratcliffe were marginal figures. Only three clergymen supported Cormack. Percival Prescott was a former Seventh Day Adventist preacher who led a tiny independent congregation. James Trainer served as a locum with the Hermitage UFC in Leith for less than a year and there is no trace of him being ordained or inducted into any major denomination. George Goodman was a minister of the UFC who served as a student pastor in Leith in 1933 before moving to Dysart in 1936.

Ratcliffe's promotional pamphlet *All About Him! By Those Who Know Him* asserts that 'The League is supported by Protestant clergymen of all Protestant denominations'. It wasn't. The only minister who supported Ratcliffe was Frederick Watson, an elderly Methodist from the north-east of England who became minister of Bellshill in 1931. As an incomer, he had no notion of the significance of what he was endorsing and quit as soon as he gained some.

The Impact of the Troubles

To move forward to the early 1970s breaks the chronology but it maintains thematic continuity because reaction to the violence in Northern Ireland shows the way in which unpopular extremism encourages moderation. Any residual sympathy for politically radical Protestantism was metaphorically killed off by the real killings in Ulster. Despite the strong family ties between Scotland and Ulster, the Troubles had only feint echoes in Scotland and the main consequence was to reinforce the view that any religion taken too seriously was dangerous.

There was rhetoric and posturing. In 1971, when it seemed that Northern Ireland was on the verge of civil war, John Adam, Grand Secretary of the Orange Order, toured Orange halls and invited men with army experience to volunteer to fight in Ulster. The idea was dropped as quickly as it was raised and no one actually went. A very few working-class Protestants joined loyalist paramilitary organisations but their contribution to the war in Ulster was slight. Some weapons were collected and shipped to Ulster but they were often poor quality. The only time a Scottish group collected a decent consignment of arms – when a young gun shop assistant murdered his manager and sold seventeen rifles and handguns to the 'Supreme Commander' of the UDA in Scotland – they never made it to Belfast. They were transported ineptly around Scotland before coming to lie in a damp cellar where they stayed for sixteen months while all those involved were lifted by the police. The low esteem in which Scots held militant loyalists can be seen in the fortunes of their bosses. Those loyalist leaders in Belfast who were not deposed by their own fractious members enjoyed the respect of their small enclaves and lived a comfortable life, which here means a decent council house and a stationary caravan at one of the popular coast parks. The Scottish UDA boss, a minor Edinburgh hoodlum, ended his days destitute. When I interviewed him in the early 1980s he was living in a squalid bedsit off Easter Road. I sat on the only chair; he sat on the bed. When his prostitute girlfriend arrived with a paying customer we had to vacate the premises and finish the interview in his car.

The UVF, the smaller of the two main loyalist terror groups, had little more success in Scotland than the UDA. It was responsible for the only major terrorist incident in Scotland. In February 1979 explosions damaged two pubs with a largely Catholic clientele: the Old Barn in Calton and the Clelland Bar in the Gorbals. Nobody was seriously injured and the police quickly arrested the men responsible. They were members of the Bridgeton UVF who had previously distinguished themselves by accidentally damaging the local Apprentice Boys hall with unstable explosives they stored there.

By 1979 Ulster loyalist terror had disabused Scots Orangemen of the sentimental attachments that eight years earlier had led Adam to propose an 'expeditionary force' for Ulster. The Order very clearly stated its rejection of paramilitary activity. Grand Secretary David Bryce, commenting on a series of severe sentences for weapons offences, said:

> The sentences will be a warning to other people who think there is something roman- tic about obtaining arms. We in the Orange Order certainly do not condone violence nor do we condone the gathering of arms. There is no place in our organisation for people like those convicted or for anyone involved in paramilitary organisations.[32]

Very small groups of Orangemen periodically made militant noises. The papal visit of 1982 was the object of attention of one such grouping that called itself the Scottish Loyalists. At the time a leading member told me: 'We have plans to stop this visit. We will smash the Mass. We will destroy the Pope's visit. We have told them this: if the police try to stop us, we will fight them; if the police want blood on the streets, we will give it to them'. The visit went ahead with no discernible disruption. The Orange Order gradually developed an effective posture toward Northern Ireland that it maintained steadfastly until the creation of the current power-sharing government. It supported the political line of the Ulster Unionist party: nothing more. Any members convicted of serious crimes were expelled: in 1990 the Edinburgh 'Pride of Midlothian' lodge had its warrant lifted for refusing to expel two members accused of fundraising for loyalist paramilitaries.

Jack Glass

Jack Glass was born into a working-class family in Dalmarnock. Both parents were committed Christians and he was converted in a Salvation Army Sunday School.[33] Like Ratcliffe, Cormack and Ferguson, he lived his religious life outside the main Presbyterian churches. He regularly attended Baptist churches and during his national service became friendly with two brothers who had been influenced by Martyn Lloyd-Jones, the Welsh Calvinist who pastored the popular Westminster Chapel in London. They introduced him to the publications of the Banner of Truth Trust which specialised in reprint- ing the works of the great puritans and he returned to Glasgow looking for a church which combined the Calvinist stress on 'sovereign grace' (that is, we can do nothing to deserve salvation; it is a free gift from God to the elect) with adult (rather than child) baptism. He could not find it. Most Baptist churches were not Calvinist; the Presbyterian churches that were Calvinist practised infant baptism. He enrolled as a private student (as distinct from a candi- date for ordination) with the Free Church College in Edinburgh and in 1965 completed his diploma in theology.

Glass's first recruits were perfect representatives of fringe Protestantism: survivors from the Tent Hall (a mission founded after Dwight Moody's Glasgow crusades in the 1870s) who had been members of Ratcliffe's SPL in the 1930s. When the Glasgow Presbytery of the Church of Scotland refused to sell him a redundant church, a group of Americans bought it on his behalf. His distinctive theological position was expressed in its name: the Zion Sovereign Grace Evangelical Baptist Church. Although Glass shared much of the theology of the Free Church, he differed in worship style. While it rejected instrumental music and 'human composition' by singing only unaccompanied metrical psalms, Glass liked the lively and vigorous hymns and choruses of the Baptist and gospel tent traditions. While the Free Church was opposed to the Orange Order, he was a youth member. He was an early supporter of Ulster Protestant militancy. He had heard of Ian Paisley as a 'dynamic gospel preacher long before he was a well-known public figure' and invited him to speak at a gospel rally in 1965. The next year he accompanied Paisley on a trip to Rome to protest against Archbishop Ramsay, the head of the Church of England, meeting the Pope. When Paisley founded his Ulster Constitution Defence Committee (a forerunner of the later successful Democratic Unionist party), Glass followed suit by founding the Twentieth Century Reformation Movement, which he described as 'a political organisation influenced by religion'. Paisley won his first election in 1970. A few months later Glass stood in a general election for the Bridgeton seat. The Labour candidate was returned comfortably but Glass's total of 1,180 votes was not far behind the SNP.

It is common for ambitious ideologues to fall out and Glass soon added Paisley to the long list of people whom he 'dis-fellowshipped'. It is tempting to suppose that Glass was envious of Paisley's political successes but the ostensible reason was Paisley's friendship with the Bob Jones family of Greenville, South Carolina. Bob Jones had founded a liberal arts university and with due humility named it after himself. Although fundamentalist, Bob Jones University was not Calvinist and it had expelled some students for the vice of 'hyper-Calvinism'. Glass asked Paisley to renounce his ties with the Joneses; when Paisley declined, Glass broke his link.

Glass also renounced Orangeism. The issue here was another unpopular principle of fringe Protestantism: temperance. Ratcliffe had condemned working-class Protestants for their drinking and Glass's father had left the Order over its failure to make temperance a criterion for membership. What prompted Glass to take up the issue was the growth of Orange social clubs and the introduction of Sunday licences. The Order's justification for its involvement in the licensed trade was that de facto Orange clubs existed anyway and by bringing them into the Union of Orange Social Clubs the Order was better able to manage them and ensure that its reputation was not damaged by rowdiness. And they were an earner: breweries offered low-interest loans to Orange halls to improve their premises and the income went a long way to paying the overheads. When those clubs began to serve alcohol on a Sunday, they added the sin of Sabbath-breaking to that of intemperance and thus became no better than Catholics. Catholics are 'keeping the Lord's *half-day*. They keep the

Lord's day in the morning. Celebrate the Mass and then enjoy the pleasure of sin for the rest of the day. Now it's your Orangemen, your Protestants, and their social clubs, drinking away the Lord's Day'.

Glass became an extremely effective preacher. He was an attractive man, articulate and quick-witted and, in his own realm, a match for Billy Connolly, the Glasgow comedian whose shows he regularly picketed after Connolly presented a humorous skit on the Crucifixion. But he failed entirely to match the success of Ian Paisley. His church never grew beyond its original congregation and a small satellite pastored by his son-in-law. He remained in the public eye only because, as he put it, he was a Protestant who remembered to protest. In his obituary, Ron Ferguson, a liberal Presbyterian, wrote: 'I admired Jack's courage. He would go anywhere to protest about the Pope, Billy Connolly, the ecumenical movement, religious satires, sexually explicit movies, bad language and tolerance of gays. He was unafraid to stand up in any company and say his piece.'[34]

Although he never planned the shift, Glass's interests narrowed over his career. Northern Ireland was given up as a lost cause early. He lost faith in any notion of a 'Protestant people' beyond the confines of his tiny congregation and found solace in the classic pietist argument that his unpopularity proved his rectitude.

> Notice there are no queues waiting to get in this morning, because the glory of God has disappeared from Scotland. Our heritage has gone because of our sin and wickedness . . . This afternoon they'll be glued to their television screens. I can't see one Orangeman this morning in this church and yet a few weeks from now they'll be marching through the streets to defend their faith. What faith?[35]

Ulster Protestants were a majority in the Northern Ireland state but they were a minority on the island of Ireland and their threatened position (and the fact that their opponents were united by a competing religion) gave them good reason to remain loyal to their religious roots. With a certain amount of mental reservation, Paisley could switch between the religious and the political meanings of the term 'the Protestant people of Ulster'. Glass had no such luxury. The Conservative and Unionist party (which under the direction of Margaret Thatcher dropped the term 'Unionist' from its title) had no interest in promoting the notion of the Scots as a religio-ethnic block. The actions of a handful of loyalist terrorists made everyone reluctant to support militant Protestantism and the violence of the Troubles was widely interpreted as proof, not of the evils of Catholicism, but of what happens when you mix religion and politics. Too few Orangemen were churchgoing Christians and too many were fond of alcohol to maintain the idea that the Order was primarily promoting Christian principles. If Glass had wanted to overlook the Order's faults, his critics would have pressed him into consistency, but he needed little pressing. His critique of the Order was clear: 'I wonder how many Protestants read the Bible. They carry it on the Orange walk in cellophane at the front. I think it stays in cellophane. It's to keep the rain out, and to keep the Orangemen out as well!'[36]

Paisley's success in combining religion and politics for fifty years eventually brought him to a position where he had to separate the two fields. When he became First Minister he enthusiastically accepted the obligation to represent all the people of Northern Ireland, irrespective of religion. And when he proved slow to appreciate what that meant for his leadership of a separatist evangelical Protestant church, his church colleagues politely pressed him to stand down from his church offices. Jack Glass always hated being called 'Scotland's Ian Paisley', in part because he believed he was a more consistent Christian preacher, but also because he knew that it was precisely the Scottish environment that prevented him from attaining Paisley's success. In his last public statement, a BBC interview shortly before his death, he said:

> I love Glasgow but it's changed . . . There was a time in the past, in this city, when 2,000 people would crowd in on a Saturday night to hear the Word of God, but today you could be born in this city, live in this city, die in this city and never hear the Gospel . . . people have never found out the real Jack Glass, but all of the protest, the preaching, the all-nights of prayer and days of prayer over the years was to try and capture the soul of the city for Jesus Christ, but people have never seen me in that light.[37]

Conclusion

Like Chapter 3, this chapter has been concerned with the ways that social divisions and religious identities combine. The enduring conflict in Northern Ireland has given its Protestants reasons, additional to the intrinsic appeal of religious ideas, for loyalty to the faith that unites them and distinguishes them from their political opponents. For all the superficial similarities between the two settings, Protestantism in Scotland never achieved the Ulster synthesis. The political flux of the 1920s and 1930s allowed a few radical Protestant movements to flourish very briefly but the climate was never encouraging. We could explain Scotland's relatively easy accommodation of a large Catholic migrant minority by a combination of obstacles that prevented bigots widening the incipient divisions: the diversity of the Scottish churches prevented a united front; Scotland's internal cultural rift between highlands and lowlands prevented anti-Catholicism becoming a national concern; and Scotland's lack of political autonomy meant that the particular concerns of Scots were overridden by British agendas. That is all true but to stop there is to allow the false impression that most Scots were bigots who only accepted the Irish migrants because they were impotent to do otherwise. Every militant Protestant movement failed not just because the social and political structures hobbled them but also because anti-Catholic animus was never strong enough to overcome such obstacles. John White used his bureaucratic skills to manipulate elements of the Church of Scotland into supporting his mania but the General Assembly eventually voted against discrimination. What the next generation thought about his campaign against the Irish can be gauged from the fact that his biographer passes over that part of White's life.[38] The voters of Scotland's two main cities had ample opportunity to support anti-Catholic parties yet the SPL and PAS enjoyed their brief success in local politics only because the re-alignment of Scottish politics that would eventually crush them first created political spaces they could exploit.

The rise of authoritarian regimes across Europe in the inter-war years shows how economic depression and political instability can encourage the scapegoating of minorities and the promotion of the idea of a 'volk' united by a common creed. Many contemporaries feared that radical Protestantism might be Scotland's fascism, but it was not and any residual appeal was killed off by a menace to the Scottish race that put White's fears about the Irish in their proper context: the outbreak of war in 1939.

Notes

1. T. Gallagher, *Glasgow: the Uneasy Peace* (Manchester: Manchester University Press, 1987), p. 72.
2. Brisby was an Ulster émigré with an independent ministry based initially in Bridgeton. When his services became too popular for his church, he held Sunday services in the City Halls in Candleriggs. He had been elected to the Glasgow School Board in 1911 but with fewer votes than the UFC minister and future Labour MP for Motherwell, James Barr.
3. J. Buchan, *Mr Standfast* (London: Thomas Nelson and Sons, 1954), p. 86.
4. *The Times*, 31 May 1927.
5. S. J. Brown, '"Outside the Covenant": The Scottish Presbyterian churches and Irish immigration 1922–1938', *Innes Review* 42 (1991), pp. 19–20.
6. J. Burrowes, *Irish: the Remarkable Saga of a Nation and a City* (Edinburgh: Mainstream, 2003), p. 143.
7. Burrowes, *Irish*, p. 148.
8. D. Ritchie, 'The civil magistrate: the Scottish Office and the anti-Irish Campaign 1922–1929', *Innes Review* 63 (2012), pp. 48–76.
9. *The Scotsman*, 24 May 1930.
10. Brown, '"Outside the Covenant" ...', pp. 36–7.
11. Quoted in Brown, '"Outside the Covenant" ...', pp. 39–40.
12. For example, Walter Elliott, Tory MP for Kelvingrove and later Secretary of State for Scotland, backed Catholic demands for an enquiry into the Belfast disturbances of 1935. As agriculture minister he urged an accommodation with the newly

installed Dublin government of Éamon de Valera and was influential in preventing a trade war with the Irish Free State; see Gallagher, *Glasgow*, p. 149.

13. *Edinburgh Evening News*, 29 September 1920; *The Glasgow Herald*, 29 September 1920.

14. W. W. Knox, 'Religion and the Scottish labour movement c. 1900–39', *Journal of Contemporary History* 23 (1988), pp. 609–30.

15. *Evening News*, 12 October 1934.

16. M. Rosie, *The Sectarian Myth in Scotland: Of Bitter Memory and* Bigotry (London: Palgrave Macmillan, 2004), pp. 128–38.

17. J. Cooney, *Scotland and the Papacy: Pope John Paul II's Visit in Perspective* (Edinburgh: Paul Harris, 1982), p. 20.

18. T. Gallagher, *Edinburgh Divided: John Cormack and No Popery in Edinburgh in the 1930s* (Edinburgh: Polygon, 1987), p. 160.

19. H. Reid, *Outside Verdict: An Old Kirk in a New Scotland* (Edinburgh: Saint Andrew Press, 2002), p. 106.

20. *The Times*, 6 and 14 August 1935; *The Spectator*, 9 and 16 August 1935.

21. Gallagher, *Edinburgh Divided*, p. 187.

22. *Edinburgh Evening News*, 2 November 1935.

23. *Edinburgh Evening News*, 1 August 1935; 6 November 1935.

24. The 1920s National Liberals should not be confused with the 1930s party of the same name: in the 1930s the issue was support for Ramsay MacDonald's national coalition. The differences are ably explained on Wikipedia.

25. F. Blundell, *Hansard*, 191 HC Deb 5s: 238; 3 February 1926.

26. Gallagher, *Glasgow*, p. 148.

27. For thoroughly detailed accounts of the Orange Order in Scotland in the twentieth century, see E. Kaufmann, 'The Orange Order in Scotland since 1860: a social analysis', in M. J. Mitchell (ed.) *New Perspectives on the Irish in Scotland* (Edinburgh: Birlinn, 2009), pp. 159–90 and 'The Dynamics of Orangeism in Scotland: The Social Sources of Political Influence in a Large Fraternal Organization', *Social Science History* 30 (2006), pp. 263–93.

28. McFarland identifies twenty-seven (out of more than 1,000) Kirk clergy appearing on OO platforms between 1873 and 1900. She adds that only nine of the twenty-seven were members of the Order and three of them were originally Ulstermen; E. W. McFarland, *Protestants First: Orangeism in 19th Century Scotland* (Edinburgh: Edinburgh University Press, 1990), pp. 115–38.

29. Details of the strange life of Hasson can be found in S. Bruce, *No Pope of Rome: Militant Protestantism in Modern Scotland* (Edinburgh: Mainstream, 1985), pp. 152–66.

30. Kaufmann, 'Orange Order in Scotland'.

31. I am obliged to Gordon McCracken for this information.

32. *The Glasgow Herald*, 17 June 1979.

33. This section draws heavily on my *No Pope of Rome: Militant Protestantism in Modern Scotland* (Edinburgh: Mainstream, 1985), Ch. 8. Quotations without

cited sources are either from Glass's sermons or from my interviews with Glass in the early 1980s.

34. R. Ferguson, 'Pastor Jack Glass', *The Herald*, 26 February 2004, p. 20. I should add that, like Ferguson, I always found Glass personally charming and extremely helpful on the many occasions I met and interviewed him.

35. Bruce, *No Pope of Rome*, p. 202.

36. Bruce, *No Pope of Rome*, p. 202.

37. BBC, 'The devil and Jack Glass', 2003. Screened January 2004. The video can be view on the tribute website *Pastor Jack Glass*; http://www.pastorjackglass.com/video-footage.html.

38. A. Muir, *John White, C.H., D.D., LL.D* (London: Hodder and Stoughton, 1958).

CHAPTER

6

THE POST-WAR KIRK

Superficially the post-war Kirk was in better shape than it had been for 200 years. The return of the Seceders and the Free Church meant that the Kirk could now claim a third of adult Scots as members, which made it more of a national church than its much larger English counterpart. Fewer than half of England's Christians supported the Church of England: the Kirk could claim two-thirds of all Scottish church members.[1] The Beveridge report of 1942 had laid the foundations for a modern welfare state which would protect its citizens from cradle to grave and that faith in government ability to produce a better world gave the Labour party its victory in 1945. The immediate post-war period was a time of confidence in institutions and social planning that allowed the national church to claim a renewed salience. The churches also benefited from a very strong desire among the demobilised service men and women and their families to return to normal.

But there were troubling under-currents. For all the desire to return to normal, the war had changed many people. It is difficult to exaggerate the extent to which settlements and settled patterns of behaviour were disrupted by six years of a war which, one way or another, mobilised most of the population. In total, around 600,000 Scots men were involved in the armed forces, the vast majority of them being moved from their home cities, towns and villages and pressed into the company of comrades from very different social and religious backgrounds. Women were also mobilised in large numbers to serve in the Auxiliary Territorial Service, the Women's Auxiliary Air Force, the Women's Royal Navy Reserve and Queen Alexandra's nursing corp. Women enlisted in the Women's Land Army and the Women's Timber Corp to fill spaces left in agriculture by the military service of men.[2] In 1942 almost 20,000 women were serving full-time in Civil Defence, with six times that number employed part-time to act as air-raid wardens, messengers, drivers, clerks and telephonists. In addition, large numbers of single women and married women without children were conscripted into industrial production: for example, 13,000 young women were sent from the west of Scotland to work in factories in Coventry.[3]

Not all the women involved in war work moved from their homes and familiar surroundings. Especially in the cities, the main impact was a change of occupation rather than a change of scenery. But even this broadened cultural horizons as many women were thrown into close contact with people from different class, region and religious backgrounds. The temporary absence of fathers, husbands and brothers was matched by the temporary presence of other young men. English troops trained in the Scottish countryside. A naval base the size of a small town was constructed at Scapa Flow in Orkney. Airfields proliferated in the flat countryside of coastal regions. Hundreds of large country houses became hospitals and convalescent homes. In an atmosphere made slightly frantic by first the fear of invasion and then the mounting casualty toll, young women, many of them released from close parental supervision for the first time, fraternised with English, American, Polish, French and Czech servicemen in NAAFI canteens and at village hall dances.[4] One Land Girl explained how she met her future husband:

> I enjoyed Quarry Court – we had dances with everybody – Polish lads, army boys, RAF, invitations everywhere . . . we had great fun, it was wonderful . . . one night I said I'd like to go to the do with the Naval Air Corp but I was outvoted so we went to the Sergeant's Mess at East Fortune and that's where I met Alex.[5]

Another Land Girl noted that her service 'opened up a whole new world for me. The long-term effect of this was a wonderful escape from the very narrow life in which I had been brought up . . . I think I learned to value people in their own right'.[6] For many the war brought tragedy. For many it brought unprecedented emotional and sexual freedom. For most it brought dislocation. My father returned to Aberdeenshire after six years of war with a Bulgarian bride, whom he had 'liberated' from a displaced persons' camp in Bavaria. My father-in-law returned to Crieff after five years of suspended animation in German POW camps. Neither of them were the people they would have become without the war and that was true for most Scots who in 1945 settled to getting back to normal.

The social disruption had its physical counterpart in the German bombing of the cities and docks. On the nights of 13 and 14 March 1941, almost 500 German bombers attacked the munitions factories and shipyards of Clydeside. Over the two days 528 civilians were killed, over 617 were seriously injured and almost 50,000 people lost their homes. The ports of Leith, Dundee and Aberdeen were also targeted.

In brief, however strong the impulse to return to the status quo ante

September 1939, neither the people nor the places were unchanged and the pieces of the jigsaw would not go back into the same spaces.

Weakening Faith

While the Church of Scotland was an institutional poster boy for a return to 'normal but better', its more thoughtful leaders appreciated that its apparent strength disguised a serious weakening of the power of religion. The re-union of Scottish Presbyterianism was made possible by declining interest in what had divided it. Some of those principles were now obsolete: there was little point in arguing about the precise status of the state church when religion was patently now voluntary. But others were still relevant and the conservatives who rejected the mergers were not wrong to see them as evidence of 'spiritual declension'. Although he was later a strong supporter of the ecumenical movement, the influential Kirk minister Archie Craig believed that 'the movement towards Church Union is less a fruit of the spirit than a business more forced upon failing institutions by the antagonism of apathy around'.[7] There was certainly a perceptible decline in churchgoing. In 1950 it was probably half of what it had been a century earlier.[8] Very many of the 1950s parish entries in the *Third Statistical Account of Scotland* refer to recent declines in church attendance.

One sign of declining commitment was – outwith the highlands and islands – the end of sabbatarianism. Farmers faced particularly strong temptation to work on the Sabbath during hay-making and harvesting because a sunny day wasted could mean the difference between a good and a bad harvest. Describing a walk to church in the 1930s with his father and grandfather, David Cameron remembered: '"A fine hairst day", the men would say stoically one to the other, not daring to make it so'.[9] The true believer would not be tempted because he trusted in the Lord to reward his loyalty. It was those whose main reason for not taking advantage of a dry Sunday was respect for community standards who were the first to break with tradition. For decades now I have asked elderly acquaintances when their fathers first started to 'cart in' on a Sunday. For most of rural Aberdeenshire the war years, when food production was at a premium, marked the first cracks. Townspeople were not tempted to work. Scotland had no legal barrier to Sunday working equivalent to the England and Wales Shops Act of 1950 but custom severely restricted economic activity until the 1980s. But Scots, rural and urban, were increasingly seeing Sunday as a day for social visiting and for recreation. The thin end of the wedge was to follow church in the morning with some wholesome leisure pursuit. Of his Sundays as a child in rural Aberdeenshire in the 1950s, David Hay wrote that his mother 'was relatively relaxed about entertainment on the Sabbath though it was hardly outrageous . . . we often took a walk to the cemetery'.[10] Visiting relatives became a common way of spending Sunday afternoon. An Aberdeen child of the war noted: 'the end of the war seemed also to signal the end of the severe Calvinism as preached in our home – we went on car rides, we went on picnics, we could read anything we wanted to on a Sunday, everything became immeasurably light in approach and content'.[11]

A less visible but nonetheless major change was the decline of family prayers. Families often augmented church services with their own Sunday rituals. Describing her East Lothian childhood in the 1890s, one woman said:

> We had prayers night and morning. We'd sing a hymn. My mother had a harmonium. In the morning we sang a song, some verses of a psalm. Then we read the Old Testament and a sermon. The servants, the cook, horsemen and nurse all came in. We used to read the Bible together and they had to read it too, poor things . . . Then we knelt and Father said prayers.[12]

Speaking of his childhood thirty years later, an Aberdeenshire man remembered: 'There was a grace said every time before a meal. We said our prayers every night when we were young. On Sunday nights there was always a chapter of the Bible read'.[13] Differing degrees of piety produced family worship of differing length and complexity but in 1900 very many churchgoing families would have ended the day with some sort of communal prayer, and the saying of a serious 'grace' before meals was ubiquitous. By 1950 all but the most perfunctory family prayers were confined to the conservative Protestant sects.

Missions and Bishops

Tom Allan came to prominence in the late 1940s as a popular minister in North Kelvinside. He also became a popular BBC broadcaster, at one point being the leading missioner in a series of 'Radio Missions' intended to be used by local church groups as the focus for their own outreach work. The Church of Scotland appointed Allan as full-time leader of 'Tell Scotland', an evangelistic campaign deliberately designed not to imitate the big-name method of American tent crusades but instead to make mission a regular part of church life which relied on the laity.[14] A three-year plan, which was strongly supported by BBC Scotland and by all the major churches except the Roman Catholics, was devised but it was immediately disrupted by precisely the sort of mass evangelism it aimed to avoid: the announcement that the American Billy Graham was due in London in 1954.

The visiting tent crusade style of evangelism was familiar to older Scots from the missions led by the American evangelist Dwight Moody in 1873 and again a decade later, and many Presbyterians did not like it.[15] Some feared that the combination of large audiences, hell fire preaching and repeated exhortation to 'choose Christ now' produced hysteria and a false expectation of spiritual excitement that made ordinary church life seem dull once the circus

moved on. Conservative Presbyterians objected to the Arminian assumption
that anyone who asked would be saved. Liberal Presbyterians objected to the
simplistic gospel that was preached. Nonetheless Allan believed that Graham
could be incorporated in the overall Tell Scotland plan and in 1955 Graham
preached in Glasgow for six weeks.

It is difficult to exaggerate the attention that was given to the event. In a
country where some goods and foodstuffs were still rationed, the tall handsome Graham with his own teeth – a rarity for adult Scots – and his smart
clothes was newsworthy. Graham's career is said to have taken off when
William Randolph Hearst (the real-life model for the Orson Welles character
in *Citizen Kane*) instructed his newspapers to 'Puff Graham!' No such instruction was required for the Scottish press, which gave Graham all the attention
he could wish. He drew a 90,000 crowd to Hampden football stadium and
every night for the six weeks he addressed a full house at the Kelvin Hall. His
Good Friday address was broadcast on BBC radio to an audience second only
to that for the Coronation. All the major Scottish Protestant churches collaborated to support the mission by bussing in congregations and by providing
volunteers to counsel the converted at Kelvin Hall and other venues which
heard the services via landlines. One way or another probably two million
Scots heard Graham. Ian Watson was among those converted.

> I used to be a terrible swearer and drinker, just like any other fellow, and I told lies,
> stole and used God's name in vain. All that stopped when I converted. It wasn't until
> I heard Billy speak that I became conscious of the fact I was a sinner. I'd always gone
> to Sunday School and was a member of the Boys' Brigade, but I didn't think too
> much about it. My father was a publican and I worked in his bar. It was when I was
> in the RAF . . . that I started going to church more often . . . I soon started to feel a
> real presence of God, asked to join the church and was confirmed. I began to think
> more about God and so, when Billy came to Glasgow, I felt compelled to go and see
> him. It was a Saturday afternoon and I was meant to be working in my dad's pub
> that night. I started singing hymns in the choir and was amazed when Billy said that
> back home in the States a barman had asked him: 'Can I be a barman and still be a
> Christian?' His answer was no. Yet here was I, supposed to be working in the pub
> hours later. When he asked people to come forward, I went to the front. I'd been con-
> firmed into the Church of Scotland when I was in the RAF so he asked if I wanted a
> reaffirmation. I said, 'No, sir. It'll be a conversion'. I instantly felt a load off my back,
> as if the burden of sin had rolled off me. I called my father and told him I wouldn't
> be coming to work that night and he understood.[16]

Not everyone was so impressed. Many liberals found the frank playing
on the emotions distasteful. The son of a Kirk minister remembered: 'I came
away from its mass excitement profoundly disturbed, indeed repelled. Mother,
brought up around evangelical fervour, was, I think, relieved to find that I

reacted as I did. The Billy Graham type of preaching, that kind of service, Mother assured us, had not been Father's style'.[17]

It is difficult to be sure what difference the crusade made to the big picture. Only 2.2 per cent of those attending made 'decisions for Christ' or gave their names for further counselling, and most of those were young church attenders.[18] But the campaign could yet have had enduring effects: church members might have found their commitment deepened and hearing Graham (and, more importantly, working for the event) may have caused Christian parents to work harder on their children. After all, Ian Watson's son became a minister. Certainly church attendance in Glasgow rose slightly after the campaign. The year before it, 6.1 per cent of Glasgow's adult population typically attended Church of Scotland services. In 1955 that rose to 7.3 per cent before settling back to 6.8 per cent the year after Graham's visit.[19]

As part of its commitment to evangelise the country, the Church of Scotland entered talks with the Scottish Episcopal Church, the Church of England and the English Presbyterian Church to bridge the gap between two traditions so as to present a united Christian front. Full merger was too much but those involved hoped that Presbyterians and Anglicans could formally recognise each others' legitimacy and allow full inter-communion. As a result of those talks, in 1959 the Kirk's Inter-Church Relations committee proposed a radical compromise of its Presbyterian principles: it would allow presbyteries (the bodies that united all the congregations of an area) to elect bishops. 'Bishops-in-Presbytery' (BIP) would thus make the Kirk episcopalian in management structure if not in high theory.[20]

Such a major change would always have been controversial but strident opposition was led by an unlikely champion: the *Scottish Daily Express*. Such interest in Kirk affairs from an English-based newspaper owned by a Canadian might seem strange but the elderly proprietor, Lord Beaverbrook, was probably the last significant link to the Edwardian fusion of religion and politics in popular unionism which was described in the previous chapter. William 'Max' Aitken was born in Ontario in 1879, the son of a Scots-born Presbyterian minister. Having made a considerable fortune, he moved to Britain in 1910 and was elected to parliament for Ashton-under-Lyme as a Unionist. He became a major force in the Conservative party, served as a government minister in both world wars and was rewarded with a peerage and appointment to the Privy Council. In his later years he was very close to Winston Churchill but his early politics were influenced by Andrew Bonar Law, who led the Conservative party from 1911 to 1923 and who has the distinction of being the only British prime minister born outside Great Britain. Like Aitken, he was a Canadian from a Scottish background whose father was a clergyman. Bonar Law was brought to Glasgow as a child after his father died and began his political career in Scotland. He was deeply opposed to Irish Home Rule – his father was an Ulsterman – and was probably the last leader of the British Conservative party who had any sentimental attachment to the idea of the Union as a primarily Protestant entity.

When he heard of the BIP proposals, Beaverbrook apparently told his editor to 'fight, fight at whatever cost even if it means losing circulation'.[21] He also gave very detailed instructions as to how the campaign should be fought:

> Please turn up the denunciation of bishops by John Knox. Then having printed it, conclude with the final sentence of the Scots Confession of 1560 . . . 'Arise, O Lord, and let thy enemies be confounded. Let them flee from the presence that hate thy Godly name: give thy servants strength to speak thy word in boldness; and let all Nations attain to thy true knowledge'.[22]

The opposition was both nationalist and classist. The proposals were denounced as the work of 'the Edinburgh professions and the fashionable Edinburgh churches . . . It was that of upper-middle-class Scotland. And the basic principle of the religion of upper-middle-class Scotland is that English institutions are U and Scottish institutions are non-U'.[23]

Why Beaverbrook in his eightieth year should have cared enough about Scottish Presbyterianism to commit his newspaper to its defence is not clear. The cynic might suppose he was trying to boost its tartan credentials to rival *The Scotsman* and *The Glasgow Herald* but his wealth and remarkable political career make it unlikely that some final business triumph was in his mind. Though he was clearly well-versed in Scottish church history, he was not particularly pious. The most likely explanation is that a wish to pay final respects to his father's culture was reinforced by resentment of the English political class. For all his success, Beaverbrook remained a distinctly chippy outsider. One weekend at his English country house, his secretary slept in and missed being driven to church with the other guests by the house chauffeur. Beaverbrook, who tellingly did not attend church, asked which church she had been planning to attend. When she said the Church of England rather than the Presbyterian church, he said she could walk then.[24]

The BIP proposals were rejected by the membership, voting in presbyteries, and by the 1959 General Assembly. We cannot know how much of that was the *Express*'s doing but we can note a subtle but important theme in its campaign. Although Beaverbrook had been a close friend of Bonar Law forty years earlier, his opposition to bishops was not based on unionism's classic synthesis of demotic Protestantism, democracy and Britishness, under the protection of the Conservative and Unionist party. The English Tories had destroyed that by rejecting the religio-ethnic foundation for their politics. What the *Scottish Daily Express* promoted was a narrower Scottish identity that opposed the largest church in England and built class resentment into its national self-image. In the absence of a Scottish parliament, the Church of Scotland was puffed as the representative voice of the Scottish people.

Public hostility to one set of proposals did not prevent church leaders continuing to work at improving relations between the churches. Beaverbrook's son Sir Max Aitken, who in an echo of his father's self-description proudly styled himself 'the minister's grandson', encouraged the *Express* to maintain its sniping at inter-church discussions through the 1960s, but matters of church structure and ethos lost salience as the cultural storm of the 1960s broke over Scotland.

The Sixties

Like the 'Swinging Sixties' of miniskirts and Mods that preceded it, the hippy era of eastern spirituality, long hair and beards, patchouli oil, cheesecloth shirts and skirts, and making love, not war, was largely a London phenomenon. The Radha Krishna Temple's recording of its Hare Krishna mantra made it to the UK top twenty in 1969 but the shaven-headed sannyasin looked more comfortable in London than in a dreich Dundee where the traditional monk's robes were augmented by anorak, bobble hat and wellie boots. But Scotland did produce one notable contribution to hippiedom: the Incredible String Band. Originally a folk trio, the departure of Clive Palmer for Afghanistan – which fifty years ago meant something very different – left Robin Williamson and Mike Heron as a duo and allowed them to develop a genuinely novel sound based on playing lengthy and musically complex songs on unusual instruments (such as the sitar and the gimbri), the lyrics of which were intended to stand as serious poetry. As the *Observer* said in the ISB's first national press coverage:

> The Incredible String Band tend to wear a strange assortment of clothes, play a strange assortment of instruments, litter their speech with metaphor, and quote at length from Robert Graves' 'The White Goddess'. But that, they say, is the way they are.[25]

Although 'The Mad Hatter's Song' from the ISB's second album, *5,000 Spirits or the Layers of the Onion*, still stands as a credible work of art, its music and lyrics ably illustrate many of the key motifs of the hippy era. It opens with Williamson chanting a classically Romantic critique of modernity over a repeated minor chord and handclaps: 'Oh, seekers of spring, how could you not find contentment / In a time of riddling reason in this land of the blind'. The consolations of religion are no longer available: 'live till you die / My poor little man / For Jesus will stretch out his hand no more'. But there is hope of spiritual enlightenment: 'But in the south there's many a wavy tree . . . In the warm south winds the lost flowers move again'. In the third section, when sitar and guitar meanderings give way to a piano blues, Williamson adds country versus city to his north/south binary divide: 'And if you cried, you know you'd fill a lake with tears / Still wouldn't turn back the years since the city has took you'.[26] There is then an elaborate metaphor of the spiritual aridity of the modern world that traces its errors back to the attempts to tame nature of the mythical Greek Titan Prometheus:

> We then cut to 'the ruined factory', a haunting image of Western modernism, where 'the normal soul insane' perceives the world completely askew and, placing material and intellectual values over spiritual ones, 'sets the sky beneath his heel and learns away the pain'.

Williamson then slips into the role of the clear-sighted seer – 'I am the archer and my eyes yearn after the unsullied sight' – and offers a positive ending: 'O prithee an fate be kind / In the rumbling and trundling rickshaw of time' for we are still 'hooked by the heart to the kingfisher's line' and like a Bodhisattva promising to lead the fallen world back to the light, he will: 'set my one eye for the shores of the blind'.

Such meanderings can easily be dismissed as the incoherent ramblings of young men overly impressed with the results of their untutored rummaging in the vast cupboards of Western romanticism and Eastern religion, but they are significant as expressions of a widespread and influential counter-culture. Instrumental striving in pursuit of goals was bad; creative self-expression was good. Rational thought was bad; feeling was good. Conventional masculinity was bad; gender blurring was good. Sublimation and sexual continence were bad; sexual liberation was good. War, especially the Vietnam war, was very bad. The nuclear family, with its confining roles for father, mother and children, was a cause of mental illness; communal living was the way to authentic relationships.[27] Deferring to authority was bad; choosing one's own lifestyle was good.

Such cultural shifts do not happen in vacuums: the cultural innovations of the Sixties were built on important social changes. By the end of the 1950s the last elements of the wartime rationing regime were finally rescinded and the economy was again growing. A combination of increased mechanisation in industry and the increasing professionalisation of white-collar service work required an expansion of education and training and the country's increasing prosperity permitted it. The result was, especially for the middle classes, the creation of a long adolescence. The school-leaving age was raised to 16 and a growing proportion of young people stayed at school until 18, when they filled the art schools and new universities. As noted in Chapter 4, the late Sixties also saw the start of what some demographers call the 'second demographic transition' or SDT. The first demographic transition is the common pattern seen as economies shifted from agriculture to industrial manufacture. The populations of pre-industrial societies were kept stable by a high death rate matching a high birth rate. Improvements in diet, sanitation, living conditions and (to a lesser extent) medical care saw the death rate fall and a sudden rise in population, followed quickly by a reduction in birth rates. The SDT is a further dramatic shift in population patterns caused largely by changes in gender roles. Equipped with effective contraception and the education required to pursue a satisfying career (either as an alternative to marriage or as a life stage before motherhood), an ever-growing number of women delayed marriage and pregnancy, so that the birth rate fell to below replacement levels.

From the late 1960s onwards all the major indexes of involvement in the mainstream churches declined.[28] The various signs of weakening commitment that had been visible in the first half of the twentieth century – the secularisation of Sundays, increasingly sporadic church attendance, the declining status and influence of the clergy – blossomed into a crisis for the churches. In 1960 the number of the Kirk's new communicants was almost the same as the number of baptisms eighteen years earlier. By 1970 it was less than a third: an abrupt failure of family transmission. When the Free Church rejoined the Church of Scotland in 1929 the re-united Kirk could claim around 27 per cent of Scots as members. After 1957 this figure fell steadily so that it was only 15 per cent by the end of the century.[29] In 1970 the Church of Scotland baptised around a third of children aged 0 to 1. In 2010 that figure was only 7 per cent.[30] Even allowing for the growth of the Catholic and non-Christian populations, this is a considerable decline. The changes in weddings is also notable. In the years immediately after the Second World War, 84 per cent of Scots weddings were religious. By the late 1960s this had fallen to 74 per cent. In 2010 it was less than 40 per cent.[31]

One of the key ways in which the churches promoted the faith beyond their own membership was through Sunday School. We have no separate Scottish data but, as modern Scots were generally more involved in the churches than the English, we can be confident that the following British figures minimally represent Scotland. In 1900 55 per cent of the population under 15 was enrolled in Sunday School. By the Sixties the figure had fallen to around 20 per cent. In 2010 it was around 5 per cent: less than the proportion of the adult population that attends church.[32] This is not because church attenders do not take their children; it is because most churchgoers are too old to have children to take to Sunday School.

One way of thinking of the post-Sixties decline is to imagine religion as the core of an electro-magnet and the people as iron filings at various distances from the core. Since probably the middle of the nineteenth century religion had been losing social power but until the Sixties the core was still strong enough for most people to have had some Christian socialisation and to be occasionally involved. Once the magnetic pull of the core fell below a certain strength, the occasional and the nominal church adherents dropped away rapidly. At the start of the twentieth century most churches had more attenders than members. By the 1970s that had reversed so that attendances were below membership levels. By the end of the century, when the number of clergy was, relative to the size of population, only half what it had been in 1900, Scotland was radically divided between a small core of church adherents and a majority of the population which had almost no contact with the Christian faith.[33] If we need an image to illustrate that change, almost any funeral of an elderly relative will make the point: most of the congregation struggle to sing even the most popular hymns.

Thus far I have been discussing the mainstream churches and the national Kirk in particular. Some data on Catholic decline was presented in Chapter 4 and the more conservative Protestant churches will be discussed in subsequent chapters. Here I want to stress that the greater resilience of those alternatives is not explained by them being in some sense more attractive to adults seeking a faith: very little of their different fates is due to adult conversion. The Baptists, the Free Churches and the Brethren held up better than the Kirk because their members were slower than the rest of the population to be affected by those changes summarised above as the Second Demographic Transition and thus had larger than average families from which to recruit. Second, because they were always more demanding of their adherents, they had less of a penumbra of occasional and nominal adherents to lose.

Clergy Status and Gender

So long as religion remained important, the social status of the clergy was always greater than their income merited. In the conventional social class divisions used by sociologists, clergy were usually placed with doctors and lawyers: a reflection of their university education, their social influence and the freedom they enjoyed in how they performed their jobs. Nonetheless income is a useful illustration of changing status. In 1914 a commercial manager earned slightly less, general practice doctors earned almost twice as much and barristers earned 2.3 times as much as a Kirk minister. By the 1930s managers had overtaken the clergy, and GPs and barristers were earning three times as much. In 2011 the typical cleric earned £22,000, the typical manager £45,000, the typical GP £67,000 and a barrister with ten years' experience could expect to earn at least £87,000, with many earning considerably more. Clergy salaries are usually augmented by rent-free accommodation, a benefit which could be worth around £16,000. This would close the gap with managers but still leave them a long way behind the doctors and lawyers who, at the start of the twentieth century, had been their peers. Another way of illustrating the change is to note that over the first half of the twentieth century, average male earnings quadrupled but typical Church of Scotland clergy salaries only doubled.[34]

Religious professionals are, of course, different. Lawyers might describe their jobs as a calling but it is not one for which we expect them to make any great sacrifice. The clergy are called by God and are not supposed to set much store by worldly matters. Nonetheless the wealth of the clergy has some reasonably consistent relationship with the power and authority of the churches. In the nineteenth century the Church of Scotland minister would usually be one of the richest people in most parishes and his class position was reflected in domestic architecture. In 1900 my Aberdeenshire parish had only three houses bigger than a cottage. The 'big house' was a mansion large enough to be converted into a maternity hospital during the Second World War. The schoolhouse was a solid two-storey structure with four bedrooms and three large public rooms. The manse was twice the size of the schoolhouse. Its stables were large enough to be converted into a house in the 1980s and its attic floor had four bedrooms for the servants. It is now owned by an oil executive. The minister (who serves four linked parishes) lives in a 1970s bungalow built in one corner of the old manse's garden.[35]

One further sign of the clergy's loss of status is that it is no longer a popular first career for men. Increasingly recruits are middle-aged people who feel unfulfilled by their secular occupations. While this shift has the benefit that newly ordained clergy have some considerable life-experience to bring to their pastoral work, it is likely to reinforce the Kirk's failure to hold the attention of young people. In 2013 the Kirk had no one in training for the ministry under the age of forty-five.[36]

It would be too cynical to suppose that women were only permitted to join the ministry because the church was running out of men but the coincidence was a happy one. For similar reasons, the two extremes of Scottish church life – the Catholic Church and the Free Churches – refuse to ordain women: not being men, they cannot represent Christ physically as well as spiritually.[37] Most of the other churches have changed their attitudes to women a little behind the general social change. The smaller Protestant churches were the first. The Pentecostal Church of the Nazarene ordained an American, Olive Winchester, in 1912 and in 1917 Jane Sharp (the wife of the founding minister of the Nazarenes in the UK) was ordained at the Parkhead, Glasgow, church; their daughter was ordained seven years later. The Baptists drifted into equal opportunities. Women had long had access to the subordinate status of deaconess and been active in missionary work. In 1918 Jane Henderson, a Stirling deaconess who had worked as an evangelist among fisher-girls in Lerwick, was called to pastor a church in Lossiemouth. In the 1930s Mary MacArthur was called to pastor the Baptist church in Tobermory. She was the daughter of a Baptist minister and, like Henderson, had worked with the Lerwick fisher-girls. As happened in more mundane occupations, the shortage of male pastors during the Second World War led to a number of deaconesses taking on full-time ministries and by the 1960s there were thirty-eight female pastors. They were given much the same recognition as male pastors but they were paid less and until 1967 they were required to resign on marrying. In 1975 the Baptist Council decided to convert all active deaconesses to ministers on the same terms and conditions as men.[38]

Close behind the Baptists came the Congregational Union. In 1928 Vera Findlay was called to Partick Congregational Church in Glasgow and a year later the Congregational Union agreed that the word minister applied equally to men and women. This did not prevent a dispute arising six years later when Findlay became a mother. Under pressure from a conservative faction she resigned but 200 members signed a petition asking her to stay and joined her in a new congregation, before following her to Hillhead Congregational Church.

The Church of Scotland was one of the first national churches to ordain women. As with the Baptists, women had initially served as deaconesses. The first woman to be ordained as a minister was Catherine McConnachie, who was ordained by the Presbytery of Aberdeen in 1969 and served as assistant minister in Tillydrone. Three years later Euphemia Irvine was ordained and inducted as a parish minister at Milton of Campsie. The rise of women through the ranks was slow. In 1996 the first woman was appointed to be Depute Clerk to the General Assembly. In 2004 the first woman was elected Moderator of the General Assembly and three years later the first female minister was elected to the post.[39]

The acceptance of women clergy was easier in Scotland than in England: there was very little concerted opposition and no congregations defected. This reflects theology rather than national character. The clergy is just not that important to Presbyterians. The minister or 'teaching elder' is distinguished from other elders by function rather than by spiritual status. Consequently the theological arguments for women ministers were the same as for women elders and the two debates were settled more or less simultaneously. The General Assembly permitted the ordination of women as elders in 1966 and as minis- ters in 1968. In contrast, the 'high' wing of the Church of England takes the Catholic view that the clergy are a special species endowed with sacramental power, which makes the argument all the more urgent to traditionalists. The Church of England also holds a hierarchical view of spiritual power which means that those who are opposed cannot avoid the issue simply by never choosing a woman priest: they may still find themselves subject to the spiritual authority of women priests when (and it is a matter of when rather than if) they become bishops. The flat power structure of Presbyterianism means that conservative congregations can maintain a private but effective veto just by not calling a female minister. The other difference is in 'reference group'. Because it wishes to keep the door open to reversing the Reformation divide, one wing of the Church of England has always opposed changes which further distance it from Rome. The Church of Scotland looks to Presbyterian churches in other countries and to other Protestant churches in Scotland and, with the exception of the Free Church conservatives, that world favours female clergy.

In this as in much else, the Scottish Episcopal Church is more 'Protestant' than the Church of England. It agreed to ordain women in 1991, a year before the Church of England, and in 2003, without any of the opposition that is currently tearing the Church of England apart, it permitted women to become bishops.

The number of female ministers in the Church of Scotland grew gradually until they now form about a quarter of the clergy in post. The pattern of distribution is interesting.[40] The presbyteries that in 2011 had the most women seem to have little else in common. Melrose and Peebles, with 61.5 per cent of its clergy female, tops the list. Second is Dunkeld and Meigle with 50 per cent. Both are sparsely populated areas, as are Shetland (42.9 per cent) and Orkney (40.0 per cent). But then half of Dunfermline's twenty clergy are women, and Dundee and Kirkcaldy (at 38.5 and 34.8 per cent respectively) are also in the top ten. There is a much clearer pattern at the other end of the scale. Of seven presbyteries with no women ministers in 2011, four (Lochaber, Uist, Lewis, and Lochcarron and Skye) are in the western highlands and islands and two (Caithness and Ross) are in the far north: all areas where the conservative Free Churches were historically strong.

It is still the case that the largest and most prestigious Edinburgh and Glasgow congregations have proved reluctant to call women but acceptance has been easier than many women feared; arguably it has been easier than has been the case in other traditionally male occupations. Women clergy have experienced no difficulty in finding a charge nor in moving on from a first charge. Most have found that local opposition has melted quickly; people who opposed 'women ministers' in the abstract lost interest in gender when they came to know their minister. My conversations with female clergy and with committed female Christians who have not sought ordination suggest that the main barrier is not congregational hostility but the job itself. A number of female ministers from clerical families told me that the strongest reservations about their career choice came from their mothers who could readily imagine the difficulty of combining motherhood with a full-time ministry. And many (especially those whose husbands had demanding jobs) recognised that their mothers had been perceptive.

There are three problems. It may seem strange to view 'the need to be religious' as a drawback to the job of minister but it does severely restrict social opportunities for single young women (and men). All couples have to reconcile or manage their differences but it is possible for a lay Christian to marry a non-believer and the number of married churchgoers who are not accompanied by their spouses suggests this is now quite common.[41] People contemplating the ministry know that their faith will shape how they are seen by potential partners to a far greater degree than if they became, say, doctors who just happened to be Christian.

The second problem is the lack of privacy. The parish clergy are expected to be perpetually on call. That was bearable for the traditional male minister whose full-time housewife spouse managed the children and acted as unpaid clerical assistant and caterer. With one exception to be mentioned shortly, childless single women ministers should find the job no more onerous than their male counterparts. But a married mother who is also a minister is in an unusually awkward position unless her husband is willing to play the role of the traditional wife.

The third problem is public scrutiny. Congregations have long treated the clergy as our mass media now treat TV talent show winners: having chosen them, they feel the right to an unusual interest in the ministers' doings. They expect the preachers of the gospel to exemplify the standards they advertise. And they still use double-standards so that the dating behaviour of young women clergy is the subject of far more critical gossip than that of their male counterparts. Raising children in the public eye is also very difficult. The minister's bairns were always expected to be angels and any shortcomings were grist to the gossip mill, but for a woman minister the problem is amplified because she will be judged by her children to an extent that is not the case with male clergy. This is a not a hypothetical concern. I know of women ministers who have moved jobs because difficult relations between their own and other children have caused ill-feeling to an extent which would not have affected a man in the same position. In short, the parish ministry is an unusually demanding occupation and until women clergy become the norm the demands will be greater on women than on men and the expectation of those pressures will still act as a disincentive.

A survey of all the Church of Scotland's female ministers asked them 'have you noticed any difference between the genders in the following areas of ministry?' The 122 respondents were evenly divided between 'yes' and 'no' when it came to preaching, committee work and vision-building, but there was a two-to-one agreement that women were different when it came to collaboration, leadership and pastoral care.[42] Although in personality, female ministers exhibit the same very wide range as men, their working styles tend to differ consistently from those of men. They are less likely to see themselves as heroic and authoritarian leaders and more likely to involve lay members of the congregation in their work: a style well-suited to an organisation which finds its staff increasingly thin on the ground.

One thing on which most of the clergy I have interviewed agree is that women ministers are generally much better than their male counterparts with children. In my youth the children's address – a short homily early in the service, after which the young children leave the congregation for the Sunday School room – was always the butt of jokes. The minister would attempt to capture the attention of the children with some toy or an intriguing tale and then introduce his often lame moral with 'Now life's a little like that, children'. Although the consequences were not as ribald as using 'As the actress said to the bishop' (or vice-versa) to turn the most innocent observation into a double-entendre, inserting 'Now life's a little like that, children' into conversations was always good for a laugh. At a 2012 church service in Kirkwall, the young woman minister left her pulpit to sit on the step that divides the main body of the church from the slightly raised altar area, gathered the children around her and chatted to them in a language they could understand about the meaning of Easter. It was clear they adored her.

Women ministers are also generally better than men at what now constitutes a large part of the pastoral role of the clergy: visiting the elderly and the infirm. Or at least they are much more practised because, as regular visitors to any hospital ward and nursing home know, women still bear the brunt of this form of social care.

The effects of the ordination of women are somewhat paradoxical. On the one hand it makes churches more normal. In a world where women can fight in the armed services, and have filled the roles of prime minister and monarch, an institution in which women are confined to the ranks is an anomaly. Whether that anomaly is God's will is for Christians to decide but all the opinion polling stimulated by the Church of England's arguments over women bishops shows that the public at large is unimpressed by the conservative case. On the other hand, ordaining women risks making the churches even more feminine. That most of the congregation is female strengthens the equity case for ordaining women but that gender composition offers little encouragement to young men to see churchgoing as a proper activity for them and having a woman preaching to women reinforces that conclusion.

Conclusion

The recent history of the Church of Scotland could readily be summarised as decline, but it is almost more important to appreciate the more subtle change in attitudes to religion that have gone along with that decline. The Tell Scotland campaign and arguments over the BIP scheme belong to a world in which many people beyond the core of churchgoers were interested in the doings of the national church on its terms; where it was normal for the BBC to cooperate in promoting the Christian gospel; and where readers of a mass-circulation daily paper might care about the proper structure for a church. By the end of the twentieth century the Kirk was just another institution to which most people did not belong. As the issue of ordaining women showed (and we will return to this in Chapter 12 when we look at gay rights), the churches are now expected to conform to social norms rather than to shape them.

Notes

1. J. Highet, 'Scottish church adherence', *British Journal of Sociology* 4 (1953), pp. 142–59.
2. Detailed sources for these data can be found in S. Bruce and T. Glendinning,

'When was secularization? Dating the decline of the British churches and locating its cause', *British Journal of Sociology* 61 (2010), pp. 107–26.

3. C. Harvie, *No Gods and Precious Few Heroes* (London: Edward Arnold, 1981), p. 53.

4. For a delightful description of these encounters from a 1941 Polish perspective, see K. Pruszyński, *Polish Invasion* (Edinburgh: Birlinn, 2009).

5. E. M. Edwards (ed.), *Scotland's Land Girls* (Edinburgh: National Museum Scotland, 2010), p. 121.

6. Edwards, *Scotland's Land Girls*, p. 129.

7. E. Templeton, *God's February: a Life of Archie Craig 1888–1985* (London: BCCI/CCBI, 1991), p. 17.

8. Highet, 'Scottish church adherence'.

9. D. K. Cameron, 'The cottar's bairn', in W. G. Lawrence (ed.), *Roots in a Northern Landscape: Celebrations of Childhood in the North East of Scotland* (Edinburgh: Scottish Cultural Press, 1996), p. 15

10. D. Hay, 'Memories of a Calvinist childhood', in Lawrence, *Roots in a Northern Landscape*, p. 51.

11. M. Swogger, 'Dramas of childhood', in Lawrence, *Roots*, p. 110.

12. L. Jamieson and C. Toynbee, *Country Bairns: Growing Up 1900–1930*, pp. 192–3.

13. Jamieson and Toynbee, *Country Bairns*, p. 183.

14. D. P. Thomson, who succeeded Allen as the Kirk's best-known evangelist, wrote and self-published many pamphlets on the Tell Scotland and subsequent campaigns. See, for example, his *Visitation Evangelism in Scotland 1946–1956* (Crieff: D. P. Thomson, 1956).

15. B. J. Evenson, *God's Man for the Gilded Age: DL Moody and the Rise of Modern Mass Evangelism* (New York: Oxford University Press, 2003).

16. G. Ritchie, 'Billy Graham in Scotland', *Daily Record*, 24 April 2010.

17. C. Maclean, *Monkeys, Bears and Gutta Percha: Memories of Manse, Hospital and War* (East Linton: Tuckwell Press, 2001), p. 128.

18. C. G. Brown, *The Death of Christian Britain* (London: Routledge, 2001), p. 173.

19. J. Highet, 'The Churches', in J. Cunnison and J. B. S. Gilfillan (eds), *The Third Statistical Account of Scotland: County of Glasgow* (Glasgow: Collins, 1958), p. 731.

20. For Archie Craig's insider account of the debate, see Templeton, *God's February*, pp. 88–99.

21. T. Gallagher, 'The press and Protestant culture: a case study of the *Scottish Daily Express*', in G. Walker and T. Gallagher (eds), *Sermons and Battle Hymns* (Edinburgh: Edinburgh University Press, 1990), p. 195.

22. Gallagher, 'The press', p. 196.

23. Prof. Ian Henderson quoted in Gallagher, 'The press', p. 197.

24. A. Chisholm and M. Davie, *Lord Beaverbrook: A Life* (New York: Alfred E. Knopf, 1993), p. 394.

25. This and all other quotations in this section are taken from R. Pendleton, 'Kindred spirits', in A. Whitaker (ed.), *An Incredible String Band Compendium* (London: Helter Skelter, 2003), pp. 68–81. For a musicologist's account that puts the ISB in the context of the changing folk scene, see R. Young, *Electric Eden: Unearthing Britain's Visionary Music* (London: Faber and Faber, 2010), Ch. 11. For their manager's account of the band, see J. Boyd, *White Bicycles: Making Music in the 1960s* (London: Serpent's Tail, 2005).

26. The 'took' rather than 'taken' may seem to be a mistake but it is demotic urban lowland Scots.

27. Scotland can claim a disproportionate contribution to the anti-psychiatry movement in the person of R. D. Laing. Educated at Hutcheson's and the University of Glasgow, Laing was a consultant psychiatrist at Gartnavel hospital before his unhappiness with the medical model of mental illness led him to train at the psychoanalytically oriented Tavistock Clinic in London. Laing's *The Divided Self: An Existential Study in Sanity and Madness* (Harmondsworth: Penguin, 1960), *The Self and Others* (London: Tavistock Publications, 1961) and *Sanity, Madness and the Family* (London: Penguin, 1964) were prime sources for the notion that much mental illness was a 'normal' reaction to abnormal relations and social circumstances.

28. C. G. Brown, *The Death of Christian Britain: Understanding Secularization, 1800–2000* (London: Routledge, 2001); H. McLeod, *The Religious Crisis of the 1960s* (Oxford: Oxford University Press, 2007); N. Christie and M. Gauvreau, *The Sixties and Beyond: Dechristianization in North America and Western Europe, 1945–2000* (Toronto: University of Toronto Press, 2013). While all commentators agree that the 1960s was a watershed, we differ in the weight we give the causes of change operative in that period as compared with earlier causes. Brown offers the clearest articulation of the 'late and abrupt' view of secularisation. I am closer to McLeod's view that the religious crisis of the Sixties involved both novel causes and the cumulative effect of weakening commitment in previous generations. For example, Brown is right that changes in demography and in opportunities for women explain the decline in women's involvement in the churches but they do not explain why male religiosity had already declined. My critique of Brown is elaborated in Bruce and Glendinning, 'When was secularization?'

29. These data come from C. G. Brown, *The Death of Christian Britain: Understanding Secularization, 1800–2000* (London: Routledge, 2001), pp. 165 and 189.

30. Baptism figures for 1930 and 1970 are from R. Currie, A. Gilbert and L. Horsley, *Churches and Churchgoers: Patterns of Church Growth in the British Isles Since 1700* (Oxford: Oxford University Press, 1977), Table B.2. That for 2010 is from the *British Religion in Numbers* website.

31. Registrar-General for Scotland, *Vital Events Reference Tables 2011*, Table 7.7; http://www.gro-scotland.gov.uk/statistics/theme/vital-events/general/ref-tables/2011/section-7-marriages-and-civil-partnerships.html. The RGS table is misleading

in that it classifies humanist ceremonies as religious. If these are added to civil marriages as 'secular', the secular/religious ratio is 60.33/39.67.

32. P. Brierley, *UK Church Statistics, 2005–2015* (Tonbridge, Kent: ABCD Publishers, 2011), table 14.4.2.

33. The 1951 figure is from Highet, 'Scottish church adherence'; the 2001 figure from Church of Scotland, *Reports to the General Assembly 2002* (Edinburgh: General Assembly of the Church of Scotland, 2002), appendix R 39/5.

34. J. Highet, 'Scottish church adherence', p. 157.

35. It is worth adding that most clergy welcome the replacement of old manses by modern houses because they cannot afford the domestic staff required to make life in a Victorian pile comfortable.

36. 'Turning a crisis into an opportunity', *The Herald*, 8 May 2013.

37. The most recent full statement is the 1976 *Declaration on the Question of the Admission of Women to the Ministerial Priesthood*, which was endorsed by Pope John Paul II in August 1988.

38. R. M. B. Gouldbourne, *Reinventing the Wheel: Women and Ministry in English Baptist Life* (Didcot: Whitley Publications, 1997).

39. For a detailed account of the campaign for female clergy in the Kirk, see M. Levison, *Wrestling with the Church. One Woman's Experience* (London: Arthur James, 1992). Mary Levison was a deacon from 1954 and in 1957 became the first woman licensed to preach by the Church of Scotland.

40. The figures were calculated from the presbytery lists in the 2012 *Church of Scotland Yearbook* (Edinburgh: Saint Andrew Press, 2012). Non-parochial ministries such as chaplaincies were not counted, nor were the ministers on the retired clergy lists.

41. The 2001 UK Time Use Survey (TUS) provides rare data on the religious activity of partners because it codes the activities of all adult members of households. Tony Glendinning and I are currently analysing this data and our preliminary work shows that only the minority of TUS diarists (43.6 per cent) who live with a partner and who are religiously active on Sundays for a period of 60-plus minutes in the company of others (that is, churchgoers) are so active with their partner. For a description of the TUS, see S. Short, *Review of the UK Time Use Survey* (London: Office for National Statistics, 2006).

42. A. T. Logan, *Ordained Ministry of Women in the Church of Scotland: the First Forty Years* (Glasgow: University of Glasgow PhD thesis, 2010).

CHAPTER

7

SERIOUS RELIGION IN A SECULAR CULTURE

This chapter is concerned with the recent tribulations of Scotland's distinctive contribution to conservative religion: the Free Church and the Free Presbyterian Church. It also considers a subtle change in outsiders' attitudes to religion-taken-seriously. The decline of Christianity in Scotland is not just a matter of fewer people going to church. As religion has become less popular it has also become less well-known and this has allowed popular perceptions of Christianity to become distorted. As the final section will illustrate, this has the strange consequence that those who take their Christianity seriously are now routinely accused of being 'unChristian'.

As explained in Chapter 1, the mergers that saw the Kirk regain its status as the home of most Protestants left behind dissident remnants. Although nationally small, the Free Church (FC) and Free Presbyterian Church (FPC) were deeply rooted in the highlands and islands. From the 1930s to the 1960s these two small bodies had actually performed relatively better than the Church of Scotland; not because they were better at recruiting adults but because they had larger families and hence more chance of keeping enough children in the faith to replace the members who passed on.

At the end of the twentieth century both the FC and FPC split. Although both schisms had particular and local causes, both illustrate two perennial features of Scots religious culture: the factionalism inherent in conservative Protestantism and the necessity to choose between separation from, or compromise with, secular society.

A Fractious Temperament?

If there were a Missus Tussaud's wax museum of Scottish stereotypes, James Mackay could qualify on two counts. Had he been raised in the highlands he

would have been a perfect 'lad of pairts': that bright son of the soil, so beloved
of sentimental Victorian Scottish literature, whose tiny rural school teaches him
so well that he rises to high office despite his lowly origins. Mackay was actually raised in Edinburgh, where his Sutherland-born father worked as a railway
signalman. But the rest fits. From a humble home, he won a scholarship to a
private school and from there he went to Edinburgh University to study maths
and physics. Another scholarship took him to Trinity College, Cambridge, for
a second maths degree. He then returned to Edinburgh University to study
law. Mackay was elected to the Faculty of Advocates in 1955; ten years later
he was appointed a Queen's Counsel and worked his way up the profession. In
1979 he was appointed Lord Advocate and took the title of Baron Mackay of
Clashfern, of Eddrachillis in Sutherland, his father's home.[1] In 1987 Margaret
Thatcher made Mackay Lord Chancellor; he was re-appointed by John Major
and served until the Conservatives lost power in 1997.

His other qualification for Scottish stereotype is his religion. A handsome
man with white hair and a stern countenance, it was entirely fitting that the
country's black-suited senior law officer should belong to one of the country's smallest Christian bodies: a church firmly associated with puritan ethics
and a literal interpretation of texts. Mackay was raised a member of the Free
Presbyterian Church of Scotland and was sufficiently committed to serve as an
elder. As he should have been, he was a strict sabbatarian who did not give
interviews on a Sunday. The synod of the FPC had repeatedly condemned:

> Communism, socialism. homosexuality, unscriptural divorce, pornography, Scottish
> nationalism, *in vitro* fertilisation, artificial insemination by donor, and Sabbath-
> robbing British Summer Time; she has advocated capital and corporal punishment.
> Always, always, fighting for the Sabbath, and always condemning the doctrines and
> practices of the Church of Rome. Rules enforced by discipline . . . condemned cre-
> mation, going to the cinema, going to the theatre, using church premises for sales of
> work or sports-clubs or *soirees*, using public transport on the Lord's Day, attending
> services of other denominations . . . and the celebration of Christmas and Easter.[2]

As a conservative Protestant organisation that still takes seriously the
principles of the Reformation, the FPC has no truck with the Roman Catholic
Church. One of the specific Romanist beliefs it rejects (as do all Protestants) is
the notion that the living can do anything to improve the salvational prospects
of the dead. Until the 1960s many mainstream Protestant churches prohibited
any kind of religious activity at the graveside in case it was misunderstood as
prayers for the dead and, when funeral services were tentatively introduced,
they were clearly intended to comfort the bereaved rather than speed the
deceased to heaven. Another Catholic belief that Protestants reject is the idea
that the clergy have supernatural power that actually transforms the bread
and wine of the Mass into the flesh and blood of Christ. Protestants will 'take

communion' or 'celebrate the Lord's Supper' in commemoration of Christ's sacrifice but they do not believe that such services involve any supernatural transformations. It is a memorial rather than a re-enactment. So a Catholic requiem mass is doubly offensive to the Protestant. The FPC has no rule forbidding members from attending Catholic funeral services but the principle is very well understood.

Lord Mackay's attendance at the requiem mass of a Catholic colleague, Lord Russell of Killowen, was raised before the Kirk session of the FPC's Edinburgh congregation in 1988; it refused to discipline him. That decision was appealed to the Southern Presbytery, which narrowly upheld the complaint and imposed suspension for six months from his eldership and from the right to take communion. The Edinburgh Kirk session appealed the Presbytery's decision to the next organisational level: the Synod. In the meantime, Mackay had attended the funeral service of Catholic law colleague John Wheatley (nephew of the famous Glasgow Labour politician). This was a lesser offence in that it did not involve a mass but it may have further antagonised his conservative critics. Mackay was asked to give a commitment not to attend further Catholic services. He refused and left the church.[3] He later reflected:

> I was rather sad but I was very clear in my own mind that there was nothing wrong in what I had done. What it did was open my eyes to a narrow denominationalism so I found myself willing to go anywhere where the gospel was preached or the sacraments administered according to what I believed to be the scriptural ways.[4]

Although Mackay did not join them, many of those who had fought his side in the arguments left the FPC and, reviving a title from the eighteenth century, constituted themselves as the Associated Presbyterian Church (APC).

The FPC was not alone in splitting over the behaviour of a leading member. The Free Church had its own schism not long after. From the mid-1980s, Donald Macleod, Professor of Systematic Theology at the Free Church College, had been questioning some of the church's distinctive liturgical and social positions. Although his challenges seem mild to an outsider, they were radical enough to create a faction within the clergy who deeply resented Macleod and his prominence as the publicly acceptable face of Scotland's Calvinist heritage.[5] That he took to writing a weekly column for the mildly left-leaning *West Highland Free Press* when he resigned as editor of the Free Church's *Monthly Record* was seen as proof of his political and social radicalism.

In 1987 there was an attempt to challenge him publicly for allegedly questioning the policy of insisting that only unaccompanied metrical psalms – acceptable because they were paraphrases of Biblical texts rather than human compositions – be permitted in worship. His principal opponent on this issue was Angus Smith, who was both a kinsman and a fellow native of Lewis. Smith had come to prominence in 1965 when he had tried to prevent the Sunday sailing of ferries from Skye to the mainland by lying down on the slipway. The local press dubbed him 'The Ferry Reverend', a mocking epithet still used by the *West Highland Free Press* thirty years later.[6] On instrumental music, Macleod proved prescient. Twenty-three years later, and in good part because the conservatives had been weakened by the schism, the Free Church allowed (though it did not require) musical accompaniment in worship.

Macleod's enemies eventually found their weapons in a body of innuendo built around a small personal indiscretion. While lecturing in Australia in 1984, Macleod had become close friends with a young woman. This became known to a number of Free Church people via Iain Murray (manager of the Banner of Truth, a well-known publisher of evangelical and puritan texts) who was then pastoring a congregation of the Presbyterian Church of Australia. Eventually Iain Murray and the unrelated John J. Murray sent a formal complaint to the Training of the Ministry Committee, which was technically Macleod's employer. Its convenor rejected the complaint and pointed out that the young lady 'unreservedly withdraws any suggestion of immorality on the part of Professor Donald Macleod'.[7] The gossip continued and when Iain Murray returned to Scotland in 1991 he and John Murray allegedly discovered 'that a young lady and communicant member had been distressed for many months on account of alleged sexual harassment' by Macleod in his Free Church College office.[8] He had apparently put his arm around Mairi MacLean, a niece of Angus Smith and a family friend. Iain Murray also heard of a second case involving a Dr Jane Hutton. She had approached the Free Church in 1987 to complain that Macleod, whom she had invited to dance with her at a conference social in Shropshire, had made a pass at her in his office when she visited a few months later. Despite this encounter she later accepted a lift from Stirling to Edinburgh in Macleod's car. She also claimed that he assaulted her on that occasion. When presented with these accusations in 1995 the Free Church courts again decided that there was no case for Macleod to answer. Now a further three young women came forward to claim that Macleod had sexually harassed them. The Church again considered the complaints and again concluded that there was insufficient grounds to try Macleod. In an attempt to bring the matter to an end, the 1995 Assembly minute stated that 'anyone now seeking to pursue it further does so at the risk of being themselves censured as slanderers'.[9]

Strongly encouraged by the two Murrays and by Angus Smith, the young women took their complaints to the police and the Crown Office decided to prosecute Macleod on six charges of assault involving five women. The case turned out to be threadbare. One claim fell at the first hurdle when it became clear that Macleod was not in Edinburgh on the date that he was supposed to have assaulted Ms Maclean.[10] Hutton's accusation of improper contact in Macleod's office was seriously damaged by the fact that she later willingly accepted the lift that was supposedly the occasion for more fondling. One of the other complaints collapsed when the accuser became confused about when she was supposedly harassed and another was rendered implausible by the fact that the complainant had stayed in close touch with the Macleod family after her averred ordeal and had, in a Christmas card to one of Macleod's sons, asked for her best wishes to be passed to his mother and his putatively assaulting father.

Overall, the case was weakened by the fact that Macleod's enemies had solicited most of the complaints, had coached the complainants and had started a fund to pay the expenses of an Australian complainant. The timing of their supposed discovery of the complaints was particularly damaging to their credibility. That three new complainants were found shortly after the Free Church had been given the legal advice that the first two were not enough seemed too convenient to have been naturally occurring. In an unusually critical summary, Sheriff John Horsburgh not only dismissed the case but also named and described as 'conspirators' the clergy who had built the case against Macleod.

> My conclusion is that the witnesses on these charges have squared their consciences on the basis that a modest degree of dishonesty on their part could be justified by the perceived resultant advantage of blackening the name of Professor Macleod and supporting his opponents.[11]

Such clear exoneration should have ended the matter but Macleod's enemies continued to pursue him through church courts on two fronts: his theology and his accusations that they had born false witness. In October 1986 the Commission of Assembly agreed to investigate Macleod's writings for signs of heresy. Macleod's supporters (grouped under the title Free Concern) persuaded a second meeting of the Commission to overturn that decision. In 1987 the conservatives re-formed an earlier organisation: the Free Church Defence Association (FCDA). In response to pleas for an armistice between the factions, Free Concern voluntarily disbanded but the FCDA continued.

As Macleod's enemies had initiated the legal process which condemned them, it seems a little rich for them to accuse him of bearing false witness but they saw themselves as blameless victims. As a relative of one of the complainants put it in a contribution to the FCDA website:

> We have all heard and read about the stress caused by it to the Professor's family but no interest has been shown in the stress and damage caused to the families of these men [his clergy accusers] and of the young women. They were all just expected to forget it and to take part in some kind of 'peace and reconciliation process'. It is no wonder the Church is in turmoil, and that some members are taking a stand for justice and truth.[12]

Considering the author was an aunt of one of the young women, the order of sufferers in the first sentence might be read as unconsciously revealing priorities: the apparently wronged clergy are mentioned before the women who were putatively the real victims.

In 1999 four ministers brought private libels against Macleod before the Edinburgh and Perth Presbytery. It refused to hear the libels. The ministers appealed to the synod which rejected their appeal and they appealed that decision to the General Assembly. When the General Assembly also refused to hear the libels, Maurice Roberts publicly reiterated the accusations, and denounced the General Assembly for its 'wickedness and hypocrisy'. He was unanimously condemned and suspended. His supporters demanded his reinstatement and refused to disband the FCDA. As a mark of Macleod's popularity it is worth noting that the same sitting of the General Assembly elected him Principal of the Free Church College. The Edinburgh Presbytery asked the General Assembly to require the FCDA to disband and 'libelled' thirty-one ministers who had signed an FCDA petition. In January 2000 twenty-two FCDA ministers were removed from their pulpits.

Most of the FCDA formed the Free Church of Scotland Continuing (FCC) and made an audacious bid to the Court of Session for the funds and properties of the Free Church. There was a precedent. When the original Free Church had merged with the United Presbyterians, the House of Lords had ended a much-appealed court case by giving all of the Free Church's extensive property to the few dissenters who had declined to change with the majority. This time there was no repeat of that generosity. Judge Lady Paton dismissed the action.

Although both had their local causes, these disputes turned factionalism into schism because they mapped on to deeper divisions. In both cases the more liberal wing was based in the lowlands and the east – Mackay and Macleod were based in Edinburgh – and their opponents were strongest in the highlands and islands, which is pretty much the same geography as underlay the 1843 and 1900 divisions.

Theory of Schism

It is often said that left-wing parties have such a fondness for ideological rectitude that they cannot see their membership reach three figures before one faction denounces the rest and forms a new party. Monty Python's *Life of Brian* had fun with the competition between the People's Front of Judea, the Judean People's Front and the Front of the People of Judea. As we saw in Chapter 1, Scottish Protestantism has a distinguished history of factionalism and schism. This is sometimes explained by two character flaws in extremists. First, they revel in unpopularity because they believe their truth so esoteric that only the blessed few can grasp it. Second, they cannot resist an argument.

No doubt there is something in both propositions but there is a more important structural explanation behind the schismatic tendency of Protestantism. The Reformation rejected the artificial unity given to Christendom by the hierarchical structure of the episcopal Roman Church in favour of the natural unity that would prevail when all right-thinking people (suitably filled by the Holy Spirit) read the plain meaning of the Bible for themselves. Their hope of a natural unity proved forlorn. Well aware of the dangers of anarchy, the Presbyterian churches constructed elaborate systems of representation to constrain enthusiastic minorities, extensively trained their ministers to ensure doctrinal rectitude, and created elaborate procedures to govern their deliberations. But as the Mackay and Macleod cases showed, no amount of bureaucracy can prevent dissidents claiming to be closer to God than the organisation when that bureaucracy, unlike the Catholic Church's hierarchy, is seen as a mere convenience.

A system which argues that each of us is equally capable of discerning the will of the Almighty and offers no theological support for any human organi-sational response to potential divergence of opinion almost guarantees that, if people take their religious beliefs seriously, they will fall out about precisely what those beliefs should be. It is not the personal psychology of Protestants which explains their fractiousness; it is the absence of any agreed divinely mandated and effective mechanism for imposing order.

Consequences of Schism

Schism is not always debilitating. In times of religious enthusiasm, the prolif-eration of competing sects has its advantages. As we saw in Chapter 2, compe-tition for followers often led to improved provision of religious offices. Once the 1843 Disruption evangelicals had decided to match the national church, they raised the money to erect churches and manses in almost every parish in Scotland, thus almost doubling the worship opportunities for Scots in the lowlands and filling many of the larger spaces in the rural peripheries. Even where competition did not add an additional church, the threat of it sometimes forced the Kirk to improve its provision. And serious rivalry, in the short term at least, deepens commitment as people feel compelled to take sides and strike antagonistic postures. If greater commitment and sensitivity to theological or ecclesiological disputes does not create many converts (and in some times and places it did), it almost certainly means that parents were more likely to impress upon their children the importance of their inherited faith.

However, factionalism and schism also has a corrosive effect. Any belief system is most persuasive when it is so firmly embedded that it is taken-for-granted. For the typical villager of the Middle Ages, Christianity was not a belief system that one could adopt or reject: it was an ever-present accurate and incontrovertible cultural account of the supernatural world and our proper relationship to it. No matter how much competing zealots may press people to choose their option, the proliferation of alternatives makes it ever more likely that some people will opt for none of them. Especially if the faith in question is already a minority concern, sub-division over what to outsiders seems trivial risks people of principle seeming to be cranks. That may not harm recruitment. Very few people not raised in the world of conservative Presbyterianism will join it. But size matters for retention in two ways: providing a satisfying way of life and providing marriage partners. The smaller any group which aims to maintain a distinct way of life for its people, the narrower the range of social interaction, the fewer the job opportunities and the more restricted a culture it can offer within its boundaries. Hence the greater the odds that its young people will be lost to the wider world. This is particularly a problem for match-making. The personal columns of the Aberdeenshire *Press and Journal* contained this rather sad advert. 'Male seeks marriage minded female. Attributes of the suitor and similarly sought would be … intelligent, professional, mature, natural beauty, aged 46–55'. Difficult enough to find. But I have omitted from that text 'a godly profession' and the heading 'Evangelical, Reformed Presbyterian'.[13] In 2010 the Free Church celebrated only eighty-nine weddings; the FCC celebrated just ten. We do not know exactly how many weddings were celebrated by the FPC or the APC because the Registrar-General only publishes figures for bodies which conducted ten or more weddings in a year. So we know it was fewer than ten. Where there was previously two small religious organisations there is now one small and three very small contending bodies and their young people are increasingly faced with the choice of not marrying at all (in which case there is no next generation) or marrying out of the community. And the second option is almost as damaging as the first because we know that broadly speaking a Christian couple, where both belong to the same denomination, has a 50 per cent chance of keeping its children in the faith and that the odds for a mixed-religion couple (even when the mix is as apparently close as Church of Scotland/Free Church, for example) are halved.

It does not take much imagination to explain that. Even if a mixed-religion couple commits to just one church, it is difficult to persuade the children that one particular faith is necessary for salvation when a loved parent belongs to another. The temptation will always be to reconcile the competing positions by moving to some tolerant 'There are many ways that lead to God' position. And if there are indeed many ways to God, then you can safely reject any one of them and before long that becomes, you can reject all of them. Thus toleration becomes indifference.

None of the four conservative Presbyterian churches is good at publishing membership data but, as can be seen from the details in the appendix (table A7.1), reasonable estimates suggest that between 1980 and 2010 the pooled membership halved. Before its split the Free Church had around 20,000 members; the FC and FCC together now have around 10,000 members, with

10 per cent of them in the breakaway FCC. Before its split the Free Presbyterian Church had just over 6,000 members; now its two successors together have some 3,000 members. As noted in Chapter 1, the conservative Presbyterians have always been strongest in the highlands and western islands and their schisms have not broadened their appeal. In 2013 the FPC, for example, had single congregations in Glasgow, Edinburgh, Aberdeen and Perth; the rest of its forty-one Scottish congregations were in its Western Isles and Skye (16) and Highlands (20) presbyteries. Although the larger Free Church has a greater presence outside its base (with three congregations in Edinburgh and four in Glasgow), its support is also concentrated: three-quarters of its 2007 congregations were in the western highlands and islands. Although this method is slightly contaminated by geographical differences in typical incomes, we can roughly identify the largest and the most committed congregations by noting which contributed more than £20,000 in 2007 to central funds. Only three of the eighteen congregations in the Northern (Sutherland and Caithness) Presbytery exceeded that figure. The figure for the Glasgow and Argyll Presbytery was four of eighteen, and three of those were in Glasgow. By far and away the best-performing presbytery was the Western Isles, where 70 per cent of its seventeen congregations (all of them in Lewis) raised over £20,000. Remarkably the single Stornoway congregation contributed more than the eighteen congregations of the Northern Presbytery and the fourteen of Skye and Wester Ross.[14]

One of the effects of the splits was to exaggerate the existing mismatch between congregations and clergy. Since the 1960s all the major Scottish churches have failed to recruit or fund enough clergy for their congregations, especially in rural areas where the sparser populations prevent rationalisation by closing small churches. Asking ministers to serve two or three congregations is common in the Kirk, and Orkney and Shetland have long had trouble filling vacancies. Before their respective schisms, FC and FPC ministers drove past each others' churches to service their outposts. After the splits this inefficiency was doubled: one small area might now contain four rival congregations, none of them big enough to fund a full-time minister. Not surprisingly, there have been tentative talks between the two more 'liberal' bodies: the Free Church has discussed cooperating with the APC over new church-planting (which is always easier than asking existing congregations to cooperate). But though they may look similar to outsiders, the four conservative Presbyterian bodies remain sufficiently committed to what divides them that extensive rationalisation will not occur until the generation that took part in the schisms has passed on.

We have no way of identifying what part of the decline described above is directly a result of the splits and what part is a 'natural' consequence of mortality on a population that has long been atypically elderly. But the details of local disputes that make it to the mass media and a number of conversations with clergy suggest that the ill-feeling created by the schisms has cost all four successor bodies members.

The Widening Divide between Religious and Secular

Christians generally use terms such as church and sect in a partisan manner. We are the true church; they are a deviant sect. Sociologists try to be consistent in the way they describe what interests them and use the terms 'church' and 'sect' to describe two polar extreme ways of organising religious life, each of which has a stable and mutually reinforcing set of characteristics.[15] The 'church' type of Christianity aims to encompass an entire people and claims to represent them to God and vice-versa. It has little notion of a membership because it practises infant baptism and claims all those it baptises as its people. Because it aims to be all-inclusive, it cannot be terribly demanding: it has to live with the religiously careless and indolent majority. The 'sect' is very different. It is a self-selecting voluntary association of like-minded believers which insists that all its members be seriously religious and which draws clear lines between its members and the 'worldly'. The Church of Scotland has generally behaved as a church: accepting, for example, an obligation to baptise, marry and bury all who reside in its parishes. The Exclusive Brethren is a sect. It makes considerable demands of its adherents and 'dis-fellowships' those who fail to meet its exacting standards. The principle of separating from the unGodly is taken to the extent of not eating with non-members (even when they are family and live under the same roof) and denying themselves job opportunities that require joining some professional body. To these two types, we can add a third: the 'denomination'. From the early nineteenth century, the decline in the number of believers, the growth of the principle of religious freedom and the success of schisms from the national churches have made the church type of religion impossible and the Kirk and the Church of England (and their counterparts elsewhere) have had to scale down their self-estimates and accept that they are just one among a number of equally legitimate bodies. Over the same period many sects have also changed. Those that last more than a generation or two tend to become more tolerant, more liberal and less strict. As we saw in Chapter 2's account of religion in Lewis, a rare combination of circumstances can allow a sectarian style of religion to become the dominant culture of an entire society: Puritan New England and Calvin's Geneva are other examples. But once those rare circumstances are lost, the sect either becomes increasingly liberal and evolves into a denomination or it shrinks and becomes increasingly alienated from its catchment population.

Being extreme is, of course, not a fixed condition but is rather a shifting function of relative popularity and the changing preferences of the majority. Those who stand still while everyone else changes may end up like the Jews in exile in Babylon who wanted to know how they could 'sing the Lord's song' in a strange land. In many small ways the increased secularisation of Scotland has made it a place of exile for conservative Presbyterians and made them seem increasingly alien. One mechanism that reinforces this vicious circle of alienation is the declining sect's ability to control its environment. Once a church (reverting now to casual usage) ceases to be representative of its local people and becomes known primarily for its ideological rigour, it attracts monomaniacs, and if it is having trouble recruiting clergy, it may well be insufficiently critical of potential supporters. For example, in 1996 an Australian was called by the Staffin congregation of the FPC. In 2000 he was dismissed for extremism. It was not so much that his doctrines were wrong. Formally they were not. But he patently lacked the ability to rub along. There is a fine line between maintaining a 'walk with the Lord' and being a nuisance. He fell out with the local Church of Scotland minister. His addresses to schoolchildren apparently involved reminding them that the unregenerate were destined to hell; the local schools banned him. He refused to attend funerals of people of other denominations, 'which ministers here always used to do'.[16] One former congregant said:

> Our family stopped attending because the minister there now has a bit of an obsession about the Roman Catholic Church, the Free Church of Scotland and the APC. There is no need for it. We have just got fed up. It's a strange form of negative Christianity. I'm afraid he comes across as a bit of a bigot. While that may seem to appeal to a minority in our Church, I'm glad to say it does not go down well with most people here in Staffin.[17]

There is an important point here about the need for sensitivity, even in an environment as culturally homogenous as the non-Catholic Hebridean islands. Evangelical Protestants often present an invidious comparison between their admirable consistency and the compromises of liberals who hold strongly to very little and are prepared to keep even that in a compartment for Sunday use only. But even committed conservatives who have many ties to neighbours who do not share their religious beliefs will learn to pick the time and place for sermonising.

Tempering and compartmentalising work both ways. Between the two polar extremes of a sect enjoying the support of the majority of its base population (Lewis in, say, 1880) and a sect being a small saved remnant (for example, the Brethren in Shetland or Edinburgh in the 1960s) there is a long period when the seriously religious and the secular cautiously co-exist. My elderly farming neighbours in Aberdeenshire recall that their fathers did not harvest on the Sabbath, not because they were sabbatarians but because they wished to avoid offending those who were. As late as the 1970s the same sensitivity was still expected from non-church people in the Hebrides and the highlands: the Northern Lighthouse Board, for example, instructed its new keepers on the need to respect local customs.

Three changes destroyed the balance of the religious ecology of the highlands and islands. The first – the growth of religious indifference – was docu-
mented in Chapter 2. The others were a decline in localism and a change in
migration patterns. The twentieth century saw a steady shift of control of both
commercial and state enterprises from the local to the international. Small
family firms became parts of national and then international concerns, driven
only by rational economic considerations and insensitive to local cultural
differences. The centre of control of state business such as education, social
welfare and policing has also shifted to London or Edinburgh. Under the original 1873 Education Act, schools could offer religious instruction as local 'wont
and usage' required. Now we have national curricula. Membership of the
European Union and other international obligations have reduced the freedom
of business people to manage their affairs in ways which protect local particu-
larities. Gay rights offers a pertinent example. While the majority of young
and middle-class Britons might be in favour of the modern equality agenda, it
seems pretty clear that most inhabitants of Lewis are not. But the modern state
rarely permits local opt-outs.

These institutional and procedural abstractions are turned into real change
by what demographers call 'counter-stream migration'. The highlands and
islands have long suffered from emigration. Between the well-known exoduses
that are mourned in poetry and song there has been a steady trickle of young
people departing for education and work. The increase of well-paid white-
collar work in local government and social services has seen some return
but the net flow is outwards. Some of the space has been filled with English
people looking to convert the capital gained from inflated house prices into a
gentler way of life. While such incomers have brought economic capital into
the fringes, the 'cultural capital' that has come along with it has been distinctly
unhelpful to the religious life of the highlands and islands. The village of
Gardenstown in Aberdeenshire is unusual in that its reputation as a Brethren
stronghold has attracted a number of English families who share the locals'
distinctive religion, but the vast majority of the cosmopolitans drawn by the
romance of magnificent scenery and simple peasant folk have been atheists
with little or no sympathy for the faith of their new neighbours.[18] Far more
likely to describe themselves as spiritual than religious, if they have any faith
it is more likely to be the New Age type discussed in Chapter 10 than the
Calvinist Presbyterianism that once coloured the highlands and islands. If
'downsizing' incomers see anything attractive in the religious culture of their
new-found idyll it is more likely to be in some fictitious construction of a pre-
Reformation 'Celtic spirituality' than in the real and recent history of the Free
Church. Fifty years ago, when they were patently a minority, unbelievers who
found themselves in the last stronghold of the pure gospel would rub along.
Now when that stronghold is crumbling, they and the more assertive of the
unbelieving locals see little reason why they should tolerate religiously inspired

constraints on their travel plans, their golf-playing or their ability to buy an alcoholic drink.

I hesitate to put a date on it but it seems clear that around the end of the twentieth century, the relative power and influence of the Godly and unGodly in the highlands and islands changed so that the latter started to view the former as a nuisance. The Calvinist Presbyterians of the highlands and islands have long been the butt of lowland jokes but those jokes used to be gentle and contained a hint of admiration for those who reminded us of our grandparents. Not any more.

God is Nice

The second-century Jewish sage Rabbi Hillel is said to have been approached by a gentile who offered to convert if the great rabbi could teach him the whole of the notoriously lengthy and elaborate Torah (or 'the law') while he stood on one foot. Accepting the challenge, Hillel stood on one leg for the time it took to say: 'That which is despicable to you, do not do to your fellow; this is the whole Torah, and the rest is commentary'. Christians have always been able to reduce their faith to the same golden rule: 'Love thy neighbour as thyself'. But there has always been a lot more to it than that: the Shorter Catechism produced by the 1640s Westminster Assembly of Divines as a simple summary of Christian doctrine contains 107 questions and answers, and editions with scriptural justifications are long books. As Christianity has become less popular it has also become less well-known and to most outsiders it has become reduced to a parody of the golden rule: God is nice, proper Christians are nice, and anyone who does or says anything which is not nice cannot be a Christian. Even within the churches there has been a visible decline in interest in the theological and organisational differences which defined the various components of our religious jigsaw. Christian unity may be God's will but it has the effect of relegating to matters of taste what were once important principles. In fairness to Rabbi Hillel, he qualified his apparently dismissive view of the Torah as 'commentary' by adding 'now go and learn it!'

The following are just a few of the many illustrations of the public misunderstanding of Christianity which I have collected over the last decade. A Scottish Sunday paper began its account of a man who had been asked to leave his Free Presbyterian congregation after his adultery became known with the summary: 'A religious hardliner has been thrown out of his church after a secret affair'.[19] The philanderer may indeed have been unco pious but it is pretty clear that the epithet 'religious hardliner' is simply a find-and-replace alternative for Free Presbyterian. Although originally developed by English charismatic evangelicals, the Alpha course in basic Christian beliefs has been used as a training programme by a wide variety of British Christians (including Presbyterians and Roman Catholics). Despite teaching nothing that is not in the creedal statements of the Christian churches, Alpha often attracts a negative press. For example, *Scotland on Sunday* ran the headline '"Danger" cult sparks mental health alert' over a story that said: 'A Christian movement about to launch a massive recruiting drive in Scotland has been accused of carrying out "dangerous and disturbing" practices by church leaders and psychiatrists'.[20] The distancing effect of the quotation marks around 'danger' is quite undermined by the full text, which uncritically repeats hysterical accusations against what is actually a rather dull attempt to teach basic Christian ideas. When pop star Geri Halliwell expressed an interest in Alpha, a Scottish Sunday paper headlined the story 'Outrage over Geri's links to anti-abortion, anti-gay group' and began it: 'Pop star Geri Halliwell has come under fire from all sides after publicly declaring that she is following a course of study with a controversial Christian fundamentalist group'.[21]

When Pope Benedict politely pointed out that very little of the flummery we now associate with Christmas is actually biblical, his comments were reported as if he had behaved badly. The *Daily Mail*'s headline ran: 'Killjoy Pope crushes Christmas nativity traditions'.[22] Clergy who refuse to provide religious offices to people who are patently uninterested in the religion in question are reported as mean-spirited. Ditto ministers who refuse to let church halls to yoga and meditation groups on the grounds that, if the original justifications for those activities are taken seriously, they are tools of the opposition.

Arguably public ignorance is a greater problem for Protestants than for Catholics because the latter have special rituals and clothes and decorations which signify 'religion' even to the ill-informed. Hence a dramatist who wishes to show some religious business can always introduce a priest, in his robes, administering the last rites. The difficulty for conservative Protestants is that their faith is largely internal. Remove the believing congregation from a Presbyterian church and, as the conversion of the parish church on the tiny island of Stroma shows, you just have a large tractor shed. Without the beliefs that made sense of them, a lot of the distinctive marks of Presbyterianism either become invisible or appear simply as pointless omissions. In 1940 the novelist Naomi Mitchison was living on the Mull of Kintyre. Her diary notes of Christmas Day: 'No special church or anything. That would be Popish'.[23] The son of a Presbyterian minister in Aberdeen in the 1940s noted that 'Though carols were sung in church services during December, Christmas was not especially religious for us or those around us . . . Some shops remained open all of Christmas Day'. Most fathers were at work and the post was delivered as usual.[24] By the 1960s Presbyterian resistance was crumbling and by the end of the century the main Scottish churches had succumbed to public pressure to treat Christmas as a special religious event: watchnight services, Christingles and all. And because very few people know or care about the Presbyterian horror of idolatry, the conservatives who resist this capitulation just seem like Scrooge or the Grinch who stole Christmas. Likewise the absence of religious business from funerals. As noted at the start of the chapter, there are good theological reasons why Presbyterians have historically been reluctant to do anything which would look like endorsing the idea that the living can change the fate of the dead post-mortem. But once those reasons are forgotten, principle is mis-read as prissiness. Once the cultural background to Puritanism is removed, all that is left is a series of negatives.

In summary, the reduction of Christianity to 'niceness' has the ironic effect of making serious Christian organisations appear mean-spirited and self-interested and, well, not Christian. There is no way of showing this statistically but there seems to have been a clear drift to the general notion that the primary purpose of Christianity (indeed, all 'proper' religion) is to promote civility. Any idea that the chief end of man might be to glorify God (as the Shorter Catechism puts it) or that loving thy neighbour might involve telling him that unless he changes his ways he will go to hell, has been quite forgotten. The net result is that the sort of condemnation which used to be levelled at the alien new religious movements of the 1960s is now often aimed at conservatives within the Christian church.[25]

Conclusion

One purpose of this chapter is to explain why a small part of a small country now has four competing conservative Presbyterian organisations. Another is to convey a sense of how Scotland's increased secularity has backed those conservatives into the awkward position of being unable to represent their principles without seeming to be unChristian. In the aftermath of the SS *Iolaire* disaster, which saw 174 Lewismen die when the ship bringing them home from the First World War foundered at the mouth of Stornoway harbour, a visiting preacher made reference in prayer to men who had been taken 'before their time'. The father of two such victims asked afterwards to see the minister privately and told him firmly: 'My sons were called by the Lord at the time He had ordained for them from all eternity, not a moment longer and not a moment before'.[26] It is hard not to admire such fortitude and conviction and it is easy to see an affinity between a belief in an all-powerful creator God and the harshness of life in the Scottish highlands and islands. For a religion to remain popular it must remain plausible, and one of the characteristics which determines plausibility is the fit between the images of the powers of humankind at the heart of the faith and in the general culture. It is not an accident that every schism in Scottish Presbyterianism since Scotland's peripheries were brought into the Protestant fold has seen the highlands and islands set against the lowlands. The two late twentieth-century schisms had their own local causes but they also illustrated two general dynamics: the fractious nature of Reformed Protestantism and the increasingly positive views of human potential found in the parts of the country that modernised and prospered first.

Notes

1. Mackay was a lord twice over: first by virtue of being a senior Scots law officer and second by virtue of being raised to the House of Lords by Margaret Thatcher.
2. J. MacLeod, *No Great Mischief if You Fall* (Edinburgh: Mainstream, 1993), p. 100.
3. For a detailed account of the case, see MacLeod, *No Great Mischief.*
4. M. Armstrong, 'A "Biblical Christian"', *Life and Work* April 2006, p. 14.
5. An undercurrent was Donald Macleod's criticism of some of the teachings of Martin Lloyd-Jones, a preacher much admired by ministers associated with the Banner of Truth Trust.
6. F. Macdonald, 'Scenes of ecclesiastical theatre in the Free Church of Scotland, 1981–2000', *Northern Scotland* 20 (2000), pp. 125–48.
7. R. Nicoll, 'A wee schism', *Guardian Weekend*, 12 October 1996, p. 34.
8. Nicoll, 'A wee schism', p. 34.
9. Macdonald, 'Scenes', p. 133.
10. Macleod's son John, whom Maclean had asserted was present in the office shortly before the putative assault, was also able to demonstrate that he was a long way from Edinburgh on the day in question.
11. Nicoll, 'A wee schism', p. 36.
12. Agnes Mackenzie, 'A lawyer's view', FCDA website active 1997–2000 but still available at http://myweb.tiscali.co.uk/theword/foundations/smlawyer.html.
13. *Press and Journal*, 30 December 2009.
14. 'Congregational remittances', *The Monthly Record of the Free Church of Scotland*, November 2007, p. 23.
15. For a detailed discussion of what sociologists mean by the terms church, sect, cult and denomination, see S. Bruce, *Religion in the Modern World: from Cathedrals to Cults* (Oxford: Oxford University Press, 1996).
16. *Sunday Mail*, 25 June 2000.
17. *Press and Journal*, 18 May 2000.
18. For an excellent anthropological study of Gardenstown, see J. Webster, *The Anthropology of Protestantism: Faith and Crisis Among Scottish Fishermen* (London: Palgrave, 2013).
19. *Sunday Mail*, 23 February 2003.
20. *Scotland on* Sunday, 20 September 1998.
21. *Sunday Herald*, 2 December 2001.
22. M. Robinson, 'Killjoy Pope crushes Christmas nativity traditions: new Jesus book reveals there were no donkeys beside crib, no lowing oxen and definitely no carols', *Daily Mail*, 21 November 2012; http://www.dailymail.co.uk/news/article-2236195/New-Jesus-book-reveals-donkeys-crib-lowing-oxen-definitely-carols-Chr istmas.html#ixzz2XW8qmSPw.
23. N. Mitchison, *Among You Taking Notes: the Wartime Diaries of Naomi Mitchison 1939–45* (London: Phoenix Press, 1985), p. 103.

24. C. MacLean, *Monkeys, Bears and Gutta Percha* (East Linton: Tuckwell Press, 2001), p. 33.

25. This argument, and its consequences for the classic church, sect, denomination and cult typology, is elaborated in S. Bruce and D. Voas, 'Secularization and typologies of religious organizations', *Journal of Contemporary Religion* 22 (2007), pp. 1–17.

26. J. MacLeod, *Banner in the West: a Spiritual History of Lewis and Harris* (Edinburgh: Birlinn, 2008), pp. 233–4.

8

FROM COMMUNITY TO ASSOCIATION:
THE NEW CHURCHES

Scotland has a reasonable claim to have invented half of the modern road. John McAdam became a trustee of the Ayrshire Turnpike in 1783 and spent ten years trying to improve road-building. Although his method of layering stones and raising the road above the surroundings was a considerable improvement, it required an American inventor, Edgar Hooley, to add the layers of tar or bitumen that gave us our modern Tar Macadam or 'tarmac'. Scotland's claim to have invented much to run on those roads is less impressive. At the start of the twentieth century the Argyll motor car, made in Alexandria, near Dumbarton, won a number of prestige races but never made the transition to mass production. Under government pressure, Midlands-based car manufacturer Rootes opened an assembly plant at Linwood (a village about 15 miles south of Glasgow) in 1963. The Hillman Imp's status as a Scottish car brought it some success north of the border but it fell far short of expected sales and there were extra costs in bringing components made in the Midlands north and sending assembled cars back south for finishing. The ex-shipyard workers had no experience of car manufacture but they did have a history of union militancy which caused an unprecedented number of strikes and stoppages. After changing ownership a number of times and limping through various schemes for state support, the plant was finally closed in 1981.

Roads and cars are important for understanding contemporary Scottish Christianity because easy travel helped undermine the parish structure of the churches and allowed the growth of 'magnet' sites. The national Church of Scotland was organised to serve people who walked to worship. The entire country was divided into parishes, and taxes on the major landowners within each parish were intended to provide a church building, a manse for the minister and a school. The assumption was that the people belonged to their parish and attended their parish church. Population shifts caused parishes to be re-organised but the national Church remains largely territorial. Major competitors pursued a similar model. After 1843 the Free Church deliberately copied the Kirk's parish structure. Even smaller Protestant denominations have aimed to provide a single building for the members of a particular area, with services conducted by a resident local minister who provides pastoral care for the congregation. In the urban lowlands the Catholic Church followed a slightly different business plan, with fewer but larger buildings in which services could be repeated by a team of clerics as often as was required for the numbers who attended. But even it divides the country into areas with their own hierarchical structures and expects that its people will attach themselves to their local church and that their priest will visit them in their homes.

The motor car is important because it freed people from an obligation to attend their local church. My neighbours drive 80 miles every Sunday, past at least twenty churches, to attend the one they prefer. 'Automobility' means that a religious provider does not need to have 300 sites to make its product available to most of Scotland; it can locate a number of large outlets next to motorways and city by-passes and invite its self-selecting clientele to come to it. One of the main beneficiaries of this Tesco superstore model has been the charismatic movement.

The Charismatics

My first experience of the charismatic movement came quite late. In 1981, I attended Dales Bible Week on the site of the North Yorkshire Showground in Harrogate as a guest of a BBC crew which was filming the event. The following is an extract from my notes of the evening service:

> The audience threw themselves into the tenth repeat of 'Awake, O Zion!' and two short stout elders hopped and jumped and twirled each other round on the stage. The man conducting the singing had his gaze fixed firmly on the asbestos roof of the hall while his right hand beat out a steady rhythm. As the final high note was reached someone began to clap and soon all of the seven thousand people were applauding themselves, each other but most of all, their Saviour. The clapping died away as people raised their arms to the heavens. There came faint humming, like the noise of bees, which grew and grew, as more and more people began to praise the Lord in tongues. The man next to us, who before the service had been acting like a perfectly efficient PR man, was now making bizarre noises. The noise became more intense as the musicians added their contribution to the droning. Sensing that the audience had peaked, the conductor sang the first line of another revival chorus and soon the hall was once more rocking to enthusiastic singing. Two middle-aged women grasped each other and hopped to the beat. A whole row from the teenagers section pogo-ed.

The first Dales Bible Week had been held six years earlier and was the work of a group of churches led by Bryn Jones of Bradford, one of a number of preachers who inspired the charismatic movement in the UK.

Purification movements are a perennial feature of the churches. Though attempts to solve the problem come in waves, the complaint is commonplace. As soon as a church becomes organised and devises set ways of presenting its services, someone will complain that it is losing its soul or its mission. There is a fairly constant tension between the roles of priest and prophet. The priest manages the church, codifies its teachings, and administers its rituals in an orderly manner. The prophet denounces its shortcomings and calls the people to return to God's original purpose. The charismatic movement of the 1970s was standard issue in its complaints about the spiritual deadness of the churches, the stultifying nature of clerical leadership and the need to re-discover the simplicity of the New Testament. Those criticisms could have been made by the Methodists in the 1820s or the Brethren in the 1880s. It was unusual only in asserting that what was missing was the charismata or the 'gifts of the Holy Spirit'. The first generation of disciples, who were personally chosen by Jesus, were held to possess a spiritual skill set – the power to heal, to prophesy and to speak in the 'tongues of men and angels' primary among them – that is now no longer available to the ordinary Christian because those gifts have been institutionalised in, or replaced by, the operations of the church.

Inspired principally by a group of male preachers from the independent fringes of Protestantism, a large number of people left the churches often to meet in small groups initially called 'house churches'.[1] Gerald Coates, one of the early leaders, coined the phrase 'new churches' as an alternative. The term 'Restoration' was also used to signify that what was being promoted was not innovation but rather the restoration of the church leadership roles identified by Paul in his letter to the Ephesians (4: 11): apostle, prophet, evangelist, pastor and teacher. Along with the critique of the existing churches came a vaguely millennialist hope that reform would reverse the decline of the Christian churches in the West and (for some) hasten the Second Coming.

As Bryn Jones told his Dales Bible Week audience, only properly constituted churches, free from human conventions and filled with the Holy Spirit, would be suitable for the showers of revival 'rain from heaven' when they came. Given the entrenched interests in the extant churches, the pioneers had to start anew. Jones knew what kind of churches he wanted: 'They would not be modelled on some allegedly perfect primitive church . . . he wanted churches "restored" to a point far further back: to all that had been in God's heart from the beginning for his church and that he had caused to be recorded in Holy Scripture for our instruction.'[2]

Some of the new groups joined in formal associations – such as Newfrontiers, Cornerstone, Salt and Light Ministries – while others grew as entirely independent congregations. Hardly surprising, given that it was led by independent evangelists with even less commitment than the average Protestant to some shared form of government, what initially seemed like a unified movement soon split into two distinct strands. One was similar to the traditional Brethren movement (but with the charismata). The other was more self-consciously modern: it encouraged women in leadership roles, it embraced the use of modern technology in worship, and it permitted casual dress, smoking and drinking.

In retrospect this now seems trivial but in the early 1980s the house church movement attracted a great deal of criticism for the authoritarian style of some of its leaders. Aware that the absence of hierarchical structure meant few constraints, and that prophesies and messages from the Lord could have come no further than the speaker's sub-conscious, the early movement leaders adopted what was called 'shepherding ' or 'covering': each would accept the spiritual direction of another. Some shepherds did indeed treat their followers like sheep: instructing them to change jobs, move house and enter or break off relationships. More common but less newsworthy was a general climate of spiritual bullying. To this day there is a significant sub-culture of former charismatics (which frequently vents on internet bulletin boards) who lost faith in the movement because they were hectored and harassed for not being spiritually up to snuff. I say that these complaints now seem trivial because the movement very quickly became institutionalised as just another clutch of small denominations and independent congregations. The commune style of small groups giving all their time and money to the cause died out and, after the initial excitement of being involved in a new wave wore off, most adherents showed little more commitment than did the typical Brethren or Baptist member.

Although new congregations were the most visible part of the charismatic movement, an equally important element was made up of congregations in the mainstream churches (particularly the Baptists and the Church of England) who rejected the Jones separatist line in favour of revitalising their own churches.

That the movement overall has the three strands of independent congregations, new denominations and congregations within the mainstream denominations makes its overall size extremely difficult to estimate. It seems likely that it grew quickest in the 1980s and early 1990s and then declined slightly, so that by the end of the twentieth century the British charismatic movement numbered roughly 400,000 people.[3]

The Pentecostalists

A friend who had been raised in a charismatic church called the movement 'Pentecostalism for the socially aspiring' and he has a point. The Holy Spirit had been similarly active fifty years earlier. That movement had been called

'Pentecostalism' after the event described in the New Testament (Acts 2: 1) as follows:

> And when the day of Pentecost was fully come, [the apostles] were all with one accord in one place . . . And there appeared unto them cloven tongues like as of fire, and it sat upon each of them. And they were filled with the Holy Ghost, and began to speak with other tongues, as the Spirit gave them utterance. And there were dwelling at Jerusalem Jews, devout men, out of every nation under heaven. Now when this was noised abroad, the multitude came together, and were confounded, because that every man heard them speak in his own language. And they were all amazed and marvelled, saying one to another, Behold, are not all these which speak Galileans? And how hear we every man in our own tongues, wherein we were born?

To drive the point home, there is then a list of sixteen language groups. Speaking in 'the tongues of men and angels' was historically held by the Christian churches to be a gift given only to the original apostles but it was a feature of a major revival which began in Los Angeles in 1906, where the ability to make strange vocal sounds was seen as proof of the believer being filled with the Holy Spirit. One reason why mainstream Christians rejected Pentecostalism was that the 'second blessing' was seen as an improper addition to what the gospel required of the saved Christian and as a form of spiritual one-upmanship. It was also suspect because of its associations with the notion of 'entire sanctification' or 'holiness': the idea that this second blessing was a necessary further guarantee of salvation and marked a signal change in the convert's character.

Pentecostalism spread widely in the USA, especially among black churches, and by the end of the century it was popular in large parts of Latin America and Africa, from where it was brought to the UK for a second time, this time by west African immigrants. At the end of the twentieth century Black Pentecostal churches formed the one section of Christianity that was growing in the UK, but in the 1920s the impact of Pentecostalism was limited. It recruited a largely upper working-class following but did not come close to the growth of Methodism 150 years earlier.[4] Pentecostalism was markedly less popular in Scotland than in England and it was largely confined to the industrial centres of the lowlands. A few congregations were established in some of the fishing towns of the north-east but it found no foothold in the highlands and islands. By the end of the 1930s it had reached its maximum penetration and there was little subsequent growth or spread. In 1959 there were seventeen congregations affiliated to the Church of the Nazarene; in 2012 there were eighteen. In 1980 the four main groupings – the Elim Church, the Apostolic Church, the Assemblies of God and the Church of the Nazarene – together had fewer than 100 congregations with a total membership of just over 4,000: about half of what it would be if Pentecostalism were as popular in Scotland as in England. By the end of the twentieth century, in places re-invigorated by the charismatic movement, there was some further spread. The Apostolic Church, for example, now has affiliates in Grantown, Newtonmore and Skye, and its Inverness congregation holds meetings in Glenelg and Brora, but these church plants are small and casual conversations suggest that a large number of the activists are English incomers.

The Dumfries River of Life

In 2012 I met Mark Smith, the pastor of the River of Life Church in Dumfries, in a setting ripe with ironies. Mark was presenting the early evening show on Alive Radio, a community radio station with a range of about 10 kilometres. The radio station was housed on the top floor of a former Catholic convent. Designed by the firm of Pugin and Pugin, it was built in 1881. According to a contemporary announcementt:

> [it] is being built for the nuns of the Perpetual Adoration, at the cost of the dowager Lady Herries. It is situated on the top of Corbelly hill, Maxwell Town, Dumfries. The site is a most beautiful one, being the highest point in the neighbourhood, and commands a view of the country for many miles. It is built with the local stone, the dressings being polished and the facings rock-faced. The colour of the stone harmonises well with the surrounding scenery.[5]

Latterly a grant-aided girls' secondary school, the convent closed in the 1970s. It was eventually bought by a Ballymena businessman who had made the buildings watertight and recouped some of his costs by selling off peripheral houses and buildings. The chapel, its distinctly Catholic decorations removed, is rented to the Apostolic Church for a token sum. Other parts of the convent were used for a Christian youth club. Apart from all the other meanings that could be drawn from the setting, there was an indirect link to the child abuse scandals discussed in Chapter 4. The main convent building was in such good and unaltered condition that it was used for the interior scenes of the 2002 Peter Mullan film *The Magdalene Sisters*, a popular if painful dramatisation of the harsh regime to which some Catholic orders subjected their child charges in the 1950s.[6]

Mark Smith is a Yorkshireman who trained as an agricultural engineer and first came to the Dumfries area in 1980 to work for the Ministry of Agriculture. Although he had attended the Dales Bible Week and had charismatic leanings, he had been raised as Methodist and he and his wife started to attend the Dumfries Methodist Church but were told when they arrived that it was due to close in six months. After sampling a number of churches in the area, they started their own house group meeting. For a while they had as their superintending pastor an ex-military man from Glasgow, but he alienated some people and Mark took over the church in 1984. Feeling a call to minister, Mark and his wife went to Sweden for a year, where they studied with the pastor of a large charismatic congregation. When they returned to Dumfries in 1987 they started the church in earnest.

The River of Life now meets in a small flat-roofed building which was once part of Dumfries railway station, but one decision in their search for suitable premises is significant. The former Greyfriars Church had lain empty since its congregation merged with another nearby in 2004. It had been bought by Andrew Crosbie, an ordained Episcopalian priest and a descendant of John Crosbie, the Dumfries provost who levied a tax on beer to raise money to build the first Greyfriars Church in the early 1700s. Crosbie said he wanted to maintain the building as a place of Christian worship and 'prevent its deterioration into either a secular use or an inappropriate use'.[7] He hoped it might be used for ecumenical services or for large exhibitions and in 2008 he offered it to Smith. River of Life turned Crosbie down because the building was so large that it would demoralise the congregation by reminding them of their relative unpopularity and because its embodiment of Victorian Christianity was exactly the association that River of Life was trying to avoid. What was obviously a church in the architectural sense would inhibit the growth of 'the church' in the sense of a worshipping people.

Building the congregation was difficult. There was notably little interest in charismatic Christianity among the natives of Dumfries. Most of the recruits were incomers: initially predominantly English but later involving two African families. The church is part of a network associated with Hillsong in London, a popular charismatic church that meets in the Dominion theatre in London's West End and attracts some 8,000 people to the five services it runs on a Sunday.

The Smiths are almost hyper-actively committed to promoting the gospel and under their leadership the River of Life has been involved in schooling, the hospitality trade, electoral politics and the electronic mass media. In Sweden their children had been taught in the independent Christian school attached to the charismatic church they attended, and when they returned to Dumfries they used the home-schooling of their own children as the core of an independent Christian school. Although non-denominational Christian schools are common in the USA, there are few in the UK. Despite widespread complaints about state schools, few parents are sufficiently wealthy, or critical, to support an independent operation and the parents of Dumfries were unreceptive. After the Smiths' children grew up, the school closed.

A more enduring spin-off from the church is its cafe. There had been a Christian bookshop in the town but it closed, and in order to keep that facility the Smiths took it over and added a cafe to the book-selling. As has been the case with many secular bookshops, the catering side prospered and overtook the book-selling. The cafe, with a small stock of Christian literature, now occupies a prime site in the town centre.

The Smiths also promoted the gospel by standing for election for the

Scottish Christian party (on which, see Chapter 12). The invitation came from George Hargreaves, the Pentecostal pastor who founded the Christian party and its Scottish off-shoot. Mark agreed to stand because he saw it as a valuable opportunity to advertise the River of Life. He polled few votes but gained a good deal of local publicity and would have stood again had he not been barred by his new role with Alive Radio. As part of the vetting process for short-range community radio licences, applicants are invited to broadcast for a number of single days. In its initial test broadcasts, the station was explicitly Christian but there was an obvious tension between being overtly Christian and serving an area in which most people have no church connection. Some of those who wanted an American-style 'televangelism' radio station dropped out and when the station did win its full community licence, it was as a secular concern. Nonetheless Smith remains thoroughly committed to it because he sees it as a valuable resource for the town.

I have spent some time detailing the River of Life because it is easy to suppose that such London 'mega-churches' as Hillsong, with its congregation in the large thousands, are typical of the charismatic movement. It is true that most cities have a couple of congregations with 300 or 400 members, but away from the large conurbations the typical New Church is not that different in scale to the congregations of the Church of Scotland.[8] For all the publicity it attracts from its cafe and the other enterprises that have borne the church's name, River of Life has about 100 members and its average Sunday attendances are between 60 and 70 people. As Smith is an extremely personable man, with a great deal of drive, it is difficult to imagine there is anyone in the Dumfries area who has not heard of his church. That so much effort has produced only moderate rewards suggests that Scotland might be particularly resistant to a movement which has enjoyed greater success in the south of England. I will return to that possibility shortly.

The Gifts of the Spirit

Any summary description of a cultural movement that has no single authoritative source or force is difficult, but the charismatic movement is distinguished by the following characteristics which, charismata aside, also describe pretty well the sort of independent evangelical church that joins the Evangelical Alliance or the Fellowship of Independent Evangelical Churches.

Being Culturally Relevant

Like the claim that the churches have lost sight of their mission, the argument over changing to keep up with the times is perennial. Do we regard a particular translation of the Bible or particular rituals as divinely inspired and thus unchangeable or do we separate a 'core' Christian message from its expressions in any particular time and place and change those expressions so that they remain culturally relevant? If such arguments have become more common in the last 100 years, that is in part because the pace of social change has accelerated. Indeed, two of the defining characteristics of modernity are the deliberate engineering of change and the perpetual expectation of change. So there is more keeping up to be done. The arguments are also now more pointed because the churches are only too well aware that they are unpopular. Old people (and people who like old things) may find comfort in repeating the formulas of the Anglican evensong service as they have been said for 400 years but the decline in the numbers of people who attend evensong undermines the argument for tradition.

The charismatic movement has been a powerful vehicle for change, especially in worship. The classic hymns of the nineteenth century, with the tunes played on an organ, have been largely replaced by modern 'praise worship' performed by an amplified band of musicians playing the instruments one would expect in a rock group. As one congregation says on its website:

> While we appreciate the rich traditions of our Christian and Scottish heritage, we are always ready to explore fresh ways of engaging with each other and encountering the living God. Multimedia, drama and contemporary music, as well as symbol, reflection and liturgy all play a part in our corporate worship. Services are planned and led by our Worship Team, who recognise the value of encouraging and developing the gifts of the church and creating opportunities for them to be used in worship, whether those gifts are in the area of communication, technology or the creative arts.[9]

The conservative Presbyterian stance of rejecting the use of 'human creation' in worship and singing only the Biblical (and hence divinely inspired) Psalms of David, unaccompanied, is logical and consistent. Objections to amplified electronic instrumentation and rock rhythms are neither. After all, when the great Victorian Free Church cleric Horatio Bonar wrote the now venerated 'I heard the voice of Jesus say', he was composing a *new* hymn, and although its usual setting, the tune Kingsfold, sounds as though it could only ever have been played on a church organ, it was actually a folk tune collected and adapted by Ralph Vaughan Williams in 1906. One only needs to read arguments about suitable forms of church music from any previous era to appreciate that the boundaries of the acceptable are always shifting. Archie Craig, a progressive figure in the Kirk in the 1950s, was raised in the pre-merger Free Church and he had severe reservations about the religious use of even classical music. Bach was acceptable but Beethoven was suspect: 'excerpts from his works might pass muster on ecclesiastical occasions, provided they were played at a sufficiently slow tempo and made to sound as much like psalm tunes as possible'.[10] That was Beethoven told.

Unable to make a consistent argument against the principle of innovation, critics of praise worship have had to argue against it in particular. When rock-and-roll first became popular in the late 1950s there were psychologists ready to argue that its 'jungle rhythms' and incessant 'beat' hypnotised and 'brain-washed' young people.[11] The same case has been made against charismatic praise worship, especially when simple choruses are repeated over and over again by people standing with their arms aloft.

Actually boredom is a greater danger than brain-washing. At the risk of sounding racist, I have to say that in the thirty-two years since I attended Dales Bible Week, I have yet to find a white charismatic congregation that comes anywhere close to the gospel singing of black Pentecostal churches. Charismatics repeat choruses but the dynamics are missing. Few white performers can manage the emotionalism of black preachers switching between speaking lines of Bible texts and singing while barely holding back tears of sorrow and joy, and the congregations are always too reserved to become lost in the experience. Like Celine Dion or Beyoncé wannabes, soloists trill and warble every note to within an inch of its life but it rarely feels like they mean it.

Modern praise worship also runs into problems with the lyrics. The advantage of traditional formulae is that one tends not to take the words literally but to read into them what one wishes to hear. The opening line of the *Nunc Dimitis* – Lord, now let thy servant depart in peace – works because it can mean many things to its diverse hearers. It may seem logical to say that every generation of worshippers should clearly express its beliefs and values in its own language but too much clarity can easily become jarring and the self-consciously modern becomes dated very quickly. One example that sticks in my memory is an updating of the harvest festival theme. As most of us are no longer involved in agriculture, convincingly celebrating the harvest is difficult. So the author instead listed a wide range of features of God's creation for which we should thank our Maker. The one I remember is 'Jet planes meeting in the skies to re-fuel'. Now in-flight re-fuelling is indeed a technical marvel but, given what we know now about the effects of fossil fuels on the environment, this feat of creation hardly seems like something to be hymned in worship. A common way round the problem of becoming dated is to stick with themes vague and abstract such as God's love for us or our love for Jesus. But when clumsily put and accompanied by a jaunty rock backing, such songs can end up indistinguishable from bad pop.

In defence of modern praise worship songs, I should cite the response to the above complaint of a friend who writes Christian rock. He argued correctly that I was not comparing like with like. It is true that few modern hymns have produced a line as potent and memorable as *Abide With Me*'s 'Change and decay in all around I see / Lord, though who changest not / Abide with me', but then most Victorian and Edwardian hymns did not produce such a strong line either. The old hymns still in use are the ones that have survived the winnowing of time and hymn book revisions and are the best of their era. Hence in faulting modern praise worship by comparing it with the work of Charles Wesley or Horatio Bonar we are mistakenly comparing the average of the present with the very best of the past.

Being Informal and Demotic

Most charismatic pastors are considerably more powerful than the clergy of the mainstream denominations because they are not beholden, either to the congregation (as they are in the Presbyterian tradition) or to a higher authority (as they are in the Catholic or Scottish Episcopal churches). However, while mainstream church clergy often demonstrate their standing by wearing a uniform of their office and by using institutional titles – who wouldn't be impressed by a 'Right Reverend' or an 'Archbishop'? – their charismatic counterparts go to the opposite extreme in their presentation of self. The smiling photographs on the websites show ordinary people: no clerical collars, no robes, no funny hats. And no pastor (or more likely 'team leader') uses a surname or a long first name: a surprisingly large number are called Dave. The website of a charismatic church in Glasgow tells enquirers: 'This Christian church is relaxed and informal, the leaders and ministers are called by their first names. You can come to church dressed casually in jeans and T-shirts, and you will often find the pastors speaking dressed down, with few formalities'.[12] Charismatics are not alone in dismissing clerical costume. Many conservative Presbyterian clergy reject the 'roman' collar because they find no Biblical warrant for clerical uniform, but they still expect congregants to dress formally because it shows due respect for the occasion. The New Church response is that there is enough that puts off the unchurched without asking them to dress up.

Experiencing Rather than Learning Doctrine

Critics assert that the casual attitude to dress is accompanied by a casual attitude to Christian doctrine. It is certainly true that, unlike the sects and denominations that pre-date the 1960s, charismatic fellowships downplay traditional lines of argument. They correctly assume that most people have no understanding of what distinguishes Brethren from Baptist; evangelical from charismatic; Presbyterian from Episcopalian. Arguably the substance of the Christian gospel is still taught, especially in the Bible study groups which core members attend. The doctrines are usually there, if one cares to look. The website of Destiny in Glasgow, for example, has an admirably clear statement of its beliefs in twenty numbered sentences. However, even there the wish to avoid giving offence is inadvertently signalled by the words which introduce the list. Instead of saying 'We believe the following defines the true Christian', it mumbles: 'Here are some of the things which are important to us'.[13]

Certainly preaching no longer has the central part it traditionally played in conservative Protestant churches. Such churches have also changed: even Free Church congregations are no longer expected to sit attentive for an hour's sermon on some point of doctrine. But many charismatic churches have gone much further in replacing the lengthy expositions of teaching, usually by a soloist bringing 'a message from the Lord in song' or the mass singing of repetitive choruses.

One area which shows the indifference of the charismatic movement (and many non-charismatic independent evangelical churches) to the historically important arguments within Christianity is its attitude to Bible translations. British conservative Protestants have until recently been committed to the 'King James' version, so-called because the translators who were summoned by King James VI of Scotland (and I of England) in 1604 prefaced their work with a sycophantic dedication to him. Traditionalists rightly value the King James version, or 'Authorised Version', for the many phrases it has contributed to general speech. Theologically aware conservatives like it because in crucial respects it is clearly 'Protestant'; that is, the translators were clear in their opposition to key Catholic doctrines. As with hymns, a reasonable case for frequent new translations of the Bible can be made. The KJV was written in the plain language of the seventeenth century so that ordinary people could understand it. For the same to be true today, we need a modern translation. But that rational case – use the version most people can most readily comprehend – misses the theological point. To the sort of congregation that paints 'King James Bible used' on its name board, the charismatic movement's indifference to the symbolic heft of the KJV is taken as a token of a broader theological laxity.

One further difference between the New Churches (charismatic or otherwise) and the traditional conservative evangelical milieu is the relative absence of life after death. Doubtless the topic is sometimes covered but it is a long time since I heard an old-fashioned 'what if you die tonight?' call to conversion. An elderly member of an independent charismatic church, reflecting on why the movement had stalled by the late 1990s, said: 'I wish we preached the gospel more strongly and had more appeals but we seem to have gone the way of most churches: afraid to preach about Hell because we might offend some'.[14] Focus on salvation in the next life has been replaced by a stress on the therapeutic benefits in this life of believing in Jesus. A rather bitter ex-charismatic derided this as 'A whole lot less God and a whole lot more Jesus-is-my-boyfriend', and he has a point. Tongues apart, the orientation of most charismatic churches is very much this-worldly: feel better and be more successful (or at least more content) in this life.

Being Unchurchy

Another innovation which is of a piece with the informal dress and the modern music is stealth naming. Many nineteenth-century chapels carved their affiliation in stone above the door. Middleton-in-Teesdale Primitive Methodist Chapel said exactly that on its front. When people did not travel much, the place name was probably redundant but the 'Prims' of Middleton wanted the world to know who they were; a sensible attitude in a society where most people would have had some idea of what distinguished a Prim from a Wesleyan. Even those chapels which did not advertise their sectarian identity nonetheless announced their Christian purpose with some Biblically resonant name: Bethel, Tabernacle, Rehoboth, Zion, Zoar, Ainon. Because they do not want to alienate the unchurched, charismatic church names tend to the abstract and high-sounding. One might guess that the River of Life and the Burnbank Living Fountain are churches but Destiny, Xcel, New Life and New Frontiers could easily be a gymnasium, a bus company, a bank or a travel company.

Because their requirements are new and because they wish to avoid the negative associations of church, charismatics have often been unconventional in their use of plant. In the early days necessity and preference coincided. Once the fellowships grew too big for houses, they met in hired premises: village halls, community centres and schools. These had the advantage that they could be the size that made the congregation feel cosy or growing rather than reminding its members that they were a small fraction of the congregation that once filled a vast Victorian church. Hired halls were heated, could accommodate a temporary stage for the praise band, and had toilets, seats that could be moved around to suit the event (rather than fixed pews), and blank flat walls against which song lyrics could be projected. The use of Powerpoint is economically rational because it reduces the need for hymn books, but it also reduces the social distance between the core members who know the songs and newcomers, who are relieved of the awkwardness of fumbling through an unfamiliar hymn book.

When they do acquire their own facilities, charismatics favour disused factories near ring roads over city centre churches because they are easily adapted. When they do buy old churches, they gut them. When they build their own, they avoid obviously ecclesiastical styles in favour of open flexible spaces. The one thing that most new churches have in common is that they do not remind people of churches.

A similar desire to avoid things 'churchy' is apparent in very many charismatic websites. The use of websites is itself something which charismatic congregations have pioneered. As well as providing all the necessary information about meeting times and places, the sites often contain videos of services, galleries of photographs, and click-on access to recordings of sermons. The value of this may seem obvious but it remains the case that most mainstream church congregations do not provide easily accessible information about service times: details painted on a board at the church are fine for people walking past but they will not help someone 10 miles away.[15] One of the advantages of affiliation with a major charismatic network is that it provides a highly professional 'generic' website which can easily be adapted by any particular congregation. But the sociologically interesting feature of many charismatic websites is the very deliberate avoidance of church reference points. They are adorned with generic stock photos of grinning people; never off-puttingly handsome but healthy and wholesome. Some even have that cliché of newspapers on the day that exam results are announced: the picture of teenagers leaping in the air, mouths wide open in elation, arms aloft. It is not too cynical to say that, at first glance, many sites could be mistaken for health tonic commercials or dating sites.

Being Socially Involved

One of the frequent criticisms made of the charismatic movement in its first few decades is that it was right-wing. This was partly a function of the times. Unlike previous Conservative administrations, which had preferred the paternalistic language of One Nation politics, the Thatcher government elected in 1979 was avowedly liberal (that is, against state interference) in economics and authoritarian (that is, for state interference) in social ethics: pretty well the opposite to the views of the typical cleric of the mainstream churches.[16] The 1980s and early 1990s was a period in which much of the post-war welfare state consensus was unsentimentally junked in favour of privatisation and a concerted attack on organised labour. Committees of the Church of England, the Methodist Church and the Church of Scotland were highly critical of much government policy in this period and Margaret Thatcher was not shy in replying. She defended wealth creation with a novel take on the parable of the Good Samaritan: 'No-one would remember the Good Samaritan if he'd only had good intentions; he had money as well'.[17] And she delivered a lengthy condemnation of Scotland's left-wing leanings in an address to the Kirk's General Assembly.[18] In that context, the inward-looking nature of the charismatic movement made it an easy target for liberal Christians.

It is doubtless the case that charismatics, like evangelical Protestants more generally, tend to be right-wing. Most are by social position middle class and their religious emphasis is on the individual, rather than the community, the people or the nation. After all, each of us must answer to God for our sins individually, not collectively. And some charismatics have been influenced by an American movement known variously as the 'Health and Wealth' gospel or 'Prosperity Theology'. As I cannot improve on it, I will simply quote the Wikipedia explanation:

> [Prosperity theology] is a Christian religious doctrine that financial blessing is the will of God for Christians, and that faith, positive speech, and donations to Christian ministries will always increase one's material wealth. Based on non-traditional interpretations of the Bible, often with emphasis on the Book of Malachi, the doctrine

views the Bible as a contract between God and humans: if humans have faith in God, he will deliver his promises of security and prosperity. Confessing these promises to be true is perceived as an act of faith, which God will honor.[19]

This is often reduced to the crude proposition that if you will give £10 to your pastor, God will give you back £100. Mainstream Christians object to this caricature of God's promises, which, apart from anything else, has the effect of making the poor and the sick responsible for their circumstances: if they had sufficient faith they would not be poor or ill. It also offends traditional puritans by removing the crucial link between glorifying God and prospering: hard work and temperate living. However, it is worth noting that Prosperity Theology is much more popular with US charismatics than with their British counterparts and, within the UK, it is much more likely in west African Pentecostal churches than among the white charismatics.

It is easy to make too much of the supposedly right-wing tendencies of the charismatic movement. Many charismatics are politically indistinguishable from non-religious people of the same social class, education and regional backgrounds. It is also easy to miss important counter-currents.[20] Many charismatic congregations have organised social programmes: providing food stores and soup kitchens, organising the recycling of furniture, and running debt advice centres are just some of the activities in which inner-city congregations are involved.

The Appeal of the Charismatic Movement

Despite the considerable efforts to which charismatic fellowships have gone to remove the historic cultural baggage which supposedly alienates non-churchgoers, relatively few people have been recruited from the ranks of the unchurched. Most charismatics have been raised in conservative Christian homes and churches but have become frustrated with their conservative doctrines, their old-fashioned styles of worship and the decline of the congregations in which they had grown up. This last point is particularly salient. Because the primary cause of the decline of the churches is not the defection of mature adults but the failure to recruit their own children at the rate necessary for replacement, as congregations have become smaller they have also become older. I often attend churches where, aged sixty, I am the youngest person in the congregation. It is not impossible to find joyful uplift in the company of twenty elderly people – Methodists, in particular, are enthusiastic singers – but it is hard. Apart from anything else, such congregations cannot support effective youth work or provide a crèche for parents with toddlers. In the early days of small house groups the sense of being in at the start of a great revival was doubtless an attraction, but for the last two decades much of the appeal has been more mundane and practical.

If there seems little mystery about the attraction of a large congregation and the facilities it can provide, there remains the issue of geographical spread. If the key attractions are a large mixed-age congregation, lively music, toilets, a crèche and a large youth club, there seems no obvious reason why Scots should find charismatic congregations less attractive than do the English. Yet this is the case. We can find anecdotal evidence in many sources. An anthropology of the Shetland island of Whalsay in the 1980s notes that an incomer from Devon started a charismatic meeting. After three years it had only six members – all incomers – and by 1991 it had ceased to meet.[21] The River of Life's failure to recruit the natives of Dumfries has already been noted. We can also see the pattern in statistics. The Toronto Blessing – so-called after the Vineyard Church at Toronto airport where in 1994 there was an outbreak of what secular observers called hysteria – is a branch of the movement characterised by extreme signs of spirit possession. Members of the congregation not only spoke in tongues but wept or laughed uncontrollably, rolled on the floor, and some cleansed their systems of sin by vomiting. In 2000 the Vineyard network had seventy-two churches or church-planting projects in the UK but only two of those (or 2.8 per cent) were in Scotland, well below par when Scotland had 8.6 per cent of the UK population. Taken together, in 2000 there were probably fifty independent charismatic churches in Scotland with a total membership of less than 5,000. That was just 3 per cent of the corresponding figures for the UK as a whole, again well below par.[22]

One explanation is demographic. Although some Catholics have been interested in charismatic renewal, it is overwhelmingly a Protestant interest. As Scotland has proportionately more Catholics than England, the part of the population available to join a Protestant innovation is correspondingly smaller. Availability may also be a consideration for non-Catholic Scots. One might guess that, with its higher churchgoing rate, Scotland has fewer people than does England who are free to join a new religious movement. However, that seems unlikely to be relevant because both countries have a vast unchurched population that in theory is available for something new. If we take very round figures for the 1980s we might estimate that 16–20 per cent of Scots and 8–12 per cent of the English were regular churchgoers, which still leaves so many unchurched people that we can hardly explain Scottish indifference to the charismatic movement by market saturation.

Nonetheless, the nature of the recently dominant religion may be a consideration. The largest part of the category of Scot that is available for recruitment to anything new – the people who appear in the 2001 Scottish Social Attitudes survey as having once attended church regularly and no longer attend but think they may go back – is ex-Presbyterian. Presbyterians are not in favour of congregational autonomy. Nor are they keen on the charismatic movement's lack of interest in dogma because neglecting the teaching of core beliefs might open the door to Popery. They are likely to find the worship styles a little too exuberant and demonstrative, and claiming the gifts of the spirit seems just too much like bragging.

There is a further explanation that involves a general feature of the way innovations of any type spread. As one common device for making the world more manageable, we often make snap judgements about some new idea or activity by looking for similarities between ourselves and its carriers. The more the promoters are like us (but better), the more likely we are to take seriously what they offer. Conversely, the wrong associations can damn some new idea or practice. The 1926 revival strongly affected the fishing communities of the Aberdeenshire coast but had little impact on farming villages just a few miles inland in good part because farmers had little interaction with, and even less respect for, fishermen. As we saw in Chapter 2, Methodism became popular in Shetland in the nineteenth century but failed in Orkney; one reason was that the first Orcadians to take up Methodism were the fishermen of Stronsay, who were widely regarded by other Orcadians as a bit strange.[23] Although there may have been little intrinsic reason why Methodism should have appealed more to Stronsay fishermen than to mainland farmers, once the association was made, it confined the appeal of the innovation. That the charismatic movement was first brought to Scotland by English incomers may itself be enough to explain its limited appeal. This isn't racism. It is just an accidental by-product of one of the ways we assess options: these charismatics do not sound like my sort of people so what they are offering is probably not my sort of thing.

Influence

That the charismatic movement has made little inroad into Scotland's mass of the unchurched does not mean that it has been without influence. Elements of the charismatic style have been widely adopted. We cannot be sure how much of that is direct borrowing of charismatic innovations and how much is others coming independently to similar conclusions, but Scottish church life in general has become less formal and more spontaneous. Even Catholic priests are no longer stern figures known only by their titles and surnames who are instructed not to fraternise with their congregants. That French expression for elite interaction with the masses – talking 'de haut en bas' or 'from high to low' – perfectly describes classic Presbyterian preaching: tall pulpits allowed the minister literally to speak down to his audience. No Presbyterian pulpit installed in the last thirty years requires congregants to strain their necks looking up, and ministers of old churches will often preach from a lower lectern than the high pulpit. Worship has become looser, with congregational involvement and personal expression replacing formality and strict adherence to prescribed forms. Decoration has become much more demotic: colourful patchwork wall-hangings made by the Women's Guild or posters made by the

Sunday School are commonly displayed on walls or large pin boards in the main body of the church. Children are now invited to make childish contributions to services rather than being forced to behave like adults. Modern praise songs have found their way into revised hymnals. Powerpoint projections enliven services. Sermons are shorter. Hard pews are replaced by comfortable chairs.

Conclusion

Although they argue about the precise dating of decline, most social scientists accept that religion has become ever less popular and explain that decline as a result of vague but nonetheless powerful changes associated with modernisation (such as greater individualism, increased tolerance of diversity and the rise of a religiously neutral state). Others, in particular Christians looking for reasons to be cheerful, prefer a cyclical view of religious change.[24] They see decline but they also see the first drops of revival rain or, if they prefer horticultural metaphors, the first green shoots of revival. In the 1980s such people seized on the charismatic movement as refutation of the secularisation thesis's assumption that decline was irreversible. In particular the obviously supernatural nature of its defining characteristic – belief in the present availability of supernatural gifts – was taken as proof that the increased secularity of our culture could be challenged by a popular religion. Twenty years ago I dissented from that reading of the charismatic movement.[25] For two good reasons, the charismatic movement is better seen as part of the secularising process rather than its antidote. The first concerns patterns of flow; the second the underlying ethos of the movement.

Despite its best efforts to remove every feature of church life that might alienate outsiders, the charismatic movement did not draw the religiously indifferent back into the realm of the Godly. Instead it provided a way for a generation of churchgoers to ease itself out of dogmatic and doctrinaire conservative Protestantism and into a faith which, while it had some unusually supernatural elements, was also in many important respects more liberal. The movement's casual attitude to core beliefs allowed young people who no longer shared their parent's theology to continue with the Jesus talk while quietly ditching what had once been defining tests of fellowship. And the relaxation of the ascetic demands of classic Puritanism – temperance, sexual continence, modesty and formality in dress codes, prohibitions on dancing, the cinema and other worldly entertainments – allowed young Christians to be less socially isolated from their non-churchgoing peers. The movement's growth stalled because the overall decline of the Christian churches reduced the pool of disaffected potential recruits and because charismatics proved no more successful at keeping their children in the faith than had the denominations and sects they left. Its compromise with secular culture was intended to draw unbelievers into the faith but, as we could guess from the relative size of the religious and irreligious populations, the pull in the secular direction was stronger. To illustrate the point with just one element of what the charismatics and evangelicals call 'cultural relevance', popular Christian rock festivals such as Greenbelt and Springfest did not attract the religiously indifferent from Glastonbury and T in the Park. Rather they allowed young Christians to attend secular festivals without feeling that they were letting the side down. In brief, the charismatic movement was not an alternative to the secular for the unchurched or for wavering Christians. The unchurched paid no attention. For some wavering Christians, the movement was a 'base camp' on the slide to the secular: a place to rest and get acclimatised before taking the next step away from conservative religion. And even those who remained committed proved no better than other Christians at recruiting their own children.

The point about underlying ethos is complicated and requires some doubtless grossly simplified theology. A Church of England vicar called the Toronto Blessing 'a mix of Gnosticism, Pelagianism, mysticism and even Arianism': a series of technical insults that I will endeavour to unpack. By calling it Gnostic, he meant that it claimed hidden knowledge. This is bad because it makes mysterious the teachings of Christ when they are plainly presented in the Bible and in the churches' historic teachings. And by making correct doctrine mysterious it inadvertently encourages the generation of falsehoods. Anyone can present any speculation as prophesy. By Pelagian, he meant that the movement emphasised self-effort in 'finding and maintaining peace, joy and fulfilment in everyday life (a recipe for mental breakdown and spiritual collapse if ever there was one)' rather than throwing oneself on the mercy of the Lord. By making contentment a product of our efforts rather than God's saving grace, it not only misrepresents Christianity but improperly blames individuals for their problems. By mystical, he meant that it stressed subjective experience over the objective truth of God's Word. And by Arian, he meant that the movement emphasised the Holy Spirit at the expense of the other two members of the Holy Trinity: God and Jesus.[26]

Whether those criticisms are valid is for Christians to debate. As an impartial observer, my interest is in the descriptive parts of the judgements and these seem reasonably accurate. My sociological observation is that they can all be traced to a common source: the increased authority of the individual. While the charismatic movement is superficially more supernaturalist than the religion of the mainstream Christian churches, its underlying ethos is secularising in that it shifts authority from the 'objective' (or more accurately the inter-subjective) authority of the Church, or of a tradition of interpreting the Bible, to the contemporary individual believer. Far from resisting secularisation, the charismatic movement has inadvertently collaborated with it.

Notes

1. For a good general history of the movement, see A. Walker, *Restoring the Kingdom: the Radical Christianity of the House Church Movement* (Guildford: Eagle, 1998).

2. D. Matthew, 'Restorationism in British church life from 1970: an insider's view', 2006; http://www.davidmatthew.org.uk/restorationhist.html. Accessed June 2013.

3. Data on congregations, membership and clergy numbers can be found in the series of *Religious Trends* publications produced by Peter Brierley; for example, *UK Religious Trends 7* (Swindon: Christian Research, 2008). In 2005, twenty-six of forty-six English counties had fewer charismatic congregations than they had in 1998. However, growth in the number of congregations does not mean growth in the total market. In the twenty-six counties where there were fewer fellowships in 2005, the number of attenders at the services of those congregations was static or growing in eight. And of twenty counties with an increased number of charismatic congregations, ten showed a decline in attendance. This suggests that the initial wave of growth, in which new fellowships were formed by a growing number of members, by the late 1990s had been superseded by a static or declining membership which nonetheless created new 'church plants'.

4. J. Highet, *The Scottish Churches* (London: Skeffington, 1960), pp. 40–1.

5. *Building News*, 25 March 1881, p. 343. Lady Herries was a member of the local aristocracy who had married into the family of the Duke of Norfolk, England's premier Catholic family.

6. There is an excellent collection of photographs of the empty convent interspersed with clips from the film at http://hera.krystal.co.uk/~urbexfor/showthread.php/11108-The-Magdalen- Sisters-Benedictine-Convent. Accessed December 2012.

7. http://news.bbc.co.uk/1/hi/scotland/7645956.stm.

8. In 1998 the average 'New Church' had a membership of 126 adults and 47 children. What distinguishes that from the average Church of Scotland or Methodist congregation is the high proportion of children. Figures were calculated from data in M. Love (ed.), *The Body Book 7th Edition* (London: Christian Research and Pioneer, 1998).

9. Bridge of Don Baptist Church homepage; http://www.bodbaptist.org.uk/about/services/. Accessed December 2012.

10. E. Templeton, *God's February: a Life of Archie Craig 1888–1985* (London: BCCI/CCBI, 1991), p. 8.

11. It is worth stressing that there is no evidence that anyone has ever been 'brainwashed' in the sense of being converted to a radical new worldview by physical and psychological pressure. The term became popular to describe techniques applied to US prisoners by the Chinese during the Korean War in order to persuade them to denounce US imperialism. Although extreme physical and psychological stress can addle the mind, no one has managed the tricky second part of the process: the implantation of cogent novel ideas. For the debate over brainwashing in 1970s

new religious movements, see D. G. Bromley and J. T. Richardson (eds), *The Brainwashing/Deprogramming Controversy* (Lewiston, NY: Mellen, 1983).

12. Destiny, Glasgow homepage; http://www.destiny-church.com/about_destiny_glasgow.html. Accessed December 2012.

13. As above.

14. Ship of Fools website discussion on the 'Decline of the UK house church movement'; http://forum.ship-of-fools.cpm/cgi-bin/ultimatebb.cgi?ubb=get_topic; f=70;t=009210#000000.

15. Over the last decade I have found many churches and chapels that give no indication of service times. In north Wales where a small circuit of dissenting chapels rotated the Sunday services between themselves, details of the next service were announced during the previous Sunday's service. When I pointed out that this effectively precluded new or irregular attenders, one chapel steward told me: 'Well, we never get any of them anyway'.

16. H. Clark, *The Church Under Thatcher* (London: SPCK, 1993).

17. London Weekend Television, *Weekend World*, TV interview, 6 January 1980.

18. For a detailed analysis of her speech and responses, see D. Brown and M. A. Morrow, 'Margaret Thatcher's sermon on the Mound: Christianity and wealth', *Journal of Communication and Religion* 33 (2010), pp. 33–55.

19. http://en.wikipedia.org/wiki/Prosperity_theology.

20. Bryn Jones and his brother both took time off from their evangelistic work to take degrees in peace studies at Bradford University.

21. A. Cohen, *Whalsay: Symbol, Segment and Boundary in a Shetland Island Community* (Manchester: Manchester University Press, 1987), p. 57.

22. Of charismatic fellowships in 2002, 93.7 per cent were in England, 2.1 were in Wales, 2.9 were in Scotland and 1.4 per cent were in Northern Ireland; P. Brierley, *UK Religious Trends Vol. 4* (London: Christian Research, 2003), Table 9.9.1.

23. H. R. Bowes, *Revival and Survival: Methodism's Ebb and Flow in Shetland and Orkney, 1822–1862* (Aberdeen: University of Aberdeen MTh thesis, 1988), p. 209.

24. I agree that religious change tends to be cyclical, with periods of stagnation being followed by periods of enthusiasm. The crucial point is that the peak of every wave of religious enthusiasm since the Reformation has been lower than the previous peak. Rather than cycles within an underlying stable demand for religion, a better metaphor would be that of a painted spot on the wheel of a wagon running down a slope. The travel of the spot creates a wave pattern but the low point is always lower and the high point is never as high.

25. S. Bruce, 'The charismatic movement and the secularization thesis', *Religion* 28 (1998), pp. 223–32.

26. P. O'Gorman, 'New blessing or old heresy?', *Churchman* 109 (1995); http://churchman.org.

CHAPTER

9

TIBETANS IN A SHOOTING LODGE

The Dumfriesshire village of Eskdalemuir sits in all the parts of its name read in reverse: the muir of the dale of the Esk, or to be more precise, two Esks – the White and the Black – which unite at the southern end of the parish and flow via Longtown to the Solway sands. The main valley is a quarter of a mile wide and 500 feet above sea level. It rises on each side of the White Esk to gloomy hills, the bleak uplands where the Edwardian upper classes shot grouse and John Buchan's fictional hero Richard Hannay fled in *The Thirty-Nine Steps*. In 1949 almost all the land was rough sheep-grazing with each farm having a few fields on the valley floor where grass and corn were grown for feed. The few houses are scattered but maps distinguish between Eskdalemuir, the site of the parish church and the school (which closed in 2005), and Davington, a few miles north.

In the early 1950s James Littlejohn, an anthropologist from Edinburgh, spent the university vacations studying sheep farmers and foresters in the area, which he anonymised as *Westrigg*. As a site for observing change in Scotland's religious climate, Eskdalemuir does not immediately seem promising. It does have an heroic past, of which a neglected gravestone in a field just north of the village offers a poignant reminder. It reads: 'Here lyes Andrew Hislop Martyr shot dead upon This place by Sir James Johnstone of Westerhall and Sir John Graham of Claverhouse for adhering to the Word of God'.

Hislop was one of the radical Covenanters who used the failure of church and state to meet the exacting standards of the National Covenant of 1638 as a reason for rejecting it and the political settlement of the uneasy mid-seventeenth century. In an age when religious dissent was political rebellion, the Covenanters were mercilessly persecuted. Graham of Claverhouse (later Viscount Dundee) was one of the leading scourges. He had come to Eskdale in May 1685 with a troop of soldiers to find Andrew Hislop, a shepherd whose reputation for preaching sedition had unfortunately spread. Claverhouse spent the night with Sir James Johnstone at his self-named shooting lodge of Johnstone House. The next day they went to find Hislop but he was out on the hills. They did find and chase his son and run him to ground in the village. Given a last opportunity to renounce the Covenant, he declined. The troopers, knowing the local popularity of the Covenanters, refused to implement the death sentence. Claverhouse shot the young man himself.

Enough of the Covenanters in the south-west survived into the age of toleration to become an only mildly deviant denomination: the Reformed Presbyterians. William Brown was Eskdalemuir's parish minister for long enough to write the area entries in both the 1793 *Statistical Account of Scotland* and its 1830s successor. Although the Reformed Presbyterians were his competition, he could say of them: 'They are a moral and religious people with whom I have always lived on most friendly terms'.[1] Finally granted a plot of land by the laird of Davington in 1836, the Reformed Presbyterians built a neat church seating a hundred or so and called their first full-time minister in 1847. James Morrison stayed for thirty-one years and shortly after his death the Reformed Presbyterians merged with the newer breakaway from the Kirk, the Free Church of Scotland. Fifty years later, the bulk of Presbyterian dissenters returned to the national Church. In the 1950s the Davington church was used for occasional afternoon services; now it is a cowshed.

The only other public building in Davington is the meteorological Observatory, which opened in 1908. It was built because the Kew Observatory in London found that the introduction of electric trams messed up its geo-magnetic measurements. In the 1950s it employed six white-collar workers, a considerable boost to an area which otherwise provided work only in minding sheep and trees. Automation has reduced the workforce to one local woman who occasionally cleans and checks the premises.

In 1900 all but three of the farms were owned by the Duke of Buccleuch, one of Scotland's richest landowners, but Buccleuch Estates gradually sold its property in the parish and by the time of Littlejohn's fieldwork, most of the valley was divided between fourteen farms and the Forestry Commission, which had covered the higher hillsides with spruce. The Observatory, school and church together provided eight white-collar jobs, and eleven women worked in mills some 15 miles outside the parish, but the land was the largest source of work. More than three-quarters of the people worked in farming or forestry.[2] Littlejohn draws a very sharp contrast between the self-contained nature of the valley in 1900 and its connectedness in 1950. It was not just the women commuting to work: the social welfare and education functions that had once been administered by the parish had been assumed by the county council. For the last two years of schooling, thirteen to fifteen, children were bussed to the neighbouring town.

Religion seems to have been of little importance to the people of

Eskdalemuir in the 1950s. Almost everyone was nominally Church of Scotland and expected to be baptised, married and buried by the Church, but few attended regularly. Doubtless nostalgia amplified the differences but the older of Littlejohn's informants presented this as a stark contrast with the piety of the past. They recalled that before the First World War almost everyone attended church on a Sunday and some walked 6 miles to do it. The Sabbath was 'then truly a holy day during which taboos were laid upon many of the weekday profane activities ... Everyone wore special clothes and refrained from gainful work. In some households no cooking was done'.[3] Whatever their private views of his religion, the Edwardian minister, who dominated the parish council and the school board, was a power in the parish, on a par with the Duke of Buccleuch's local agent.

The period after the Second World War saw a rapid decline of such outward respect for religion as keeping the Sabbath. In June 1950 the wife of a farmer remarked that 'the manager came to me in great agitation one Sunday and asked if I minded if he led in that day [i.e. carted sheaves of corn from the field]. He said he'd never done it in his life before but didn't like to miss such a fine day'.[4] Preventing crops being damaged might at a stretch be justified as a work of necessity. Not so socialising. The parish minister explained 'apparent apathy or indifference to the ordinances of religion' by 'the tendency to use the Sabbath ... to do chores or entertain visitors or go visiting'. He also blamed material progress. Tracks had become roads and grocery vans now visited the outlying farms and cottages. Buses had 'made people less inclined to walk than they were in a former generation and, with no buses on a Sunday, this has had an adverse effect upon attendance at church, especially for those members who have a long way to come'.[5] The motor car removed that excuse but it did not produce any religious revival and by 2010 Eskdale shared a minister with three neighbouring parishes and its fortnightly services rarely involved more than ten people.

Samye Ling

The church architecture of Eskdale neatly symbolised power and popularity. The Reformed Presbyterian chapel was a rather pleasing single-storey, red sandstone building but it sat on low land some distance from the road. The parish church, a two-storey building with a tall spire, sat prominently at the junction of the valley's two roads. Now the chapel is a cowshed and the parish church is dwarfed and made dowdy by its exotic neighbour, the largest Tibetan Buddhist monastery in Europe.

Close by the road is the three-storey high white Stupa (from the Sanskrit for 'heap'), a monument in which are placed relics, sacred texts, and the ashes of former residents of Samye Ling. In a U-shape around the base of the Stupa is a low stone building which houses prayer wheels. Cross the garden, with its ponds, Buddhas and prayer flags, and you come to the substantial old house. Behind that is a quadrangle surrounded by a cement-block building, which would look like a 1970s comprehensive school were it not that one side has a long porch supported by red-painted columns, is edged in bright blue, yellow and red tiles, has stained glass in its windows and is topped by a two-storey yellow-roofed pagoda.

Samye Ling was not originally a Tibetan project. Johnstone House, the large nineteenth-century building on the site of Sir James Johnstone's original shooting lodge, was sold by Buccleuch Estates shortly after the Second World War to Sir Gordon and Lady Kate Lethem. In 1964, after Sir Gordon's death, it was bought by a trust set up by Theravadin Buddhists in London looking for a remote retreat centre.

Like Christianity, Buddhism has been fragmented by age and geographical dispersal into a large variety of traditions and schools. Theravada Buddhism (the Buddhism 'of the elders'), the oldest tradition, is rooted in monastic life and is found mainly in India, Burma, Thailand and Sri Lanka. Mahayana Buddhism is the Buddhism of the great way or the great ox-cart, so-called because it is generally more moderate and aims to encompass the common people, and is found in China, Japan, Korea and Vietnam. The Buddhism of Tibet (and Nepal, Sikkim, Bhutan and Mongolia) belongs to the Vajrayana or 'Diamond' strand. Among its distinguishing features are a greater stress on the esoteric knowledge of rituals and a belief that enlightenment (and hence release from the burden of rebirth) can be achieved in one lifetime rather than being the endpoint of a gradual improvement over many rebirths.

British engagement with Buddhism has a complex history. Much of it came through the intellectual interests of colonial adventurers and administrators such as Sir Edwin Arnold, who in 1879 published a biography of the Buddha in the form of the epic poem *The Light of Asia*. Arnold's interest had been sparked during his seven years as Principal of the Government Sanskrit College at Poona. Much of the interest was scholarly, rather than religious, and it had one important result. T. H. Rhys Davids, a civil servant in Ceylon who finished his career as Professor of Comparative Religion at the University of Manchester, founded the Pali Text Society in 1881. By 1922, when Rhys Davids died, the Society had issued ninety-four volumes of Theravadan Buddhist sacred texts in roman script and in English translations.

A major source of religious interest in Buddhism was the wealthy Russian émigré Madame Helena Blavatsky and her Theosophical Society, which she and Colonel H. S. Olcott founded in New York in 1875. It was initially intended to study and explain the work of spirit mediums and the strange phenomena they could apparently produce – a great fascination for the Victorians – but it broadened its scope when Olcott and Blavatsky moved to India to pursue their growing interest in Eastern religion. The Society's modest objectives were eventually codified as the formation of the core of a universal brotherhood of humanity without distinction of race, creed, sex, caste or colour; the study of comparative religion, philosophy and science; and the investigation of the unexplained laws of nature and of the powers latent in man.

The Theosophical Society was just one of many Victorian-era organisations which, like the Masons, were structured in lodges and which claimed hidden knowledge of the true nature of the world which was gradually revealed to members as initiation rituals and tests elevated them through grades of membership. It inspired many imitators, including the Hermetic Order of the Golden Dawn, which numbered Aleister Crowley, the founder of modern Black Magic, among its members.[6] Another member was a man who went to Ceylon in 1898 as C. H. Allan Bennett and returned as Ananda Metteyya, the first Englishman to be ordained as a Theravadan Buddhist monk.

In 1924 Christmas Humphreys, a barrister who later became a judge, formed the London Buddhist Society, initially as a lodge within the Theosophical Society. This was the first enduring organisation in Britain to provide a platform for all schools and traditions of Buddhism. A slow trickle of Westerners travelled to Asia to take monastic ordination, mainly as Theravadan monks, and a few Asian monks came to live in Britain. In his day job Humphreys was responsible for the prosecution of Ruth Ellis, the last woman in Britain to be hanged, but his hobby did much to popularise Buddhism. Van Morrison's song *Cleaning Windows* mentions reading 'Christmas Humphreys' book on Zen' between shifts in 1960s East Belfast. Humphreys was also responsible for inviting Ananda Bodhi (who had been born George Dawson in Canada) to head the small Buddhist centre in London, and it was Bodhi who bought Johnstone House as a meditation and retreat centre.

Among those invited to teach at Johnstone House were two young Tibetan lamas: Akong Tulku Rinpoche and Chogyam Trungpa Rinpoche. For the informed, their status was signified in their names: 'tulku' signifies an 'enlightened being' and a reincarnation of the Lord Buddha. 'Rinpoche' means 'precious great being' and is a title conferred on respected teachers. Even when the biographies produced by followers are stripped of their thick layers of hero worship, their story is dramatic. Raised from childhood as incarnate lamas, they were heads of their respective monasteries in Dolma Lhakang and Surmang.[7] In 1959 the Chinese markedly tightened their control over Tibet and the monastic leadership – which was also the Tibetan government – decided to flee to India. As the Chinese army controlled all the lowland routes, the lamas had to traverse mountain terrain and a journey that they expected to take three months took ten. They were often lost, ran desperately short of food, and close to the end of their journey most of the party were captured when they tried to cross the Brahmaputra river. Of the 300 people in the party who set out in April 1959, only fifteen made it to India.

At the receiving refugee camp in Assam, Akong and Trungpa were befriended by Freda Bedi, an English woman who worked for the Indian Civil

Service. Bedi put them in charge of a school for tulkus in Dalhousie, where they learned English. She also arranged for Trungpa to study comparative religion at St Anthony's College in Oxford. In 1963 the two young Tibetans arrived in London, where they were met by Ananda Bodhi[8] and various British Buddhists and supporters of Tibet. While Trungpa studied, Akong worked as a hospital orderly.

Helped by a BBC radio profile and by the publication of *Born in Tibet*, an account of his escape, Trungpa gradually developed a reputation for teaching which led to invitations to Johnstone House, and then an offer to take over the enterprise, which had been losing money. In March 1967 control was passed to the Tibetans.

Peace, Love and Understanding

The timing could not have been better. 1967 was the 'summer of love', the year that the US anti-Vietnam War protests and the hippie movement of long hair, psychedelic music, free love, communal living, and peace, love and understanding burst into the public consciousness. In January 1968 the Beatles went to Rishikesh in India to learn from Maharishi Mahesh Yogi, the founder of Transcendental Meditation. For a few short years Eastern religion was tremendously hip, and though it is difficult to separate truth from later embellishment, Johnstone House became something of a celebrity magnet. There is no doubt that Leonard Cohen lived nearby at Garwald for a few months; he later became a Zen student. John Lennon and Yoko Ono are reputed to have visited, as apparently did members of the Incredible String Band's entourage.[9] Before his career as first a Space Oddity and then Ziggy Stardust took off, David Bowie apparently seriously contemplated becoming a monk. He stayed for a couple of weeks in late 1967 or early 1968.[10]

The hippie interest in Buddhism seems to have been rather unhealthy for the young Tibetans. Akong's younger brother Jamdrak later reformed and became a senior figure in Samye Ling but as an adolescent he 'threw himself headlong into the hippy hedonism of that time',[11] as did Trungpa. Trungpa drank heavily and had casual sexual relationships with a number of his female students. What part alcohol played in it is not clear but he was seriously injured when he crashed a car.

Diana Pybus was the daughter of a wealthy family that had once owned Denton Hall (now the home of the Catholic bishop of Hexham and Newcastle). By her own accounts a disturbed adolescent, she had heard Trungpa lecture in London and felt so drawn to him that she pressed her mother into taking her to Samye Ling. Her mother's disapproval – they left after two days – did not dampen her enthusiasm and she ran away from her Cambridge boarding school to return to Trungpa. By the time of this second visit, arguments between Akong and Trungpa about the latter's promiscuity and drinking had led to Trungpa being asked to leave Samye Ling and he was staying with friends nearby. They made love on Pybus's first visit and only a month or so later, in January 1970, they were married in Edinburgh. In her published biography, Pybus says she was sixteen when they first had sex but in an interview with a sympathetic journalist she says, 'to tell you the honest truth, I don't think I was 16 yet, I think I was still 15'.[12] Akong disapproved of the marriage and although the couple were accommodated in Samye Ling, relations between the two lamas continued to deteriorate.

> One day some major donors were coming to Samye Ling. Rinpoche was very turned off to the idea that Akong was putting on a fake front for these wealthy people so that they would give money. He didn't feel that genuine spirituality was being practised at Samye Ling at that point, and he thought the whole situation was corrupt. Just before the donors arrived, while Akong was downstairs waiting to great them, Rinpoche went into Akong's bedroom upstairs and completely destroyed Akong's personal shrine with his walking stick. Then he went and urinated all over the top of the stairwell, after which he lay down and passed out at the top of the stairs.[13]

Not long after their wedding, Pybus and Trungpa left first for Canada and then for the USA. Trungpa's departure marked a turning point in Samye Ling's development. Akong was both more traditional and more adept at building positive relationships with local and national figures whose approval was crucial to Samye Ling's long-term growth. Trungpa went on to attract a large devoted following in the United States. Like many a guru, he developed delusions of grandeur: he re-branded himself as a 'king' and had his students support him as courtiers and servants. In his final years he even had them wear military-style uniforms. His alcoholism and promiscuity were scandal enough but worse was the behaviour of his appointed 'regent' and successor Osel Tendzin (aka Thomas Rich). Although he knew he was HIV-positive, Tendzin had unprotected sex with a number of young men in the Shambala community.[14] The American counter-culture of the 1970s was large enough to support every kind of guru but it is difficult to imagine that Samye Ling could have survived Trungpa's continued presence.[15]

The celebrity phase had passed by the spring of 1971 when Tim Goulding of the Irish psychedelic folk band Dr Strangely Strange visited. When I asked him about the rumours of celebrities at Samye Ling he replied: 'There was no one "of note" that I know of during that time. But there was a motley crew of serious students of Tibetan Buddhism, people on a rest cure from a hectic social life in London and one or two burned-out drug casualties'.[16] He and his girlfriend had gone to Samye Ling to get married:

> as we both thought that Buddhism was the most realistic of the World Religions. I had been a bit of a spiritual detective already and was attracted by the non-theistic

nature of the teachings of Gautama Buddha plus his practical approach to suffering and its relief. Oddly enough there was a 26-year-old Japanese Zen monk, Gendo, visiting and I spent most of the month with him; five hours a day of Zazen [sitting meditation] punctuated by a little bit of sliding on tea trays in the snow (his black robes billowed in the wind). He give me one of six paintings that his Master had given him before he left Japan which I still have.

Like most visitors, Goulding was impressed by 'a lovely monk called Sherab who painted Tibetan Tankas' and by 'Akong the abbot who seemed somewhat shy but helped to cure people by walking up and down on their backs'. It turned out that the monastery could not perform a marriage ceremony so the Gouldings were married in the Registry Office in Lockerbie and then had a 'belsing' ceremony at Samye Ling: 'Akong said he had no wedding ceremony in their tradition but that he could do a ritual for the undertaking of a new project. It was a belsing as he could not pronounce blessing'. He summarised his stay in Eskdalemuir: 'So I came away knowing very little about Tibetan Buddhism, a tiny bit more about Zen practice, and a lovely warm glow from seeing a picture of Ramana Mahareshi on the front of a book from the library. I made a small watercolour of that'.

Tim Lewis was a Warwick University student who first visited Samye Ling in 1972 at the invitation of a friend. He then had no great interest in religion. He had been raised in a vaguely Church of England household but had never actually believed in the Christian God. A number of people on the fringes of Samye Ling had bought or rented shabby smallholdings in the valley and Lewis stayed with one such couple, attended teachings in the monastery and became intrigued. He returned to Warwick to finish his degree but visited a number of times and when he graduated he decided he wanted to study with Akong and joined the community. At that time the resident population fluctuated between ten and thirty people. Lewis spent a year living in a damp caravan and looking after the monastery's small herd of cattle – 'I became quite good at that' – and started to dabble in woodwork. Akong had decided to build a proper Tibetan temple and suggested that Lewis be responsible for the joinery. He trained for six months in London and then returned to work on what became a thirty-year project. Along the way he became a Buddhist, built his own house in the village and created a successful joinery business in Lockerbie.

Growth and Acceptance

Forty years after he took over Johnstone House, Akong reminisced: 'Now people accept us but in the early days it was difficult. We had been pushed out of our own country and now other people were trying to push us out'. He attributed the hostility to misunderstanding: 'They thought we were doing some kind of black magic. It upset us because we always tried to do positive things and not do any harm'.[17] It is true that the Scottish tabloid press leaped on the Trungpa-Pybus story and was perpetually interested in the potentially potent mix of alien religion and hippie promiscuity, but a detailed reading of the local papers and conversations with a few elderly locals suggests there was actually little opposition in Eskdalemuir, probably because depopulation had left few locals to oppose anything. The one major public row concerned Akong's wish to build an incinerator to cremate the dead and, somewhat ironically, the opposition came not from the few local farmers but from English incomers who were concerned about the threat to the unspoiled environment that had attracted them to the valley.

In one important respect Tibetan Buddhism's presence in the West was very different to that of its Zen cousin. The promoters of Zen were simply advertising a religion that had a secure base in its homelands. The Tibetans were exiles who feared that Chinese occupation would destroy the religious culture of Tibet and so were intent on reproducing what they could so as to preserve it. Hence Sherab's art, Akong's medicine garden and the building of the temple. As well as constructing the physical plant, Akong spent the first decade after Trungpa's departure creating a sustainable social structure. Key to a firm identity was sorting out the notion of membership. Now those who wish to become monks and nuns are first taken as paying guests for a month. If still interested (and judged suitable) they become trainees for six months. Then they can sign on for three one-year periods of monastic life and at the end of each the Abbot and the candidate review progress, which allows Samye Ling and candidates to part company without any great drama. Only after that lengthy probation does the Abbot administer life-long vows. For the really serious there are closed retreats at the nearby Purelands site: in 1984 nine women and seven men were separated from the outside world for four years of intensive meditation and study.

With the monastic core firmly established and the temple in place, Samye Ling could diversify into running a wide variety of weekend and week-long courses in various aspects of Buddhism and Tibetan culture. And it attracted tourists. The website encourages the curious to visit the temple and the Tibetan Tearoom offers a good cup of coffee and a decent line in the high-calorie home-baking required by the itinerant Scot of a certain age.

At the same time as purifying the core membership by becoming more rigorous in recruitment, Samye Ling worked to improve its public profile. A crucial early supporter was the Liberal politician David Steel. Steel, who lived close by, epitomised respectability. For over thirty years from 1965 he was a member of the Westminster Parliament. He led the Liberal party until its merger with the Social Democrats. He was a major mover in the campaign for devolution and he became the first Speaker of the re-formed Scottish Parliament in 1997. When he joined Tai Situpu, one of the most senior figures in the Kagyu order, in formally opening the new temple building in August 1988, he did so dressed in the uniform of a Queen's Privy Councillor.[18]

Holy Isle, about a mile long and half a mile wide, lies just east of the island of Arran, in Lamlash bay. It was owned by a Mrs Kay Morris, a devout Catholic, who (according to the Samye Ling version of events) dreamed that Mary the Mother of Christ instructed her to offer the island to the Tibetan Buddhists.[19] She persuaded Lama Yeshe (Akong's reformed brother who had come out of twelve years of secluded retreat to run Samye Ling while Akong was abroad) to visit the island. He was impressed by its beauty and its history as an ancient site of pilgrimage and set about raising the money to renovate the farm and former lighthouse buildings. With a good sense of public relations, the project was presented not as an expansion of Buddhism but as the promotion of non-sectarian spirituality. In the spirit of the times, the new buildings were to be eco-friendly.[20]

It is a mark of the extent to which alien cultures have become accepted in Scotland that, in much the same way as attracting arts centres and the gay community is now seen as a regeneration strategy for rundown parts of Western cities, Buddhist spirituality is now promoted as socially uplifting. When Alex Duncan, a former rock musician who had played with Supertramp and Atomic Rooster, returned to his home town of Dundee as the Venerable Karma Jiga, the Lord Provost opened the new Rokpa centre and announced that the project was 'a natural progression for Dundee, which this administration is making strenuous and so far successful strides to rid of its former drab and depressed image'.[21]

Scottish local councils have traditionally sought religious legitimation, with a church service to mark the first meeting of a newly elected council and perhaps prayers before every council meeting. Such rituals were initially confined to the Kirk and then broadened to accommodate Christian minorities, but since the 1970s non-Christians have been sometimes invited to confer divine approval on local government. In December 2007, and in recognition of its importance to the local economy, Dumfries and Galloway council invited nun Ani Tsultrim Zangmo to mark Samye Ling's fortieth anniversary. She chanted for 30 seconds and then delivered a brief homily on the importance of being in harmony with nature and the elements.[22] Three councillors pointedly absented themselves and the press coverage clearly implied that they were being mean-spirited and narrow-minded.

Buddhism's Appeal in the West

Although there are far fewer Buddhists than Muslims in Scotland, Buddhism has a better conversion rate. The vast majority of Hindus and Muslims are immigrants who brought their faith with them or the descendants of such immigrants, but half of the 7,000 Scots who described themselves as Buddhist in the 2001 census did not have Buddhist parents.[23]

It is not hard to see the appeal of a diluted philosophical Buddhism. As a friend flippantly but perceptively put it: 'It's the best of all the religions without the silly bits'. Reincarnation allows us to keep the idea that our selves survive the death of our bodies without getting bogged down in the Christian problem of just where those who enjoy the 'bodily resurrection' reside. The desire for some sort of community, without the awkwardness of being part of any actual community, is served by the notion that, in some sense, we are all one. That all beings and indeed everything in the world is all part of the same essence fits nicely with the contemporary stress on environmentalism. There is a strong ethical thrust in the code for living. The Five Precepts – not killing, not stealing, not lying, not using intoxicants and not engaging in sexual misconduct – are arguably harder to quibble with than the Christian Ten Commandments. And the idea of karma (or moral consequences) allows us to think that bad people will get their comeuppance without the Christian problem of why a supposedly just God allows bad things to happen to good people. Karma explains the apparent lack of just deserts: if good things happen to bad people (and vice-versa) they must have deserved it from a previous life. That can, of course, get a bit sticky when applied to real situations. In May 2008 the actress Sharon Stone explained the earthquake that killed at least 80,000 Chinese people as being a deserved consequence of the Chinese treatment of the Tibetans. She said, 'I thought, "Is that karma?" When you are not nice, bad things happen to you.'[24] A much clearer example of karmic consequences followed immediately when Stone was sacked from her lucrative modelling contract with the Dior fashion house. But for all its difficulty of precise application, the idea of some supra-mundane system of rewards and punishments is appealing.

Buddhist meditation techniques also have an obvious appeal. Clearly many Westerners are unhappy with their lives in ways which are best addressed not by changing their circumstances (after all, they are vastly better off than their grandparents) but by changing their reactions to those circumstances. Anxiety, depression, insecurity, neuroticism and insatiable desire can all be addressed by cultivating detachment through meditation. Especially in its Zen form, which is more philosophical and less ritualistic, Buddhism can quite readily be secularised into a self-help therapy that offers a drug-free way of addressing the minor discontents of modern life.

Of course, Buddhism in its original setting is far more than a code of ethics or a cure for anxiety. Especially in its Tibetan form it is a supernaturalistic religion. Its rituals are not psychological exercises: they are magical ways of accessing real supernatural power. Samye Ling does not shy away from imputing supernatural powers to its leaders. Of His Holiness the sixteenth Karmapa performing the Black crown ceremony, the official history says that it produces 'benefits for all beings' and that 'This sacred rite performed exclusively by the lineage of the Karmapas, bestows tremendous blessings on all those who are fortunate enough to witness it'.[25] The author also gushes about the

Karmapa's 'radiant presence'. Just as the Catholic Church believes that the ritual of blessing the bread and wine is qualitatively different when performed by a properly ordained priest and by a good actor, so the rituals performed by reincarnate lamas are held to confer, actually rather than metaphorically, spiritual power. Hence the importance of the lineage, which is established at the start of teaching sessions by reciting the list of the incarnations of the monastic order's leaders back to the Buddha. One can understand Buddhist principles by reading the sacred texts but one only gains the power when the teachings are delivered by embodiments of a previous Buddha or those who have been instructed by such a person. Chogyam Trungpa was not just himself: he was the embodiment of all the previous Trungpas. Akong played a major part in the disputed identification of the embodiment of the deceased sixteenth Karmapa and did so with a classic 'sign' story. Apparently he had asked the dying Karmapa if he could have one of his teeth after he had been cremated; this wish was granted but the relic never delivered. When Akong met the young child who was putatively his old master re-born he said to him, 'You have something for me' and the young child fished out a milk tooth from under a rug and gave it to Akong.

The official Samye Ling history offers unashamed hero worship of tulkus. Photographs of the current head of the lineage are displayed in prominent positions at all centres. The lineage prayer is recited at the beginning and end of all sessions other than public lectures. A lama reinforced the importance of lineage at a public lecture: 'If you want to check the authenticity of a group then all you need to do is check the lineage. Any legitimate school should have a lineage that traces back to the Buddha himself. If they do not have that then it most probably is not a good school and could be dangerous'.[26]

Samye Ling still believes in magic. In 1977, during his second visit, his Holiness the sixteenth Karmapa walked around the site of what would become the Purelands meditation centre with Akong and Sherab Palden. There were many large rocks along the path, 'one of which His Holiness said was a par-ticularly nice rock. Akong Rinpoche replied that it was just a rock but that if his Holiness would make a footprint on it then it would indeed become a special rock'. His Holiness stepped on the rock. 'There was no footprint to be seen and everyone forgot the incident until some years later when the rock had to be moved during the building of the retreat centre. Some people wanted to get rid of the rock altogether but Rinpoche told them to keep it and when Sherab's nephew Gyamtso washed the mud off it he discovered the clear imprint of His Holiness's foot'.[27] And the official history has a photograph of what does indeed look like a footprint in a very large rock.

Religious rituals can always be interpreted in a secular fashion. An atheist can find benefit in reciting the collects of the Book of Common Prayer: they may make him mindful of others and remind him of his obligations to his fellows. Samye Ling believes that prayer works supernaturally. When

prayers in the temple end, a monk moves around with a notebook, recording the number of mantras each monk and nun has recited. These are added
together: a record of the merit which has been spread by the group for the
benefit of all 'sentient beings'. The turning prayer wheels are not just ethnic
kitsch. Those who inscribed them and who ensure they turn believe that the
words are heard by divine beings who are thus encouraged to improve the lot
of humankind.

What most obviously sets Samye Ling against the spirit of the age is its
decoration. A certain Zen aesthetic – no furniture, monotones, plain screen
walls – fits easily with Western modernism. One can imagine the Bauhaus
architects or Frank Lloyd Wright as Zen Buddhists. But Samye Ling's style is
the lurid reds, golds and purples of a loud Indian restaurant. The logic is that
of Florentine or Venetian Christianity: the buildings of God provide the stark-
est possible contrast with the colourless poverty of the common people and
testify to the richness of the divine. Tim Lewis, who helped build the temple,
confessed that he found the colour scheme a little brash and pointed out that
the later stupas were 'a little less screaming', but he recognised the importance
to the Tibetans of trying to preserve their culture. And, to return to the fundamental rift between Akong and Trungpa, preserving its Tibetan roots is what
prevents Samye Ling's Kagyu school of Buddhism losing control of the beliefs
which define it.

Accommodating the West

The modernising model for selling the East to the West had been pioneered
by Mahareshi Mahesh Yogi with the marketing of his brand of Hinduism
as Transcendental Meditation or TM. TM was first presented in the West
in explicitly religious terms and with the full cultural context that expected
devotees to commit themselves entirely to the movement, as yogins would in
India. In that form it attracted a lot of attention but very few members: it could
only recruit single young people without family responsibilities and few of
them stayed for more than a few months. Even those who found it rewarding
were drawn away from full-time commitment by the wish to marry and have
children. By the early 1980s TM had radically changed its approach 'largely
on marketing grounds'.[28] TM now stressed three things in its advertising.
Its meditation techniques were of practical benefit in this world: meditation
would make you a happier, better and more effective person. Second, TM was
not disruptive: only twenty minutes a day would work wonders and that could
be easily slotted into a busy life. Third, you did not have to subordinate yourself to anyone else's demands: you remained in control of your commitment.
This is vital because, although a few seekers after spiritual enlightenment are
looking for an authoritarian world which will provide them with certainty and
direction, most are autodidacts with a rather high opinion of their own critical

faculties. Indeed, one of the common characteristics of modern seekers, the trait which expresses their modernity, is that they claim the right to decide for themselves what they will believe.

Although TM could not prevent a 'cash-and-carry' response – sign up for the basic meditation course, learn the technique, then move on – it maintained cohesion by having an inner circle of full-time adepts who mastered more arduous forms of meditation such as 'yogic flying', the levitation that looks to the rest of us like bouncing.

Like TM, the Buddhists of Samye Ling evolved a layered strategy to deal with their move from being leaders of the established religion of their country to being the teachers of an exotic faith in a strange land. Unlike the Friends of the Western Buddhist Order, a movement which has stripped away most of the Eastern cultural accompaniments, Samye Ling has preserved (exaggerated even) its esoteric magical faith, and the Tibetan art and music that goes with it, but at the same time it also presents more appropriate faces to peripheral audiences. The Holy Isle project presents an inclusive form of generic spirituality. The Rokpa Trust and its international charity work promote social and economic improvement in deprived parts of the world. In open public lectures, Tibetan Buddhism is presented less as an exotic alien religion and more as a philosophy of compassion that can provide techniques for making life more manageable. In its outer layer of engagement with the public, it stresses its lack of interest in converting and recruiting outsiders, its ecumenical openness to all religions and forms of spirituality, and its respect for individual conscience. At a lecture in Discovery Point in Dundee a lama advised, 'I am not here to tell people what to believe and what to do. That is your responsibility. You need to find things out for yourself and take responsibility for your own behaviour. If you try to leave that responsibility to someone else then you will never make progress or learn anything'.[29] A middle-aged mother of three who studied Buddhism for eight years before requesting ordination told her audience: 'One of the most important teachings of the Buddha was "Don't believe anything just because I'm saying it". The philosophy is "Go out there and find out for yourself if it works"'.[30]

The obvious problem with stressing the individual's right to decide what works is that it clashes with Samye Ling's wish to maintain the tradition. Lama Yeshe said of his charges:

> Always impatient. And they don't really like to be told anything by anybody. Everybody feels they must be individual. Consequently, there is this lack of discipline, lack of commitment and very often, great instability. My monks and nuns, they will all be happy and committed for one or two days, and then they become depressed for a while because they are maybe thinking, 'What have I done, what is it I really want?' It's a constant battle. And it requires discipline.[31]

Conclusion

At its most superficial, Buddhism is popular. People who have no religious beliefs beyond a vague hope that the self lives on after the body, and the principle that we should not destroy the planet, may describe themselves as Buddhist. The cultured middle classes of Edinburgh's New Town or Glasgow's West End may casually describe their vague thoughts about the meaning of life as 'a Zen thing'. Buddhas and prayer flags are popular decorations with the same people who have reduced Feng Shui from its Chinese roots as serious necromancy concerned with placating the souls of the dead to an interior decorating style.

It is hard to gauge the number of Scots who take Buddhism seriously. We get little help from the Scottish press which effortlessly presents any story about Samye Ling as proof of Scotland's 'spiritual hunger' without noticing that most of the people involved in Samye Ling are not Scots. Samye Ling is in Dumfriesshire for the same reason that black magician Aleister Crowley bought Boleskine House near Inverness: the property was cheap, the scenery beautiful, and the population sufficiently thin for opposition to exotic incomers to be weak. Samye Ling is a joint English–Tibetan project with an international clientele. When poet Kathleen Jamie visited in 2001 the three monks she met were an Italian, a Yorkshireman and a Scot; the visitors she met were four Finns and an Ulsterman. Thom McCarthy, who later owned three gift shops on Edinburgh's Royal Mile and raised much of the Holy Isle money, was American. The nationality of twelve of the thirty-one non-Tibetans credited in the official history with a role in the early days can be identified: seven were English, two were French, and there was one Scot, one Dane and one Dutch woman. This influx of dynamic young people has been a huge boost to Eskdalemuir. Two young men who helped build the monastery went on to run successful construction businesses. The impact of Samye Ling on Eskdalemuir is clear. Of 175 residents in the 2001 census, two-thirds were born outside Scotland: the average for Scotland as a whole was 13 per cent.[32] Almost half were English. Such new blood has been very good for Eskdalemuir but as the monastery is recruiting internationally its growth can hardly be taken as a sign of Scottish 'spiritual hunger'.

Samye Ling has influence far beyond its resident population because it is a transit camp and a teaching centre. Far more people pass through than stay, not because they lose faith in Buddhism but because they conclude (often because they want a family) that monastic life is not for them. One young woman was drawn to Samye Ling after taking meditation classes. She was ordained within a few weeks and for five months enjoyed the life of a nun until she found herself attracted to a lay resident.

It was the one thing I never thought would happen. We were both determined to be good, not to let it get out of hand. But I'd keep getting told off for talking to him.

It was absolute hell for five months, until he left the community. By that time I'd decided to finish the year, then give the relationship a go. I knew if I stayed I'd regret passing up the chance of maybe meeting my soul mate, and all the other romantic things you think about all the time when you're in robes and can do nothing about.

She had no regrets about leaving or about having joined. It was like 'having a sabbatical. It was taking a year out to think "what do I want to do with my life?" It was definitely the best thing I ever did, and I couldn't have gone back to what I was doing before because something profound has changed in me.'[33]

Notes

1. W. Brown, 'The parish of Eskdalemuir', *New Statistical Account of Scotland: County of Dumfriesshire* (Glasgow: William Blackwood and Sons, 1835), p. 413; http://stat-acc-scot.edina.ac.uk/link/1834-45/Dumfries/Eskdalemuir/.
2. J. Littlejohn, *Westrigg* (London: Routledge and Kegan Paul, 1963), p. 11.
3. Littlejohn, *Westrigg*, p. 51.
4. Littlejohn, *Westrigg*, p. 68.
5. R. Wilson, 'The parish of Eskdalemuir', in G. Houston (ed.), *Third Statistical Account of Scotland: the County of Dumfries* (Glasgow: Collins, 1962), p. 418, Ch. 49. Although published in 1962, the Eskdalemuir entry was written in 1952, when Littlejohn was doing his fieldwork.
6. There is a Scottish connection: from 1899 to 1913 Crowley owned Boleskine House, on the south side of Loch Ness.
7. They are part of the Karma Kagyu sect, one of the four main traditions of Tibetan Buddhism, the others being the Nyingma, Sakya and Gelug. The Dalai Lama is the head of the Gelug tradition and until the Buddhist leadership fled the country the Dalai Lama was also Tibet's temporal leader.
8. Leslie Dawson used the name Ananda Bodhi when he was head of the tiny Theravada Buddhist community in London. He returned to Canada in 1964 and later shifted allegiance to Tibetan Buddhism, renamed as Venerable Namgyal Rinpoche; http://en.wikipedia.org/wiki/Namgyal_Rinpoche.
9. Incredible String Band involvement is quite likely. The band and members of the dance troupe that accompanied them rented cottages at Glen Row near Peebles, a 36-mile drive from Eskdale.
10. http://music.aol.com/artist/david-bowie/biography/1003166.
11. A. R. Khandro, *Kagyu Samye Ling: The Story* (Eskdalemuir: Dzalendara Publishing, 2007), p. 24.
12. D. Mukpo, *Dragon Thunder: My Life with Chogyam Trungpa* (Boston and London: Shambhala Press, 2006); S. Silberman, 'Married to the guru', *Shambala Sun*, November 2006, pp. 41–51.
13. Mukpo, *Dragon Thunder*, pp. 88–9.
14. L. P. Eldershaw, *Collective Identity and the Post-Charismatic Fate of Shambhala*

International (Waterloo: University of Waterloo PhD thesis, 2004), pp. 228 and 230.

15. It says much about the forgiving spirit of Akong that the Samye Ling bookshop stocks all of Trungpa's publications, including the biography in which he criticises Akong.

16. This and subsequent quotations without cited sources are from interviews and email exchanges conducted between 2010 and 2012.

17. *The Scotsman*, 3 March 2007.

18. The Queen is notionally advised by her Privy Council. Members are senior figures of the political establishment.

19. Khandro, *Kagyu Samye Ling,* p. 86.

20. Holy Isle is not the only Clyde coast island to be owned by an Eastern religious organisation. In 2009 Little Cumbrae was bought by disciples of Guru Baba Ramdev for use as a meditation and yoga training retreat; 'Baba Ramdev buys Scottish island', *Hindustan Times*, 28 September 2009.

21. *The Scotsman*, 6 February 1998.

22. 'Councillors snub Buddhist ceremony', *Dumfries and Galloway Standard*, 16 November 2007.

23. D. Voas, 'Religious decline in Scotland', *Journal for the Scientific Study of Religion* 45 (2006), pp. 107–18.

24. BBC, 'Anger over star's quake remarks', *BBC News*, 28 May 2008; http://news.bbc.co.uk/1/hi/entertainment/7423089.stm.

25. Khandro, *Kagyu Samye Ling*, p. 28.

26. I am grateful to John McKenzie for this quotation from his postgraduate field-work. See J. McKenzie, *ROKPA Scotland: a Sociological Account* (Aberdeen: University of Aberdeen PhD thesis, 2008).

27. Khandro, *Kagyu Samye Ling*, p. 37.

28. R. Wallis, *The Elementary Forms of the New Religious Life* (London: Routledge and Kegan Paul, 1984), p. 34.

29. Again I am obliged to John McKenzie for this quote.

30. M. Brown, 'The Buddhists of Eskdalemuir', *Daily Telegraph*, 4 October 1997.

31. Brown, 'The Buddhists of Eskdalemuir'.

32. Calculated from data available at Scotland's Census Results Online; http://www.scrol.gov.uk/scrol/common/home.jsp.

33. Brown, 'The Buddhists of Eskdalemuir'.

CHAPTER

10

THE ENGLISH ON THE MORAY RIVIERA

When Yeshe Losal wanted to publicise Samye Ling's plans to develop Holy Isle as a spiritual retreat and to display various designs for the new centre, he did so with a press conference at the Findhorn Foundation near Forres, on the Moray coast.[1] This was a sensible choice because it connected Samye Ling to an international network of the sort of people who attended spiritual retreats on remote islands. Now one of Europe's oldest New Age centres, Findhorn had its inauspicious origins in the 1962 sacking of three English people from their jobs running the Cluny Hotel in Forres.[2] Peter and Eileen Caddy and their friend Dorothy Maclean moved into the cheapest accommodation they could find: a shabby caravan on a holiday park.[3]

The Caddys and Maclean had a long history of involvement in the English fringe milieu of alternative spirituality, esoteric knowledge, plant spirits and Venusian UFOs. Rosicrucians (or the people of the 'red cross') claim access to an ancient body of secret knowledge about the nature of the material and spiritual worlds which supposedly dates from the Middle Ages but which like most of such things is a modern invention. As a young man Peter Caddy joined the Rosicrucian Order Crotona Fellowship, a group barely larger than its name that met in a pub in Christchurch to study esoteric subjects from lectures, plays and correspondence material prepared by their inspired master George Sullivan. Peter also attended meetings at the Pimlico flat of Sheena Govan, whom he married in 1948. Govan is an interesting fringe character. She was raised in an evangelical home by a father, J. G. Govan, who founded the Faith Mission, a non-denominational organisation which missionised rural areas of the British Isles.[4] Govan believed in intuitive insight into the divine, which she encouraged in her small but devoted band of acolytes by a combination of hectoring and bullying intended to remove such blockages to enlightenment as emotional associations with others. Govan had a caravan in Glastonbury and her followers were familiar with the various groups that saw it as a place of particular spiritual power.[5] Caddy's career as a catering officer in the RAF allowed him to visit India and Tibet where, like the Theosophists before him, he found themes to borrow for his own personal bricolage. It also led him to meet Eileen, who was then married to another RAF officer with whom she had three children. Her affair with Peter cost her that family and, although Sheena accepted Eileen (who was by then pregnant with Peter's child), she regularly forced the couple to part for their own spiritual good. Maclean was also part of the Govan circle. It was Govan's decision to move to a tiny isolated cottage in Glenfinnan that brought the Caddys and Maclean to Scotland. After a few years of unemployed poverty, all three found work running a large hotel in Forres. Although by their own account they turned a white elephant into a popular and profitable concern, their employers – who had been disturbed by sensationalist coverage of Sheena Govan's circle in a number of popular Scottish papers in 1957 – moved them to the Trossachs for a season and then fired them. That led to the three spending what they assumed would be a temporary sojourn on the Findhorn caravan park. Desperately poor, they began to grow their own vegetables.

> Dorothy had had messages come through to her in meditation, to feel into the nature forces such as the wind, and then the higher nature spirits of clouds or vegetables. She had discovered to her surprise that her entry into that realm was welcomed by those spirits. At Peter's request that she ask for help with growing the vegetables, she found she was able to attune to the essence of the garden pea . . . In focusing on the essence of the pea plant and approaching it with deep love, she had found the doorway into the intelligence within the plant.

What Maclean called 'devas' (after the Sanskrit for 'shining ones') apparently held the archetypal pattern for perfect growth.

> She explained the process of their work as vital lifeforce directing energies through a vibrationary interplay of what we humans would recognise as sound and light, in order to materialise all life into form. And their way of working was through love, an all embracing if impersonal love, which expressed itself through a free, unburdened joy in communicating what needed to be done in the gardens.[6]

Initially Eileen was the least assertive of the trio but she had a gift which Peter lacked: having first heard an 'inner voice' in a Glastonbury church, she became a channel for regular messages of spiritual guidance.

> I could sit and meditate for a long time and nothing would come, but as soon as my pen touched the paper it was like switching on an electric current. The words flowed. I was told: 'I work through each of you in different ways. You know when you need

guidance from Me, you can receive it instantaneously. Like a flashing of lightning it is there. You can find the answer immediately; therefore you hold great responsibilities in your hands'.[7]

She initially regarded her revelations as coming from God, rather traditionally conceived. Later she saw the source as her higher self: 'There is no separation between ourselves and God, there is only 'I am'. I am the guidance. It took me so many years to realise this'.[8] The Caddys had frequently used Eileen's divine guidance in managing hotels. Marooned in a caravan park, they had less to decide but Eileen regularly received her guidance in the only place she could find solitude: the park's unheated communal toilet block.

The Caddys first attracted attention for their spirit-assisted gardening prowess: 'stories of plants performing incredible feats of growth and endurance: 40-pound cabbages, 8-foot delphiniums, and roses blooming in the snow'.[9] That reference to snow shows how ignorance breeds myths. Foreigners and southerners assume that because Forres is very much 'up north' it must be cold and hence successful horticulture must be miraculous or at least unusual. Actually that part of the coast used to be described, with only the mildest sarcasm, as the Moray Riviera. Average temperatures in July are 19 degrees centigrade, summer days are long, and the warm coastal waters prevent winter averages falling below zero. Without any help from devas, Forres has won the Scottish Town in Bloom award many times.

Gradually like-minded people were drawn to the caravan park. The first were elderly long-term habitués of the cultic milieu, but the trickle turned into something of a rush in the late 1960s when the hippie counter-culture produced an interest in communes. We now know that the radical Sixties would lead to eighteen years of Conservative government but for a time it seemed to many that the world was about to change abruptly and that individualistic capitalism was about to be replaced by communal living. Even some sociologists were attracted by the idea that communes offered a viable model for the future of the West and that one such was being pioneered in a caravan park near Forres.[10]

In 1969 the caravan park had about 600 visitors and in 1970 the group grew from seventeen to forty-two adults and nine children. In the spring of 1973 the BBC ran a prime-time documentary about the growing community and the publication of Paul Hawken's entirely flattering portrait of the group in 1975 brought it to the attention of an international audience.[11]

The modern community owes much to two changes: the Caddys' conversion to optimism and the input from an American couple. Official histories play down the Caddys' early ideas but they seem to have seen themselves as a protected remnant in a largely bad world. Peter Caddy's interest in Venusian spaceships seems to have been fuelled by a Cold War vision of the world as something from which we would be rescued by alien spacemen. The appointed day was Whitsun 1966.

a group of about sixteen carefully selected people (plus a few gatecrashers) gathered with us at Findhorn. We had been told to expect an attempted landing by our space brothers, so we all assembled on the beach at the landing site we had prepared and built up in our meditations over the years. Those with inner sight actually described a spaceship as it came in and hovered overhead; I saw nothing, of course, but when Roc was told to stand in the centre, where a beam of light would be focussed on him to 'raise his vibrations', even *I* saw him disappear briefly! It gave me quite a shock, yet while nothing else seemed to happen afterwards – according to the sensitives, the spacecraft flew off again – all of us there were filled with a tremendous feeling of upliftment, as if something very profound had changed and things would never be the same again.[12]

There are two common reactions to the failure of such predictions. One is to argue that salvation has been delayed by a lack of faith. In 1786 a small group of followers of the prophetess Joanna Buchan built wooden platforms on Templand Hill near Thornhill, discarded their possessions, cut off all their hair except for a small tuft by which the angels would catch them up, and gathered on the hill for their ascent.[13] At the end of the day the company retraced their steps to the shabby barn in which they had lived for a year. Buchan tried to persuade them that the angels had delayed their ascent to heaven because their faith was not yet strong enough, but her re-interpretation was not convincing and the community slowly disintegrated. The other common response is to argue that actually something really did happen on the appointed day and that the prophet had just misunderstood the signs. The Seventh Day Adventists and the Jehovah's Witnesses have successfully re-interpreted the failure of their end-times prophecies in such a way and grown faster after the failure than before. The Caddys took the second option. Eileen's inner voice announced:

Let none of you have any feeling of disappointment regarding last night . . . All was in preparation for something far, far greater than any of you have ever contemplated. Raise your thinking and you will raise your living to an entirely new level. Do it this instant, going your various ways, knowing that this is actually happening to you. Rise together.[14]

The guidance went on to say that sufficient Light had been anchored on the planet (presumably by the work of the Caddys and like-minded souls) so that destruction was now no longer inevitable: 'the spacecraft that had come, as we thought, to arrange . . . evacuation had in fact "popped in" to tell us that everything was all right'.[15] Clearly there might be a lot of retrospective re-writing in this account produced thirty years after the event but Peter Caddy thought of the 1966 spacecraft visit as 'a turning point in human history'.[16]

The second significant change was the arrival of David Spangler, a young American who has a reasonable claim to have been one of the founders of the

'New Age'. Active in psychic circles in California since 1965, Spangler first visited in 1970 and moved permanently to Findhorn in 1973. He and his wife Myrtle Glines put the educational work of the community on a firm footing and encouraged the expansion which in 1975 saw the purchase of the Forres hotel which the Caddys had managed when they first arrived in Morayshire. In 1983 the community's base was secured when it bought the caravan park. It was also gifted the tiny tidal island of Erraid off Mull and a house on Iona, both of which are run as outposts of the Findhorn community.

To present its growth as proof of the virtue of its spiritual ethos, approved histories of the Findhorn community often describe it as self-generating and miraculous: proof that the Caddys' philosophy of manifestation – identify your real needs and present them to the spirit world and they will be met – worked. The same material can be read in a more rational fashion. Peter Caddy was already acquainted with some of the key figures in the English world of esoteric knowledge and he assiduously cultivated others. Robert Ogilvie Crombie (known as 'ROC') and Sir George Trevelyan of the Wrekin Trust were friends.[17] He acquired the mailing list of well-known psychic Liebe Pugh and used it to advertise the publication of *God Spoke to Me* – a collection of Eileen's spiritual guidance – and to solicit donations. Essentially what Caddy did was to garner publicity by exaggerating Findhorn's size and achievements, commit to expansive building projects the community could not afford, and hope that enough people would be attracted and large enough donations sent to cover the costs and to make the exaggerations realistic.

With the Caddys' marriage in trouble, Peter began to spend more time advertising the community abroad and he left it finally in 1979. Eileen also retreated from active involvement in day-to-day running of what was now a considerable operation.

Since 1979 Findhorn has been re-structured a number of times as ambitious growth plans brought debt problems and its reluctance to adopt a strong management structure caused repeated difficulties in determining its purpose. But it has survived by clearly separating its strands and by making its purpose more mundane but sustainable. As the revolution for which it was the catalyst never occurred, it settled for providing a base for spiritual education for a largely transient population. There is a core of about 150 staff which services a regular programme of instruction for visitors: about 5,000 a year in the 1990s, perhaps 2,000 a year in 2010. Much of that instruction is delivered in Experience Week: visitors arrive in cohorts and spend a week in group meditations and instruction classes. They also do much of their own housekeeping and work with staff in such domestic tasks as gardening and food preparation. For many, Experience Week is enough; they go home and add what they have learned to what they gain from the wide range of other spiritual practices. A few will come back for further and longer periods and a handful who are acceptable to the core staff will be invited to join the staff and become permanent resident members. By creating a clear and controlled route into membership, the Foundation resolved the swamping problem of the early days when there were no formal mechanisms for rejecting unsuitable people who wanted to join. In 2005/6 income was £1.6 million, with three-quarters of that coming from fees and the rest from trading activities and donations.[18]

In addition to the staff core, there are perhaps 300 or 400 sympathisers and ex-staff who live in their own properties in Findhorn village and in the surrounding area, and who provide some services to the Foundation and support its activities. The Phoenix is a large organic and wholefood store and bookshop. The Apothecary supplies homoeopathic and herbal medicines. The Universal Hall provides a large modern auditorium for music and dance events. One strand of work that has proved particularly attractive to the wider world is ecologically sensitive development. To Peter Caddy's interest in organic horticulture, later generations of residents and associates have added sustainable forms of electricity generation, waste-water purification and house-building.

Exactly what is taught at Findhorn has varied over the years with the interests of the residents and of the wider New Age community. Some elements have provided controversial and divisive. Under the leadership of Craig Gibsone (1989–93) the holiotropic breathwork style of psychotherapy popular at the Esalen Institute in California was promoted. This involves beliefs about the importance of birth experiences for later psychological development and uses hyperventilation to help the psyche cure itself. It was suspended after complaints led to a critical report from academics.[19] For a short time crystals were in vogue but many residents had little sympathy for the grandiose claims made for the power of crystals to channel power from Atlantis.[20]

Insofar as there has been an enduring core, it is a combination of environmentalism and personal growth psychology. A variety of rituals (for example, using dance, meditation and music) offer participants ways of transcending their personal problems and becoming happier, more effective people. This emphasis on personal growth rather than on social revolution has allowed a rapprochement with capitalism. The hippies who saw Findhorn as an alternative to 'The Man' have been replaced by professionals who boast of selling their services as consultants in conflict resolution to oil companies and accountancy firms.[21] In 2004 Eileen Caddy was awarded an MBE for services to 'spiritual enquiry'.

Alternative Spirituality

Although David Spangler entitled his first Findhorn Press publication *Revelation: Birth of a New Age*, the 'New Age' label is now largely shunned, though no one has yet produced a better short phrase.[22] The term is important because it explains the otherwise obscure combination of being highly critical of many aspects of the modern world (especially the nature of modern relationships) and being extremely optimistic about the possibility of improvement. Astrologers divide the history of the world into Great Years, consisting of twelve 'months', each of which is 2,160 years long and is represented by a star sign in the Sidereal Zodiac. Stonehenge dates from the start of the Age of Aries. The birth of Christ marks the start of the Age of Pisces. Now, as the hit musical *Hair* put it, we are at 'the dawning of the Age of Aquarius'. As William Bloom, a doyen of New Age philosophy, put it:

> We are passing out of 2,000 years of Piscean astrological influence into the influence of Aquarius, which will affect all aspects of our culture, as we move from Piscean structures of hierarchical devotion to more fluid and spontaneous relationships that dance to an Aquarian rhythm.[23]

One reason for disdaining the New Age tag is that it implies the superficiality of fashion; another is that many of its practitioners draw on what they regard as ancient cultures for their rituals and therapies. I put it like that because the ancient lineage claimed for their ideas, practices and rituals is always better public relations than good history.[24] Much of contemporary Wicca, for example, dates no further back than a series of books written by retired colonial civil servant Gerald Gardner in the 1950s.

Precisely characterising the world of alternative spirituality is difficult because, unlike many of the new religious movements of the 1970s, it is, in sociological terms, cultic rather than sectarian. Most providers do not claim that they and only they have the truth and do not recruit a loyal following that must subscribe to specific beliefs and dogmas. Instead they suppose that there are a large number of equally valuable spiritual paths and that each of us should decide for ourselves what we will believe. That basic difference in underlying ethos is reflected in organisation. Most New Age activity does not have members: it has clients and audiences.[25] The client cult is structured around the bond between producer and consumer. Typical is the alternative therapist who advertises his or her services (and it usually is a 'her') in an appropriate magazine or website, or on the notice board of a health food shop, and provides individual consultations for a fixed fee. Thus a classified advertisement in *Fortean Times* invites one to: 'Make the pilgrimage to Middle Earth – Tarot, crystals, oils, lava lamps, jewellery, incense, cards, tarot readings by appointment' and then gives the address and phone number to call to arrange such a reading.[26] Audience cults are structured around the mass distribution of the word: spoken and printed. The circulatory system of the New Age body was initially made up of books, magazines, audio cassettes and public lectures; now the internet performs the same function, though personal presentations in lectures and workshops remain popular. Promoters of particular revelations or techniques use New Age magazines and websites to advertise their meetings. They present their insights and therapies and move on. New Life Promotions, which organises the annual Mind, Body and Spirit conventions in London, also arranges national tours for prominent New Age teachers.

As there are no boundaries to the cultic milieu and anyone is free to offer horoscope readings or advertise the spiritual benefits of Tibetan overtone chanting, it is difficult to summarise the beliefs of the holistic spirituality milieu but there are some obvious common threads.

First, there is the belief that the self is divine. The major world religions assume a division between the Gods and the people they created. God is good; people are bad. People only became good by subjecting themselves to God's will and God's commandments as instructed by his representatives on this earth. Religion provides rituals, therapies and dogmas to control the self and shape it into a valuable object. The cultic milieu does not have that division of God and his creation. Instead it supposes that we have within us the essence of holiness. The human self is essentially good because it is essentially God. If it is bad then that is a result of our environment and circumstances. The aim of many New Age belief systems and therapies is to strip away the accumulated residues of our bad experiences in order to release our potential. Although not always recognised by practitioners, who prefer to claim the authority of ancient wisdom, such a view obviously borrows heavily from psychology from Sigmund Freud onwards.

Second, there is no authority higher than the individual self. How could there be if we all possess the essence of divinity? We can learn from others (and some spiritual seekers have an unfortunate fondness for corrupt and exploitative gurus) but the final arbiter of truth is the individual. As an American 'neo-pagan', with some difficulty, explained:

> Gnosis, direct knowledge. Uh, books can give you hints and directions to where you might look, but you gotta do it . . . I have a hard time believing anything without some form of personal proof, it – now it doesn't have to be objective, it can be subjective, for me, but if I've experienced it, then to me, it – it – I can accept is as true, but if I don't experience it, I can't – I have a very hard time accepting it. I have to check it out myself.[27]

He got there in the end! In the world of holistic spirituality one does not accept authority; what matters is what works for you.[28]

That self-assertiveness explains the third thread: eclecticism. As we come from a wide variety of backgrounds and no two people experience the world alike, we all have different notions of what works for us and this is reflected in the enormous cafeteria of cultural products to be found in the cultic milieu. A simple way of illustrating that range is to consider the subjects covered in the 1990s in a popular series of books called 'The Elements of . . .'. The nouns that followed included: Alchemy, Astronomy, Buddhism, Christian Symbolism, Creation Myth, Crystal Healing, Dreamwork, Earth Mysteries,

Feng Sui, Herbalism, Human Potential, Meditation, Mysticism, Natural Magic, Pendulum Dowsing, Prophecy, Psychosynthesis, Shamanism, Sufism, Taoism, Aborigine Tradition, Chakras, Goddess Myths, the Grail Tradition, Qabalah, Visualization and Zen.

> I do follow a lot of different spiritual paths. I don't consider myself – I call myself a witch but I'm not Wiccan. I study tantric techniques but I'm not a tantric Buddhist. Uh, I do dreamwork techniques, but I don't really follow that original path. Um, I look into Native American studies and at what they have, but I don't consider that my path. I'm very eclectic – I like this idea of pulling from all different sources to find what works for me . . . diversity is the key.[29]

This is the simultaneous sampling of one person. There is also a great deal of sequential sampling. Even those new movements of the 1970s such as Scientology and Transcendental Meditation that would have liked to be sects and whose cadres privately believe that they have the truth and everyone else is plain wrong have been forced by market pressures to accept the eclecticism of the cultic milieu. Instead of recruiting loyal followers, they market their services to people who will take a course, attend some events, acquire the important knowledge and then move on to some other revelation or therapy. As a consequence, the milieu is rich in its diversity.

Fourth, eclecticism requires a particular attitude to knowledge. Many New Agers do not look closely at the compatibility of various revelations and therapies but move between them with the aid of shallow analogies. A lecture on the theory of angels (we all have one apparently) talked of travels in Australia. The speaker skipped from ley lines to Ayurvedic anatomy to spiritual hotspots: 'Just like we have chakra points in our body so the earth has chakra points and if you go to one of those you can tap the energy flows'.[30] If analogy does not allow every idea to lead to every other, then they find philosophical reconciliation in the Eastern notion of a fundamental unity behind apparent diversity. It is all really cosmic consciousness. The claim to be 'holistic', which in alternative medicine can just mean paying attention to all the circumstances that might cause an ailment, becomes a reason not to look closely at how different ideas might clash.

My final observation is probably the most important for this general review of religious change in Scotland. In one respect New Age spirituality and much modern Christianity are similar. All the major world religions promise that if we follow their teachings we *may* be happier and healthier people, but those therapeutic benefits are always secondary to the primary purpose of glorifying God and never assured. Medieval Christians followed the instructions of the Church because that is what God required. While they might hope for a good life, it was always possible that God's inscrutable providence destined otherwise. In the contemporary cultic milieu, as in much of liberal Christianity, therapy is the primary, not the secondary, function: the purpose is to feel better and to be happier in this life. Although those interested in contemporary spirituality often portray it as an alternative to worldliness, in operating ethos it is individualistic and in purpose it is largely this-worldly. Which is why Findhorn can market its personal effectiveness strategies to capitalist corporations.

How Popular is New Age Spirituality?

That the Findhorn community has survived for over fifty years despite its individualistic ethos and consequent difficulties with the idea of management is testimony to the resilience of those involved but it tells us nothing at all about the popularity of the New Age in Scotland. Its founders were English, subsequent leading figures have been American, French, Australian and Canadian, and its clientele is international. Lost somewhere in between personal and planetary transformation, local transformation has been almost entirely missed. Almost all of the sympathisers in the local area are incomers. While the local tourist board appreciates the Foundation's boost to the local economy, its neighbours are often less than complementary, especially about expansion plans. One local described it as having gone from a benign community which 'believed in fairies in the garden' to a commercial venture 'feeding upon trusting people'.[31]

Gauging the popularity of New Age spirituality is difficult, though I should immediately add that the practical difficulties do not justify the grandiose claims that are commonly made for it. As a self-description, 'spiritual' is certainly more popular than it was in my father's day, when it meant ethereally pious, with just a whiff of incense or smelling salts.

Table 10.1 shows how the 2001 Scottish Attitudes Survey sample responded to the question 'Whether you attend services or not, are you religious, spiritual

Table 10.1 Self-description as Religious, Spiritual or Neither, Scottish Social Attitudes Survey 2001

	Whether you attend services or not, are you . . .	%
18–34 years	Religious	15
	Spiritual	13
	Neither	72
		100
35–54 years	Religious	28
	Spiritual	18
	Neither	54
		100
55 and over	Religious	54
	Spiritual	12
	Neither	33
		100

or neither?' As we would expect, the 'religious' description is strongly associated with age, with only 15 per cent of Scots aged 18–34 but more than half of those over 54 choosing it. The 'spiritual' tag is not terribly popular with any age group but its pattern is suggestively different to that for 'religious'. The youngest and the oldest age groups are almost the same: 13 and 12 per cent respectively. The self-description is more popular with those aged 35–54, which suggests something of a fashion. Half of those people were young adults in the early 1970s, when Scots rather tentatively dabbled in hippiedom.

To analyse further the importance of New Age spirituality, the 2001 survey asked people if they had ever tried a variety of arguably New Age activities, and how important were these in their lives.[32] As can be seen from table 10.2, most Scots had never tried any of the things we suggested. The most popular things were the least obviously spiritual: forms of alternative or complementary medicine which we defined by the prompt 'such as herbal remedies, homeopathy, or aromatherapy'. And they had been tried by only 45 per cent of the sample. Yoga and meditation, staples of the cultic milieu, had been tried by fewer than a quarter of Scots. When one adds in filter questions for how important the respondent thought the activity, one finds that only 5 per cent of Scots consulted horoscopes in newspapers and magazines and thought this practice important; only 6 per cent of Scots found more serious forms of divination (such as 'Consulting a tarot card reader, fortune teller, or astrologer') important, and only 10 per cent of Scots judged yoga or meditation to be important in their lives.

It is likely that many of the Scots who had tried yoga or meditation or forms of complementary medicine were conventionally religious churchgoers. In order to isolate a distinctly 'alternative spirituality' constituency, we can ask what proportion of those who said they had tried forms of divination and found them important also described themselves as 'spiritual'. The answer is just seventeen people from a sample of over 1,600, or about 1 per cent of the population. Various other ways of analysing the results produce similar results.

There are, of course, many reasons to be sceptical of survey results, especially when the survey is trying to tap complex attitudes, but grounds for being confident that the figure of 1 per cent is in the right ballpark can be found in data produced by a very different style of research. Colleagues from Lancaster University spent two years collecting information about every sort of activity in the small town of Kendal that could arguably be called 'New Age': from attendance figures for group activities such as the yoga classes at the local college to individual client numbers collected from face-to-face practitioners. They concluded that 1.8 per cent of Kendal's population was regularly engaged with what they called 'the holistic spirituality milieu'. Arguably they cast their net too wide: it includes therapeutic massage, for example, that could be entirely physical in purpose. And many of those who take yoga classes do so for entirely mundane reasons. One yoga instructor whose booking for

Table 10.2 Experience and Salience of the New Age Activities, Scottish Social Attitudes Survey 2001

	Horoscopes^ %	Divination+ %	Yoga or meditation %	Alternative medicine~ %
Never tried	59	70	78	55
Tried and believing it to be				
very important	1	2	3	5
Quite important	4	4	7	15
Not very important	21	13	9	20
Not at all important	15	11	4	5
%	100	100	101	100

^ Consulting horoscopes in newspapers and magazines.

+ Consulting a tarot card reader, fortune teller or astrologer (excluding horoscopes in papers and magazines).

~ Alternative or complementary medicine, such as herbal remedies, homeopathy or aromatherapy.

the church hall was rejected by the Catholic priest because it was a Hindu religious activity protested: 'I tried to explain that my yoga classes were not religious at all'.[33] Fortunately we need not argue about such inclusions because the researchers asked their respondents if they saw their activity as 'spiritual' or not. Just over half said it was not. Hence the proportion of the people of Kendal engaged in holistic spirituality activities for spiritual reasons is 0.9 per cent, much the same as the 1 per cent that Tony Glendinning and I estimated from the very different methodology of our Scottish survey.

It is worth stressing a point that may have slipped from sight. The alternative to conventional religion is not Wicca or paganism or angel guardians or spiritual seeking, all of which are extremely rare. Most of what little New Age activity we find in Scotland is much more closely related to psychological and physical well-being than to alternative religion.[34] It is an extension of the gym and the self-help therapy manual rather than an alternative to churches and church-going.

A final thought: one reason to be sceptical about the popularity of spirituality is that the notion plays a valuable part in allowing the promoters of conventional religion to convince themselves that a change in style will provoke a revival. A Church of Scotland minister said: 'people were clearly looking for spirituality but not within the old institutional authority structure'.[35] It is certainly true that those people who are interested in matters religious and spiritual are much less likely than their grandparents to accept the church or sect type of religion which insists on conformity to a divinely approved package of beliefs. But the first part of the sentence is misleading because it suggests that such seeking is common.

Gender and Spirituality

The gender gap in the churches has been mentioned. The gender gap in the world of holistic spirituality is considerably greater. The Kendal study found that 80 per cent of those actively involved were women.[36] A similar gap can be found in the 2001 Scottish survey. At the entry level of having tried any of the activities at least once, the difference was 30 percentage points: 85 per cent of women but only 55 per cent of men had dabbled. As we move up through the layers to more serious involvement, the totals go down and the gender gap becomes proportionately larger. So 24 per cent of women but only 10 per cent of men had tried something more than once or twice, had paid for it, and 'thought it important in living their lives'.[37] Because it becomes important later on, it is worth noting that the most popular activities were forms of complementary medicine. When we try to identify a clearly 'spiritual' New Age sample by isolating those respondents who describe themselves as spiritual and have any serious engagement with either yoga and meditation or divination, we find only 7 per cent of women but that is still more than twice the 3 per cent of men.

Whether Scots are interested in any form of alternative spirituality has a lot to do with social class, education and occupation: it is largely a preserve of graduates working in the caring professions. Men and women who worked in social, education and health professions were more likely than other professionals and people in skilled and unskilled manual occupations to be sympathetic towards holistic spirituality and to have tried yoga, meditation and the like. The greatest difference between men and women of similar social backgrounds is not in general attitude toward the spiritual but in the later stage of deciding whether to continue with some spiritual practice after tentative engagement or exploration. When asked to choose between describing themselves as 'religious', 'spiritual' or 'neither', 14 per cent of the male respondents and 16 per cent of female respondents chose 'spiritual', an insignificant difference. But as we move through each level, from thinking of oneself as spiritual, to initial experimentation, to regularly engaging in alternative practices and finding them important, we see that more men than women drop out.

Survey data does not tell us why initial male sympathy does not translate into regular engagement at the same rate as that of women but we can hazard a guess: much of the holistic spirituality milieu is designed by women for women. The practitioners of Dianic witchcraft (that is Diana the Goddess, not Diana the British princess, although that would be more fun), for example, 'emphasise women's oppression and point to the European Witch burnings as a "women's holocaust" ... and they denounce injustices done to women in the name of patriarchy'.[38] The 'Mists of Avalon pilgrimage to England' organised by Sacred Journeys for Women, an American group, is 'open to all

women who would like to spend a week in the beautiful English countryside'
but closed to pastorally inclined Anglophile men.[39]

There is a more subtle type of closure. When a therapist announces that
she is 'Working primarily through feminine energies and combining ancient
knowledge with contemporary therapies',[40] she does not reject men as clients
but is hardly likely to attract many. An advertisement for a St Brigdhe (or
St Bridie) Goddess conference in Glastonbury promised:

> We will be honouring all Her aspects, especially those connected to Her four fires,
> the fire of inspiration and poetry, the fire of love, the fire of healing and the alchemi-
> cal transforming fire of smithcraft. We will walk Her sacred swan landscape here in
> Glastonbury, join in local Bridie ceremonies, make pilgrimage to Bride's Mound, and
> visit the holy wells where She is honoured here today.

The flyer concluded, 'We will make Bridie Dolls and Bridie Eyes. Bring
ribbons, beads and materials to decorate yours. We will also make a healing
girdle to wear when we offer healing in Her name' and 'There will be a special
ceremony for those who wish to dedicate themselves as a Priestess of Brigdhe.
Please bring white ceremonial clothing, veils and headdresses.'[41] That a large
part of the world of alternative spirituality constructs itself around gender is
no surprise. After all, one of its themes is the rejection of patriarchy, especially
in the form of the idea that the divine creator is male.

Slightly less inherently gendered are ideas and activities that are closely
related to something in the secular world that already has a clear gender preference pattern: group singing and dancing is more popular with women than
with men and that alone would explain why women are more likely than men
to be attracted to spiritual growth practices that involve singing and dancing.
Much the same point can be made about that range of therapies often called
'bodywork'. Men might be attracted to a locker-room style of massage administered by strong men who smell of liniment. They are unlikely to be attracted
to forms of massage and healing therapy that are presented as extensions of
the health spa: 'Pampering4life is a lifestyle of pampering all aspects of one's
life. It is the ultimate indulgence of pampering your mind, body, and freedom.
... Relax and feel your desire to live the life God has given you after all,
Pampering4life is a celebration of you . . .'[42]

A final thought is also relevant for the gender gap in the churches. I can
illustrate the point from years of observing how my students choose option
courses. Sign-up sheets for the sociology of sport, sociology of law, sociology
of religion and the like were mounted on the department notice board and
remained for a week so that students could alter their choices once they had
sorted out other timetable commitments. Year after year we found the same
pattern of changes. At first a few women would sign up for the sociology of
sport and a few men would sign up for the sociology of gender. Once the lists

started to show a clear gender difference, deviant early enrollers would return and change their choices so that by the time the courses first met, the sport option was male and the gender course was female. Students very quickly took the fact that the vast majority in the class were of the other gender as signifying that this course was not suitable for them.

This is not at all unusual. What we have learned from decades of studies of the diffusion of innovation, of interpersonal influence and of religious conversion is that a sense of similarity between promoters and potential converts is important in persuading people that something new is worth trying. People in the evangelism business appreciate that if you want to appeal to young people, you use a young evangelist. When the Moonies first arrived in the USA from Korea, they recruited only very slowly: the Korean missionaries had trouble attracting serious interest from white Americans. Only once they were able to deploy young, white, middle-class Americans did they start to recruit young, white, middle-class Americans. Even when the innovation in question is technical (a new seed variety, for example) and might best be promoted by an expert (in this case an agronomist), the farmers being targeted proved more open to being persuaded by like-situated farmers than by experts. The simple point is that in many situations of choice people are more likely to trust those who are in crucial respects like them than people who are different. What the good evangelist does is present himself as being very much like his audience except that, since conversion, his life is so much better. The similarity point is important because he has to convey the impression that this product will 'work for you'. The guru, the founder of the movement, can be different. Indeed, if she or he is claiming some charismatic authority it helps to be exotic, but the local sales rep for the new life, the new persona, the new idea must be someone in whom the targets can see themselves.

Gender is one of the most obvious social markers. Whatever its origins, once a skewed gender pattern is established it tends to be self-reinforcing. Men simply look at the existing participants and think, 'These people are not like me so this is probably not my thing'. Organisers then respond by accepting that their clientele is female. They portray the activity accordingly: the posters for aerobics in my local gym exclusively feature women. They also schedule accordingly: the aerobics classes are during the day when the crèche is available.

Romancing the Stones

One of the recurring features of New Age thought is a romantic preference for the ancient over the modern. Probably every civilisation has thrown up its romantics who accept that the 'modern' centre has brought material benefits but assert it has cost people their souls. True humanity is to be found in the undeveloped fringes of a society. For William Blake, William Wordsworth and Samuel Taylor Coleridge in the early nineteenth century, it was the lakes of north-west England or the Welsh hills that provided the antidote to urban industrial life. Now that much of 'England's green and pleasant land' is under tarmac, the modern romantic has to look further afield or further back. Hence the preference for borrowing themes and rituals from the cultures of Tibet and Nepal, aboriginal Australia, ancient Egypt and pre-conquest American Indians.

Scotland still offers opportunities for romantic exploration. It has large areas of wild primitive countryside: some of it never developed, other parts reverted to nature after the subsistence farmers were cleared from the land. Kilmartin in mid-Argyll offers a particularly rich prehistoric landscape with over 350 burial cairns, standing stones, cists and other structures and monuments the purpose of which remains obscure.

That our knowledge of our pre-literate past is scant does not stop modern spiritual seekers making extravagant claims about it. Consider the example of Frank MacEowen, a Canadian shaman and healer who, in an article entitled 'Rekindling the Gaelic hearthways of *Oran Mór*', describes becoming 'a neo-Celtic practitioner reviving the ancestor-based spirituality of his own Gaelic heritage'.[43] MacEowen believes in a cosmic consciousness that allows shamanic practices of previous civilisations to be 'remembered' centuries after they had disappeared. He began his 'journey' by being drawn to North American shamanism and then to the medical practices of other indigenous peoples before an experience during a Sun Dance revealed that his task was to 'remember' the ways of his ancient Scottish ancestors. The 'shrilling of eagle-bone whistles' was converted, he says, to highland bagpipes, as he danced with his ancestors, and experienced their sufferings. This led him to search within his 'cell memories' for ancestral knowledge [and] to discover himself as . . . a descendant of hereditary seers.[44]

MacEowen's search apparently led him to Kilmartin and to a mis-described 'Pictish' grave where he had visions of Bride's Well, which visit produced, at least in part through sound, humming that reverberated from the walls of the grave and cairn, resulting in his learning double-voiced or harmonic chanting, drinking from the 'fifth stream' of wisdom, and finally experiencing *Oran Mór*, which he translates as the Great Song.[45]

There is much more of this pillage of themes from the folklore of many cultures in a justification of his status as a healer. That MacEowen locates Kilmartin in the Western Isles (rather than on the Scottish mainland) and describes the village as a 'town' are just two of the reasons that an anthropologist who shares MacEowen's interests doubts he actually visited the place. His mis-representation of many of the monuments suggests that, if he did visit, he did not bother to consult the educational displays in the excellent museum. And his notion that the knowledge possessed by ancestors can be biologically inherited provides a convenient alternative to actual historical research. The advertisement for one of his books says:

For all those who have felt the tug of memory or a connection to some time and place that came before, this book explores the depths of one's connections to ancestors, to the land, to the mysteries of life . . . the author brings readers along as he journeys to Ireland for a shamanic conference and shares his experiences and how they tie in to the meanings of Celtic traditions. Readers recognize connections to other spiritual traditions and shamanic teachings of other indigenous peoples. They also discover ways to reconnect with their own heritage and to cull the good teachings and incorporate them into their personal spiritual practices.[46]

MacEowen's justification for his current claims as a healer is an extreme example of the New Age pick-and-mix approach to culture, but something similar is remarkably (and for a serious historian, distressingly) common and we can readily extract its functional themes. It is difficult to analyse this sort of material without sounding cynical, so I will not try.

First, there is the romantic contrast: modernity is fine for some things (if he did visit Kilmartin he would have flown to Scotland and even romantics like their planes to be well-serviced) but for the truly human spirit we must search for the simple and the primitive. Second, ancient is better than modern, for healing the soul, if not for heart by-pass operations. Third, new products and justifications are constructed by weak analogy. MacEowen works his way from American Indian shamans via a wide variety of traditional healing practices to 'Celtic' healers, with crucial links in his identification of unity-underlying-diversity resting on nothing more than one word looking like or sounding like another. Fourth, ancient allows you to avoid facts. If you try to appropriate elements of religions that are still alive and well, you will find yourself arguing with representatives of those religions. As there are no Pictish shamans around now, you can say what you like about them without fear of contradiction.[47]

Not all spiritual use of the past is quite as promiscuous.[48] Part of Kilmartin's real history links to the (actually western) island of Iona, where in AD 563 the Irish monk Columba established a church and monastery. The Abbey was substantially rebuilt in the fifteenth century but was abandoned after the Reformation and fell into ruin. That it is now in use again is due largely to the generosity of James Lithgow, Glasgow shipbuilder, and entirely to the energy of one of Scottish Presbyterian's most remarkable figures, George Fielden MacLeod.[49] The son of a cleric, MacLeod was decorated for bravery during the First World War and afterwards trained for the ministry. Ordained in 1924, he became increasingly concerned about social inequality and in 1930 he left his wealthy Edinburgh parish for Govan Old Parish Church in one of the most deprived parts of Glasgow. In 1932 he suffered a mental breakdown and spent some of the following year in Jerusalem recuperating. While worshipping in an Eastern Orthodox Church on Easter Day he underwent a profound spiritual experience. His gradual shift toward socialism and pacifism (he was active in the Peace Pledge Union in the 1930s and in the Campaign for Nuclear Disarmament in the 1950s) led him to found the Iona Community. The idea was to bridge the gap between the dispossessed working classes of Glasgow and the Church of Scotland by having clergy and unemployed men work together on the rebuilding of the Abbey and associated buildings. Initially the Iona Community reported to the Church of Scotland but its current status as an independent ecumenical body better reflects MacLeod's interest in promoting a non-denominational spirituality. Rebuilding the Abbey not only gave unemployed workmen something positive to do; it also allowed MacLeod to promote a version of Christianity that, by pre-dating it, transcended the great Reformation divide of Protestant and Catholic.

Iona and Columba are real enough and the serious historian can know a great deal about the Celtic Christian Church but, as with the Mayans and the Hopi, Celtic Christians are sufficiently remote and obscure that popular culture can attribute almost any characteristic to them. In common with the romanticism of the New Age, such attribution supposes that whatever one dislikes about this world is 'modern' and was absent from Celtic Christianity.[50] The failure of the Church of England in November 2012 to approve the legislation that would have allowed women bishops provoked a flurry of commentary. One comment that caught my eye was the assertion that 'Women bishops existed before. I'm pretty sure the Celtic Church had them or at least figures of equivalent status'.[51]

Conclusion

It is the social scientist's job to describe and explain, but some judgement, when it is little more than drawing attention to elements of description that are often overlooked, seems appropriate. For all their talk of love in the abstract, the founders of the Findhorn community were poor at managing their personal lives. Peter Caddy broke up Eileen's first family, used his status at Findhorn to enjoy sexual relations with young female members of the community, and was married five times. Although his biography tries to re-interpret this patent failure as a success by saying that each new relationship represented a step in personal growth, Caddy is himself more honest about the distress he caused Eileen. All too frequently the insights gathered by meditating and channelling spirits seem to be much the same as the outcomes lesser mortals achieve by behaving selfishly and regarding others as opportunities to satisfy their desires.

Given that the number of Scots who seriously pursue the courses of spiritual development offered by centres such as the Findhorn Foundation is tiny, the attention given to alternative spirituality in this chapter needs some justification, beyond the obvious point that the exotic is more interesting that the mundane. The justification is that, while holistic spirituality is not popular, it is arguably symptomatic of a feature of modern Western culture that has considerable implications for religion. As I have already noted in a number of places, a major cause of secularisation is our contemporary insistence on the individual's right to decide what to believe. This contrast involves massive simplification but it does not distort the record: pre-modern societies laid much more store by the community (be that the family, the tribe, the clan) than by the individual. Until the Reformation (and for some time later in Catholic and Lutheran countries), the Church claimed to represent the entire people to God and vice-versa. The Reformation inadvertently gave a considerable boost to individualism by arguing against the transfer of merit from one person to another, and against the magic powers of the clergy to change our salvational fates. Initially Reformation individualism involved responsibilities rather than rights. Each of us had to answer to God for ourselves, severally rather than, as in the model of the medieval church, jointly. But to exercise that responsibility the common people had to be accorded certain rights: to be literate, to read the Bible and to understand church liturgies in their own languages. The Reformers were not democrats but accidentally they promoted the social changes that would see the individual displace the group. The net result is a polity in which individuals have the right to select their governments and an economy in which, within the limits of what they can afford, individuals have the right to consume what they wish. If people can choose their washing machines and choose their political leaders, why should they not also choose their Gods?

Notes

1. *Press and Journal*, 12 February 1994.
2. I am grateful to Liz Dinnie for interesting me in Findhorn and to the various members and officials I have met on my visits. For a sympathetic account of Findhorn which concentrates on the organisational difficulties of maintaining a community founded on an individualistic philosophy, see E. Dinnie, *Managing Individuality: an Ethnographic Study of the Findhorn Foundation Community, Scotland* (Aberdeen: University of Aberdeen PhD thesis, 2008). See also S. Sutcliffe, *Children of the New Age: A History of Spiritual Practices* (London: Routledge, 2003). Insider's accounts include C. Riddell, *The Findhorn Community: Creating a Human Identity for the Twenty-First* Century (Findhorn: Findhorn Press, 1991). Most accounts of Findhorn have been produced by sympathisers. For a critical alternative, see Kevin Shepherd's Citizen Initiative website: http://citizeninitiative.com/index.htm and A. Roberts, 'Saucers over Findhorn', *Fortean Times*, December 2006; http://www.forteantimes.com/features/articles/saucers_over_findhorn.html.
3. A. Rigby and B. S. Turner, 'Findhorn Community, Centre of Light: a sociological study of new forms of religion', *Sociological Yearbook of Religion in Britain* 1 (1972), pp. 72–86; A. Rigby, *Alternative Realities: a Study of Communes and their Members* (London: Routledge and Kegan Paul, 1974).

4. T. R. Warburton, 'Faith Mission: a study in inter-denominationalism', *Sociological Yearbook of Religion in Britain* 2 (1973), pp. 75–102.

5. For a detailed account of the contemporary Glastonbury New Age milieu, see R. Prince and D. Riches, *The New Age in Glastonbury: the Construction of Religious Movements* (Oxford: Berghahn, 2006).

6. H. Fisher, 'Tuning into nature', *Nova: Australia's Holistic Journal*, 2008; http://www.novamagazine.com.au/article_archive/2008/08_09_turningintonature.html. Note that the web address really does say 'turning' rather than, as it should be, 'tuning'.

7. E. Caddy, *Flight into Freedom: the Autobiography of the Co-Founder of the Findhorn Community* (Longmead, Dorset: Element, 1988), p. 87.

8. J. Slocombe and E. Ward, 'Willing to change: an interview with Eileen Caddy', *One World: The Findhorn Foundation and Community Magazine* 12 (Winter 1993/94), p. 9.

9. P. Hawken, *The Magic of Findhorn* (London: Souvenir Press, 1975), p. 1.

10. Rigby, *Alternative Realities*.

11. P. Caddy, *In Perfect Timing: Memoirs of a Man for the New Millennium* (Findhorn: Findhorn Press, 1996), p. 301.

12. Caddy, *In Perfect Timing*, p. 261.

13. For the most detailed account of the Buchanites, see J. Train, *The Buchanites from First to Last* (Edinburgh: Blackwell, 1846).

14. Caddy, *In Perfect Timing*, pp. 261–2.

15. Caddy, *In Perfect Timing*, p. 262.

16. Caddy, *In Perfect Timing*, p. 262.

17. There is an old connection between rural Scotland, New Age spirituality and fringe educational ideas. Trevelyan had taught at Gordonstoun, the spartan school founded in 1934 by Kurt Hahn, and attended by Prince Philip and Prince Charles, and Govan taught there briefly in the 1960s; Sutcliffe, *Children of the New Age*, p. 81.

18. Dinnie, *Managing Individuality*, pp. 5–10.

19. In 1993 the Scottish Charities Office, having received complaints concerning its use at the Findhorn Foundation, commissioned Anthony Busuttil, Regius Professor of Forensic Medicine at the University of Edinburgh, to investigate Breathwork. His opinions caused the Findhorn Foundation to suspend the programme.

20. The crystals period and the hostile reactions to it are detailed in Riddell, *The Findhorn Community*, p. 87.

21. In 2002 Findhorn proudly announced contracts with BP and with PWC (one of the world's largest accountancy firms) to provide training services; T. McDonald, 'Findhorn is open for business', *Scotland on Sunday*, 9 June 2002.

22. This contained 'channelled messages' from Spangler's source which he called 'Limitless Love and Truth'; D. Spangler, *Revelation: Birth of a New Age* (Findhorn: Findhorn Press, 1971).

23. William Bloom, *The New Age: an Anthology of Essential Writings* (London: Rider/Channel 4, 1991), p. xviii.

24. For an introduction to the academic literature, see P. Heelas, 'The New Age in cultural context: the pre-modern, modern and post-modern', *Religion* 23 (1993), pp. 103–16, and the other essays in that issue.

25. On audience and client cults, see R. Stark and W. S. Bainbridge, *The Future of Religion: Secularization, Revival and Cult Formation* (Berkeley: University of California Press, 1985), pp. 27–9.

26. *Fortean Times* 67 (February/March 1993).

27. Quoted in J. P. Bloch, 'Individualism and community in alternative spiritual "magic"', *Journal for the Scientific Study of Religion* 37 (1998), p. 293.

28. Matthew Wood makes an interesting distinction when he argues that there is not a single 'New Age' milieu committed to epistemological individualism. His alternative description is of a world where people have so many ties to a variety of sources of authority that none of them can be formatively authoritative; M. Wood, *Possession, Power and the New Age: Ambiguities of Authority in Neoliberal Societies* (Aldershot: Ashgate, 2007), p. 11.

29. Quoted in Bloch, 'Individualism and community', p. 295.

30. I have to apologise to this now anonymous speaker at the 1993 Mind Body Spirit festival in the Floral Hall, London. Although I took detailed notes, I forgot to record her name.

31. Interview with Sir Michael Joughin, April 1996.

32. Further detailed statistical analysis can be found in S. Bruce and T. Glendinning, 'New ways of believing or belonging: is religion giving way to spirituality?', *British Journal of Sociology* 57 (3), pp. 399–413.

33. 'Priest bans yoga for "being incompatible with Catholic faith"', *Daily Telegraph*, 26 September 2012; http://www.telegraph.co.uk/news/religion/9567412/Priest-bans-yoga-for-being-incompatible-with-Catholic-faith.html.

34. It is worth noting that Paul Heelas, who did more than most social scientists to argue that we are witnessing a 'spiritual revolution', shifted to talking about 'well-being spirituality'; compare P. Heelas and L. Woodhead, *The Spiritual Revolution: Why Religion is Giving Way to Spirituality* (Oxford: Blackwell, 2005) with P. Heelas, *Spiritualities of Life: New Age Romanticism and Consumptive Capitalism* (Oxford: Blackwell, 2008), pp. 60–78.

35. Quoted in H. Reid, *Outside Verdict* (Edinburgh: Saint Andrew Press, 2002) p. 47.

36. Heelas and Woodhead, *Spiritual Revolution*, pp. 94–5.

37. Bruce and Glendinning, 'New ways of believing'.

38. T. G. Foltz, 'Women's spirituality research: doing feminism', in N. Nason-Clark and M. J. Neitz (eds), *Feminist Narratives in the Sociology of Religion* (Walnut Creek, CA: AltaMira Press, 2001), pp. 89–98.

39. Sacred Journeys website; http://www.sacred-journeys.com.

40. Patricia Dancing Elk-Walls website; http://its-about-energy.com/.

41. K. Jones, 'Brighde's Blessing Retreat'; http://www.kathyjones.co.uk/retreats/bridie_retreat.html 2008.

42. http://wellnessindustry-bunny.blogspot.com/2011/04/divine-healing-spirituality-and-your.html.

43. J. Blain, 'Shamans, stones, authenticity and appropriation: contestations of invention and meaning'; http://www.sacredsites.org.uk/papers/Blain_J-perm.pdf.

44. Blain, 'Shamans', p. 50.

45. Blain, 'Shamans', p. 50. Translated mundanely, 'Oran Mór' means simply big song or big music and it usually refers to bagpipe music; poetically it means all of music or the fundamental nature of the universal.

46. F. H. MacEowan, *The Spiral of Memory and Belonging: A Celtic Path of Soul and Kinship*; http://books.google.co.uk/books/about/The_Spiral_of_Memory_and_Belonging.html?id=Io6WJPWZ-WAC.

47. Even trained historians may prefer the obscure religion of the distant past to that of the real recent past. Catherine Czerkawska spends more than a third of her account of Gigha on its pre-historic remains and asserts that: 'Mostly [the early Celtic Christians] sought to convert with a light touch . . . It is a pity that successive and much-more heavy-handed proselytisers on Gigha, no less than elsewhere, seemed set on destroying what had endured for so many hundreds of years'; C. Czerkawska, *God's Islanders: a History of the People of Gigha* (Edinburgh: Birlinn, 2006), p. 99. James Hunter wrote about nineteenth-century evangelical Calvinism in 'The emergence of the crofting community: the religious contribution 1798–1843', *Scottish Studies* 18 (1974): pp. 95–116 but the subject is absent from his later *Scottish Highlanders* (Edinburgh: Mainstream, 1992), in which he prefers Columba and pre-Reformation Christianity as the foundation of a distinctive Highlands identity.

48. For a romantic view of Argyll's pre-history that is much more realistic, see M. Campbell, *Argyll: the Enduring Heartland* (Kilmartin: Kilmartin House Trust, 2001).

49. C. Harvie, *No Gods and Precious Few Heroes: Scotland 1914–1980* (London: Edward Arnold, 1981), p. 83.

50. From Engels onwards, Marxist anthropology pioneered this Arcadian method of discovering pre-capitalist societies to be in almost all respects superior to capitalist ones. On the recent invention of Celtic spirituality, see M. Bowman, 'Reinventing the Celts', *Religion* 23 (1993), pp. 147–56 and R. Probert, 'Chinese whispers and Welsh weddings', *Continuity and Change* 20 (2005), pp. 211–38.

51. 'Comment is free: Women Bishops', *Guardian* website, 21 November 2012.

11

SCOTS MUSLIMS

On the afternoon of 30 June 2007, a dark green Jeep Cherokee was driven into the front of the terminal building at Glasgow airport. Security bollards stopped the car breaking through the doors. There was a series of small explosions but the blasts and the subsequent fire were contained within the Jeep. Five members of the public were slightly injured, some hurt tackling the terrorists. Police identified the two men apprehended at the scene as Bilal Abdullah, a British-born doctor of Iraqi descent working at the Royal Alexandra Hospital in Paisley, and Kafeel Ahmed, also known as Khalid Ahmed, a Cambridge student. It was quickly established that the two men had been responsible for a failed bomb attack on London's West End a few days earlier. Ahmed died of his burns. Abdullah was sentenced to thirty-two years in prison.

The initial reaction to the airport attack was shock at what Scots took to be the latest atrocity in a sequence that started with the Twin Towers in 2001 and included the 2005 London tube bombings. But once it became clear that the sole fatality was one of the terrorists, the tone changed quite noticeably. John Smeaton, a baggage handler who weighed into the fight between a policeman and one of the terrorists, became a celebrity, not just for his prompt action in joining the fray and pulling clear an injured civilian, but also for his curt description of his actions: 'So I ran straight towards the guy, we're all trying to get a kick in at him, take a boot to subdue the guy'.[1] He told ITV News: 'Glasgow doesn't accept this. This is Glasgow; we'll set aboot ye'. That quickly became a key motif: Southern softies might be intimidated by terrorist numpties but Glaswegians would not stand for any of that nonsense. Some commentators added a note of exasperated superiority by using the 'taking coals to Newcastle' metaphor for the absurdity of trying to import a new line of religiously inspired violence to a place which was already famous for sectarian conflict. Importantly, many public figures deflected hostility from

Scotland's Muslim population by pointing out that neither of the terrorists were Scots and that Bilal Abdullah was only in Scotland because of his short-term post at the Paisley hospital. Thus a jihadi attack that could have inflamed anti-Muslim feeling in Scotland was re-interpreted in ways that allowed Scots of all religions and none to embrace their preferred stereotype: we are harder than the English. But behind the 'wha's like us' bluster, there are real differences between England's and Scotland's Muslim populations and in responses to those minorities.

Origins and Numbers

Work on merchant ships brought small numbers of South Asian Muslims to the ports of Glasgow, Leith and Dundee but the bulk of Scotland's Muslims migrated here in the late twentieth century.[2] The first accurate measure came with the introduction of a religious identity question in the 2001 census. There were then 42,577 Muslims in Scotland, just less than 1.0 per cent of the Scottish population. To set this in the right context for considering, for example, changes to Scottish culture, it is worth noting that Scotland had ten times as many residents who had been born in England as it had Muslims.[3] Almost half of Scots Muslims were born outside the UK and two-thirds described their ethnicity as Pakistani. The rest were Bangladeshi, other South Asian and African, with about 8 per cent describing themselves as 'White British'.[4]

Like other migrants before them, new Pakistani Muslims tended to settle in areas which already had a sizeable Muslim community, hence the highly concentrated settlement pattern. In 2001 none of Scotland's Muslims lived in thirteen of Scotland's thirty-two local authorities and between 1 and 7 per cent could be found in seven authority areas: the vast majority of Muslims lived in the two main cities. Edinburgh had 16 per cent, and 42 per cent lived in Glasgow.[5] But even in Glasgow there were too few Muslims to maintain an entirely segregated way of life, even if it had been desired. Almost all Scots Muslims attend state schools. As of 2011, Scotland had only one Islamic primary school, the private Qalam Academy in Glasgow. Two other small private primaries, in Glasgow and Dundee, closed after damning inspection reports. There are no Muslim secondary schools. Various focus group studies suggest that Scots Muslims generally mix well with fellow pupils who do not share their faith but close friends are likely to be Muslims. As one young man put it: 'I talk to everyone but like I feel more comfortable talking to people like with my same background, the same as you, like the same religion and stuff'.[6] One constraint on inter-religious mixing is the pressure on Muslim pupils to attend after-school classes in Islam run by mosques or Muslim associations. A Muslim youth worker said:

I remember finishing school at 4pm, going to Madressah and returning home to do my homework. After that, there wasn't time to do anything but go to bed. We have

to help integrate young people and activities such as playing football with other
children helps that process. A lot of my non-Muslim friends did that, but I wasn't
able to.[7]

In an interesting echo of the Irish Catholic experience of being snubbed
by old Scots Catholics, a number of recent migrants claimed to receive a distinctly cool reception from longer-established Muslims: 'I think people who
are from here the [British] Pakistanis, they treat [us] like bad [more] than the
Scottish people. The Scottish people never treat me like that'.[8] That there may
be an objective base to such impressions is suggested by research which shows
that Muslims born in Scotland were more likely than recent migrants to be
concerned that an increase in Muslim numbers would make integration more
difficult.[9]

In 2001 over three-quarters of married Muslims – 79.7 per cent to be
precise – had a Muslim spouse. Sikhs (at 75.7 per cent) and Hindus (68.9 per
cent) were similarly likely to have married co-religionists. In contrast, only
42.3 per cent of married Catholics have a Catholic spouse.[10] Part of that is
explained by lack of opportunity: only one-third of 'majority' or native Scots
know a Muslim and only 15 per cent have a Muslim friend.[11] Partly it is a function of how seriously many Muslims take their faith; they know that marrying
out will bring difficult decisions about how to raise their offspring. But one of
the most frequently mentioned obstacles to greater mixing is one that has not
previously been an issue for inter-ethnic relations: alcohol. Traditionally most
Muslims do not drink alcohol. Equally traditionally much of Scottish social
life revolves around pubs, clubs and bars. As one non-Muslim explained: 'You
can't very well go "Right, we'll go for a pint". You never see, even if the guy
was just in for an orange juice, you never see them, not many I've ever seen
inside a bar'.[12]

One obvious contrast with the reaction of Scots to Irish Catholics in the
first decades of the twentieth century is that there is no significant organised
political opposition to Muslims.[13] In the 1920s it was common for people of
all social classes and political persuasions to think in terms of races and, in
a moderate form, the animal husbandry metaphor of 'preserving the breed'
was commonplace. The Nazi attempts to eradicate Europe's Jews abruptly
consigned the language of race and racial purity to the realms of the unspeak-
able, if not the unthinkable. For the declining proportion of Scots who worry
about such things, Scotland's Christian heritage is threatened far more by the
growing number of the religiously indifferent than by the small number of
the religiously different. Economic competition has been insignificant. A large
proportion of the Muslim migrants started small businesses (typically in catering and retail) which needed little start-up capital and could be built by family
members working long hours. In many towns and cities the Asian corner
shop and the Indian take-away (which was usually Pakistani) became valued

parts of the commercial landscape and by the end of the twentieth century a successful business class had developed.[14]

One Asian Scot noted that 'quite a few hundred families from England' were attracted to Scotland by its reputation for 'less prejudice and little racism'.[15] Certainly surveys show a generally benign attitude toward Muslims. Muslims were viewed less favourably than any of the other religious groups asked about but, nonetheless, two-thirds of respondents had a favourable opinion toward Muslims, three times as many as those with an unfavourable opinion. One survey also found that 46 per cent of those questioned think that Muslims living in Scotland were loyal to the country while 33 per cent thought they were not.[16] Not surprisingly, given that they share the same reservations about preserving the faith in a mixed-marriage as Muslims, religious Scots were markedly more 'unhappy to acquire a Muslim relative', an attitude expressed by 47 per cent of Presbyterians and 33 per cent of Catholics. However, what is more important given the growing secularity of Scotland, this was a view shared by only 18 per cent of Scots who did not claim a religious identity.[17]

One of the favourite Scots self-images is that, in comparison with the southern English, they are friendly and welcoming. Superficially this is supported by detailed comparison of Scots and English attitudes toward Muslims.[18] A less self-serving explanation is that a happy coincidence of objective differences between Scotland and England make relations between Muslims and non-Muslims less of an issue north of the border. The difference in numbers has already been mentioned. Add to that Scotland's prior saturation with Protestant–Catholic conflict. And then figure in the tension caused in England by the anti-Salman Rushdie protests in the 1990s, riots in north-west towns in 2001 and the terrorist attacks in London.

Unfortunately there are still enough uncultured Scots hooligans to provide Muslims with unpleasant experiences. An example is the man who tore the veil of a young Saudi woman walking to Glasgow's Central Station to get a train.[19] Many respondents in focus-group research mention being insulted in public; some mention being threatened. But it is heartening to note that some also mention non-Muslims intervening to counter bad behaviour and that very few respondents asserted that they faced deep or common hostility. Women who wore veils or head scarves reported occasionally feeling uncomfortable at being stared at but some of them also noted that they could hardly complain about attracting attention when one of their purposes in wearing distinctive dress was to signal their Muslim identity.[20]

Politics: from Labour to SNP

Like the Irish before them, Pakistani immigrants strongly supported the Labour party, despite their generally conservative social values. Until David Cameron tried to shed it of those features which caused a leading Conservative to describe it as 'the nasty party' and UKIP rose to claim the votes of racists and xenophobes, the Conservative party was much more hostile to immigrants than Labour. The main difference between the Irish and the Pakistani support for Labour was that in the first case economic interest led the Irish to support the labour movement, and the Scottish Labour party and the Irish came to power together. Scotland's Pakistanis supported the Labour party despite a lack of economic interest between a community of self-employed shopkeepers and the party of organised labour and because it was already in power. By the 1970s any community leader in Glasgow or Edinburgh who wanted to advance the interests of his or her people had no choice but to support Labour.

The shifting political allegiances of Scots Muslims can be illustrated with brief biographies of three leading Muslims: Bashir Maan, Mohammad Sarwar and Bashir Ahmed. Maan was born in the Gujranwala district of British India (now modern-day Pakistan). As a student, between 1943 and 1947, he was involved in the campaign for independence of the Indian sub-continent and for the creation of Pakistan. Following this, he organised the rehabilitation of Muslim refugees from India to his locality. He settled in Glasgow in 1953 at the age of twenty-six. Starting as a door-to-door salesman, he went on to open one of Glasgow's first shops to sell alcohol at heavily discounted prices. He subsequently sold this part of his business concerns because he became concerned that profiting from the sale of cheap booze was not compatible with his faith, but by then he was a wealthy man and his wealth and community activism saw him become convener of the Muslim Council of Scotland, president of the Islamic Centre in Glasgow, chair of the Scottish Pakistani Association and president of the Standing Conference of Pakistani Organisations in the UK and Eire. His status in the Muslim community translated into appointed public offices. In 1968 he became the first Asian or Muslim Justice of the Peace in Scotland. In 1977 the Home Secretary appointed him a deputy chairman of the Commission for Racial Equality and he was elected president of the Scottish Council of Voluntary Organisations. He was also active in electoral politics. In 1970 he became the first Muslim elected to a public office in the UK when he was elected as a Labour councillor for the Kingston ward. He stayed on the council for thirty-three years. He allowed his Labour party membership to lapse in 2004 when it became clear that the public had been misled by those in favour of joining the US war on Iraq.[21]

The second noted Glasgow Muslim was also a self-employed businessman who supported the Labour party. Mohammad Sarwar was born in 1952 in the Toba Tek Singh district of Pakistan and educated at the University of Faisalabad. He made his fortune in Scotland from the family wholesale cash-and-carry business, United Wholesale Grocers, which Sarwar and his brother founded in 1982. Already a local councillor, Sarwar's political career enjoyed an unexpected boost in 1993 from a reform in the Labour party's structure and a constituency boundary re-organisation. As the party's main funders, trade unions were allowed a disproportionate degree of influence through the device of the 'block vote'. Union representatives were allowed to claim their entire membership as party members, even though many union members did not even vote Labour. During his short term as Labour leader – he died unexpectedly in 1994 just two years after becoming Leader of the Opposition – John Smith replaced the block vote with OMOV, the euphonious acronym for 'one member, one vote'. With trade union influence reduced, Sarwar supporters (many of them suspiciously new recruits to the local branch) were able to displace an old Irish Catholic Labour hack as the candidate for Glasgow Govan and Sarwar was duly elected to Westminster in the 1997 election that saw Tony Blair come to power.[22] He was re-elected at the 2001 general election and when the 2005 general election saw further boundary changes in Scotland, he fought and won the new constituency of Glasgow Central. At Westminster he had the distinction of chairing the Scottish Affairs Select Committee from 2005 to 2010. When Sarwar retired, he was succeeded by his son Anas.[23]

Our third illustrative figure is Bashir Ahmad. Born in India before partition, he arrived in Scotland aged twenty-one. He worked as a bus conductor and bus driver before buying his own shop. He subsequently owned shops, restaurants and a hotel before retiring from business. He was elected five times as president of the Pakistan Welfare Association.[24] Unlike Maan and Sarwar, Ahmad was a Scots nationalist. In 1995 he founded Scots Asians for Independence, and became a member of the SNP's national executive committee in 1998. In 2003 he was elected as councillor for the Pollokshields East ward of Glasgow City Council. He was elected as an SNP member of the Scottish Parliament for the Glasgow region and Scotland's first and only Asian MSP at the 2007 election.

Since the restoration of the Scottish Parliament in 1999 there has been a significant change in Scottish politics. In 1999, at the first elections to the Scottish Parliament, Labour was easily the largest party, with fifty-six seats to the SNP's thirty-five, with the Conservatives taking eighteen and the Liberal Democrats seventeen. Four years later the results were much the same. The major parties came in the same order, the main difference between that Labour and the SNP lost seats to minor parties and independents. However, 2007 saw a major shift with the SNP (with forty-six seats) displacing Labour as the largest party, and in 2011 the SNP won an absolute majority of seats: sixty-nine to the fifty-nine of the other parties combined. Having few seats to lose in the first places, the Conservatives suffered least: they lost only two seats. Labour was reduced to just thirty-seven seats, nineteen fewer than a decade earlier. The Liberal Democrats were punished for forming a coalition with the Conservatives at Westminster and were reduced from seventeen to five seats.

As Table 11.1 shows, the switch in voting preference among Scots of Pakistani ethnicity (who were overwhelmingly Muslim) was far greater than among Scots at large and it happened earlier.[25] Among the population at large

Table 11.1 Voting Preferences of Scots of Pakistani Ethnicity and All Scots, 2001 and 2003

	Westminster Election 2001		Scottish Parliament 2003	
	Scots Pakistani %	All Scots %	Scots Pakistani %	All Scots %
Labour	74	44	28	35
SNP	13	20	47	24
Liberal Democrat	6	16	15	16
Conservative	5	16	1	17
Other	2	4	9	9
Total	100	100	100	100

Source: A. Hussain and W. Miller, *Multicultural Nationalism: Islamophobia, Anglophobia and Devolution* (Oxford: Oxford University Press, 2006), p. 164.

the Labour vote fell between the Westminster election in 2001 and the Scottish Parliament election two years later from 44 to 35 per cent, but the Muslim Labour vote dropped from 74 to 28 per cent.

This radical shift in Muslim preferences had two causes. The positive 'pull' was the hard work that the SNP had put into cultivating the Muslim vote in Glasgow; in particular the party was successful in persuading Scots Muslims that supporting the SNP allowed a religio-ethnic minority a way to keep their religious distinctiveness while showing their commitment to their new home.[26] The negative 'push' was the Labour government's decision to support the USA in the invasions of Iraq and Afghanistan. Even those who have no fondness for military dictatorships and barbaric medievalism could suppose that it was not the West's responsibility to intervene.

The Paradox of Multi-culturalism

There are two radically different ways in which the modern state can deal with minority populations. It can, as the USA and France do, ignore them and insist that all citizens have an equal right to representation through conventional political parties and the democratic process. Or it can suppose that people who share some objective distinction which activists claim to be the basis for a shared communal identity (for example, sexual orientation, gender, ethnicity) should be treated as members of 'blocs' and encouraged both to celebrate their distinct identities and to claim rights for that putative identity. This multi-culturalism was popular with Labour-dominated English local councils in the 1980s. Instead of promoting equality by ignoring all differences that were not relevant for the matter in hand – the traditional view of what equity requires – multi-culturalism supposes that distinct groups have a right to 'their' identity (even though the extent to which the groups favoured by progressive Labour councils actually had much in common can be doubted) and that ignoring differences is oppressive.[27]

Scottish Labour councillors have usually been so thoroughly 'Old' Labour that the 'identity politics' of the 1980s had little impact north of the border: there was far less funding of women's groups and minority sexual orientation bodies. And there was less courting of religio-ethnic minorities. There were few council seats (and only a handful of Westminster seats) where Muslim votes would make a difference, so there was far less of the English practice of parties cultivating self-appointed 'community leaders' who could deliver the votes of their extended family networks in return for access to local government grants for community centres and the like. However, elements of that system began to appear after 2001 when the Westminster government turned its attention to the problem of Muslim radicalisation and decided to promote 'moderate' Muslim voices. The Scottish government followed suit.

One paradox of multi-culturalism is that it tries to solve the problem of Muslims' apparent lack of commitment to British democratic values and procedures by the entirely undemocratic procedure of accepting the claims made by self-aggrandising individuals and tiny organisations to represent the interests of Muslim communities. An example of a career built on claims to represent an ethnic bloc is that of Osama Saeed, who founded the Scottish Islamic Foundation in 2008 and persuaded the Scottish government to use it as a vehicle for dealing with the Muslim community.[28] SIF was given over £400,000 to distribute for youth projects (such as 'developing Scouts groups that cater for Muslim religious sensitivities' and 'the development of local madrassas'). When it was reported that 60 per cent of all grants given by the Equality Unit in 2008 had gone to just five Muslim bodies, Christian groups complained about the inequity of courting Muslims with taxpayers' cash.[29] The complaints shifted from inequity to inefficiency when it transpired that the SIF went bust four years after its creation with little to show for its funding other than promoting a few individuals (such as Humza Yousaf, who became an SNP MSP and within two years was a junior minister).

The second paradox of trying to improve the integration of minorities by giving their representatives a distinctive voice is that those voices are then encouraged by their role to be distinctive. If one is supposed to represent 'Muslims', the tendency is to be 'uber'-Muslim. This in turn generates small differences which a malign press can exaggerate into a major scandal. A fine example of this process can be seen in the depressingly predictable tale of the Dundee police dog. To advertise their new phone number, the Dundee police produced an advert featuring a cute-looking Alsatian puppy sitting in a police cap. The only Muslim member of Dundee City Council, who was also a member of the Tayside Joint Police Board, criticised the advert: 'My concern was that it's not welcome by all communities, with the dog on the cards. It was probably a waste of resources going to these communities. [The Police] should have understood'.[30] The *Daily Mail* picked up the story and ran it under the headline 'Muslims outraged at police advert featuring cute puppy sitting in policeman's hat' despite there being no evidence that anyone, not even the Muslim councillor, was 'outraged'. The story was picked up by other mass media outlets and web blogs which ran it as proof that Muslims were crazed bigots. Experts then pointed out that some Muslims do keep dogs as pets: the Saudis in particular are fond of the Saluki breed of hunting dog. Islamophobes condemned Dundee Muslims; other Muslims condemned the Islamophobes; and so it goes. The unfortunate councillor was pilloried for making a fuss about trivia but had the reasonable defence that his critical comments had been extremely mild and that he was simply doing what the multi-cultural model required him to do: representing minority sensibilities.

How Religious are Scots Muslims?

There are three reasons to expect that Scotland's Muslims will be generally more religiously observant than its Christians: place of origin, migrant status and nativist hostility. Pakistan is considerably more religious than the UK and so, if those who migrated to Britain were merely typical of their former neighbours, they would be considerably more pious than the typical Scot. But as we saw in Chapter 3, migration itself can be an unsettling experience which may encourage a strong attachment to elements of the culture. In the old world the mosque is just one of many social institutions that support a person's way of life. In the new world it is one of the few places that can both provide familiar experiences and aid the transition. It is the place where migrants can find people like themselves and people who are already well-established and can help adapt to new circumstances. For Hindus and Sikhs of both genders, the temple and the gurdwara can be important community centres; the mosque really only plays that role for Muslim men. The few mosques that welcome women separate them in a 'sisters' gallery' and many mosques do not welcome them at all. However, both migrant men and women can react to being in an alien environment by making more of their religious identity than would have been the case had they remained in a place where it was taken for granted. As one young Muslim woman put it: 'because we are all inherently part of migrant communities we tend to hold on to identity a bit more'.[31] The shift from conventional expressions of an unremarkable characteristic to a deliberate embrace of something distinctive may also be inadvertently encouraged by hostility. There is little evidence that Scots Muslims are reacting to occasional reminders that many non-Muslim Scots find them strange (and a few find them threatening) by embracing radical jihad. What I am identifying is a much milder reaction: a degree of dogged determination. The logic is this. These people think I am a bit odd to wear a head scarf. I could wear a head scarf or not. If I were in Egypt, I probably wouldn't. But I do not want to let the side down by seeming to hide my religion. So I will cover my head. Or I will make a point of praying at the set times. Or I will keep Ramadan strictly.

But none of this should cause us to forget that the social-psychological forces pressing in the other direction are extremely strong. There is a great deal of silliness (and some paranoia) in the press reporting the tiny numbers of native Scots who convert to Islam without making any serious attempt to assess how many people raised as Muslims move in the other direction. In the long run, religious minorities generally change so as to reduce what distinguishes them. We could put it negatively as pressure to conform. We could make the same point more positively. Young Muslims can see much about secular society that is attractive. It offers freedom from traditional constraints on consumption and on sexual expression. It offers opportunities for life-enhancing relationships with people of other religions and none. It offers a chance to make one's own choices instead of following one's parents' wishes. As the experience of the Exclusive Brethren or the Free Church shows, remaining distinctive means foregoing opportunities and not everyone will do that. In brief, it would be foolish to suppose that Scots Muslims have uniquely found the cure for religious drift and are managing a 100 per cent record in the reproduction of their religion while committed Christians manage only 50 per cent.

However, theorising is not evidence and we are short of reliable evidence about how successful Scots Muslims are in raising their children in the faith and about how rigorously Scottish Muslims observe the requirements of their faith. There is no equivalent for non-Christians of Peter Brierley's censuses of church attendance and Scottish mosques either do not keep records of attendance or do not belong to over-arching organisations which collate and publish such information. Moreover, if such data existed it would tell us a lot less about Scottish Muslims than church attendance tells us about Scots Christians because most Muslim women are not expected to attend prayers at the mosque and because, for Muslims of both genders, other aspects of the faith are as or more important than attending communal prayers. Most of the research on Scots Muslims has been of the focus-group variety, which tells us a lot about a small number of people but gives us no grounds from which to generalise to Scots Muslims as a whole. So we know why some young Muslim women wear the veil and others do not but we have no information about their relative proportions in the population, nor about such obvious issues as the differences between migrant and Scots-born Muslims. We are left trying to make sense of snippets such as the claim made by Faisal Hussein, who worked for the SIF, that some 10,000 young Scots Muslims attend voluntary after-school classes on Islam: in 2001 there were only 11,000 Scots Muslims aged 5–19.[32]

It is obvious that not all children born to Muslim families follow in their parents' faith. Although it is not normally what we have in mind when we talk of assimilation or integration, one feature of Scottish culture that has been adopted by some young Muslims is juvenile criminality. The murder of Kriss

Donald in 2004 brought to the public's attention the existence of a small but vibrant sub-culture of Asian gangs in Glasgow and East Renfrewshire. As the judge said in sentencing the perpetrators:

> You have all been convicted by the jury of the racially aggravated abduction and murder of Kriss Donald, a wholly innocent 15-year-old boy of slight build. He was selected as your victim only because he was white and walking in a certain part of the Pollokshields area of Glasgow when you sought out a victim. This murder consisted of the premeditated, cold-blooded execution of your victim by stabbing him 13 times and setting him alight with petrol while he was still in life.[33]

The press interest sparked by the Donald murder generated numerous detailed accounts of Asian gang life. Left-wing sources tended to portray gangs such as the Young Shield as an understandable response to poverty or to racist attacks, but both claims are hardly sustainable.[34] Many of those convicted of crimes (Imran Shahid, for example, Donald's chief assailant) are the children of successful businessmen and, as gang members themselves admit, violence, drug use and sexual predation are stimulating alternatives to the puritanical lifestyles their parents wish them to adopt. Furthermore, Asian gangs feud with each other, which looks more like standard gang behaviour than defence against racism.

As an aside, it is worth noting one small benefit of the multi-cultural 'big man' method of doing local politics. Although in party politics terms Mohammad Sarwar was just a rank-and-file MP, he was able to use his status in the Pakistani community to play a crucial role in bringing to justice Donald's killers. After the murder they had fled to Pakistan, which has no extradition treaty with Britain. Through his political connections Sarwar was able to negotiate a one-off extradition.

Of course one cannot use the tiny number of people of any background who commit murder to represent any larger population but we do know something about Muslim criminality overall. The Scottish Prison Service does not keep systematic records on inmates' religion but it does note ethnic origins: in 2010, 1.2 per cent of the male prison population was South Asian.[35] Given the relative sizes of Indian, Pakistani and Bangladeshi populations in Scotland, almost all of those prisoners will be Muslims by heritage, if not practice. Unless we suppose that the Scottish police forces and courts are unusually harsh in dealing with religio-ethnic minorities, this suggests that Scots Muslims form about the same proportion of the prison population as they do of the population at large. There are two inferences we can draw from this: not all nominal Muslims are religiously observant, or being religiously observant no more guarantees a blame-free life for Muslims than it does for Christians. In either case it is a useful corrective to the view that Muslims are all that different to Christians.

It is inevitably the case that those who are unusually committed to their faith stand out far more than those whose commitment is slight. We can hardly notice, let alone count, those Scots from Muslim families for whom religion is of little or no importance. What is certain is that very many Scots Muslims are hardly more religious than many nominal Christians. If we have to try to put a figure on it, we can start with the surveys which show that two-thirds of Muslims claim to be religiously observant, allow for some exaggeration, and suppose that perhaps half of Scots from Islamic backgrounds are not particularly religious.[36]

The Relevance of Religion

For many Scottish Muslims, Islam is not just a religion; it is an important part of their family background and of their shared community identity. Especially in an environment that is mostly uncomprehending and sometimes openly hostile, open criticism of the faith is difficult because it is felt as disloyalty. Nonetheless many Scots Muslims struggle with the same problem that confronts Christians: how does one separate the essence of the faith from its transient cultural trappings so that it can be modernised and kept relevant?

The point is well-made in a critical report by a German Muslim, living in England, of visits to Scottish mosques:

> A few months ago I took a new Scottish Muslim convert to the mosque in Dumfries for Friday prayers. The address before prayer was entirely in Urdu, except for a few incoherent English words thrown in . . . never as much as even half a sentence though, making the content completely incomprehensible for the non-Urdu speaker. Having said that, understanding Urdu did not help much either, since the subject matter was almost completely irrelevant to living in Britain. This was followed by a brief sermon in 'Arabic', made up only of standard phrases commonly used as a framework for this purpose over the centuries and fleshed out with nothing else. The experience felt very foreign and, except for the compulsory nature of attendance at Friday prayers, a complete waste of time.

They tried again at Easter, this time visiting the Central mosque in Glasgow.

> The service started with an address in Urdu, as if that was the lingua franca of Scotland. Part of this was then translated into English, none of which contained any references to the lives the attending worshippers live in Britain. Then followed a run-of-the-mill Arabic sermon read from a script which, whilst coined in flowery poetic language, made no reference whatsoever to current affairs or the situation of Muslims locally or anywhere else in the world.

The visitor witnessed a revealing clash at the Glasgow mosque:

During prayer a couple of babies could be heard crying from the sisters' gallery at the back . . . After completing the prayers [the Imam] made an announcement that it was an outrage for women to bring children to the mosque and let them cry in order to disturb the brothers' prayers. I am told this wasn't the first time such an announcement was made. But for the first time there was an unexpected response . . . one of the sisters made her way right through the crowd of male worshippers leaving the mosque in order to question the Imam . . .

Outside the Imam's office the mosque administration sprang into action. It would not be possible to speak to the Imam. He was too important to be summoned, you would have to go to him. She tried, she said. No, not her, a man would have to speak to him on her behalf, it was not acceptable for a woman to speak to him. His staff eventually suggested a later appointment could be made, one woman only, accompanied by a man through whom she would speak.[37]

Although the episode might seem foreign to the Christian reader, the three main points of contention – the proper language for worship, clerical authority and gender relations – all have their Christian corollaries. The mosque conducts its service in two languages that distance its message from its audience: Arabic as the traditional language of Islam and Urdu as the language of Pakistanis. The Christian parallel would be a Gaelic Catholic congregation in Glasgow conducting the mass in Latin. The right of congregants to challenge their imam has its obvious parallels in Christian debates about the authority of the priesthood. And the Christian churches have had their own struggles coming to terms with women who object to male chauvinism.

When my great aunts and uncles migrated to Canada, Australia and South Africa in the 1920s their ties with their Aberdeenshire kin were reduced to Christmas cards and the occasional photograph of a new family member. Now cheap flights and telecommunications allow migrants to remain in easy contact with their homelands. That they can retain one foot in the old country itself means that Scots Muslims are unlikely any time in the foreseeable future to assimilate entirely to the culture of their new home. But it is equally unlikely that their religion will remain dominated by Urdu-speaking old men. There are two possibilities. The one promoted by radical Muslims is the creation of a trans-national Islamist identity: a worldwide people committed to the restoration – creation might be a better term – of Muslim rule. The other is the gradual evolution of more liberal and flexible interpretations of what Islam requires in a modern secular society. Despite the press attention to the small number of young men radicalised by Abu Qatada and the like, there is little sign of this option becoming popular in England and even less in Scotland. 'Throughout the focus group discussions none of the participants spoke about a sense of belonging with a global Muslim community'.[38]

There are good reasons to expect the liberalising option to dominate. A key demographic change is the introduction of Muslim women to the labour force. In 2001 almost half of Scottish Muslim women aged between sixteen and fifty-nine, as compared to 6 per cent of all Scots women, had never 'worked'. That figure probably over-states the domesticity of Muslim women because the definition of work would omit many women who served in the family business and lived 'above the shop'. Nonetheless it testifies to the very strong preference for traditional gender roles. But the census also showed that Muslims are far more likely than Scots Christians to be full-time students: 17 per cent of Muslims aged over eighteen, as compared to under 5 per cent for the population as a whole. Almost half of those students are women and their qualifications will give them access to the world of professional work. The children of the shopkeepers and curry house owners are becoming doctors, accountants, chemists and lawyers. The Sarwar family can illustrate that social mobility. Mohammad made his fortune in retail; his son Anas was educated at the prestigious Hutcheson's Grammar School and the University of Glasgow and worked as a dentist before becoming an MP. Currently Muslim families are markedly larger than the average; that will change as young Muslim couples appreciate the benefits of two professional incomes. As family size falls and as professional work outside the home replaces the family business, the pressure on women to remain domesticated will reduce. As more Muslim women become involved in the public sphere the influence of the home will reduce, as will the pressure to remain religious in the style of their grandmothers.

Conclusion

The migration of Muslims to Scotland, like that of Hindus and Sikhs, has added to the range of Scottish Gods but it has hardly broadened the options for the native religious seeker because, unlike Buddhism, Islam has attracted very few converts. That is readily explained. Islam, like Christianity tradition-ally conceived, is an authoritarian, demanding faith and the Scots who have lost interest in one authoritarian, demanding faith are unlikely to be attracted by another, especially when it requires major changes in lifestyle. There is also the point I made in chapters 9 and 10 about the ease of creative pillage. Buddhism has so slight an actual presence in Scotland that Scots can treat it as a cafeteria of options from which the most attractive and flexible elements can be selected and re-interpreted to suit private tastes. Although the number of Scots Muslims is small, they form a living community, parts of which represent the faith in a way that discourages creative borrowing.

Arguably the greatest impact of Islam has been to hasten secularisation. There are two strands to that argument: one concerns 'church–state' relations and the other concerns public attitudes to religion. One obvious effect of Islam has been to call attention to unfinished business in the evolution of the state's stance on religion. I made the point in Chapter 1 that the gradual marginalisation of religion in British public life was not driven by militant atheists: it was an accidental by-product of religious schisms producing religious minorities that tried to protect their own interests by reducing the privileges of the state Church of Scotland and Church of England. Because the Free Church and the Seceders were only interested in their own standing as against that of the Kirk, they stopped short at the point where all churches had achieved rough equality in the eyes of the state. Unlike the French, the British did not insist on a radically secular state; they settled for a series of fudges. Religion was allowed to retain a number of privileges (such as state-funded schools, a guaranteed presence on the BBC, seats as of right in the House of Lords, prayers at the start of council meetings, laws protecting Christianity against blasphemy) on the understanding that these would not be used in a partisan fashion. The arrival of Islam called all such accommodations into question because this new and serious faith wanted to be included. In some cases it was: hospital, military and prison chaplaincies, for example, were broadened to include non-Christians. In other cases, drawing attention to the inequity of native religions enjoying privileges that were denied to the new faiths led to disparities being resolved in a secular direction. For example, when Muslims complained that only Christianity was protected by the blasphemy laws, the government considered broadening them to protect all religions but decided instead to repeal them. Now that the majority of the population has no religious faith, any claims that non-Christian religions are the victims of discrimination because they do not enjoy some historic privileges of the Christian churches will result in those privileges being withdrawn rather than extended.

The second and more subtle way in which Islam hastens secularisation is by fostering the general impression that religion taken too seriously is trouble. Muslims and liberals who complain of Islamophobia are often both right and wrong simultaneously. Many British people are only accidentally Islamophobic: they are actually opposed to all religion that is not confined to the domestic hearth and the leisure sphere. As we will see in the next chapter, there is a general consensus that religion in the abstract is a good thing but that fatwas on authors, demonstrations against films, shariah courts and demands for halal meat are a nuisance. What makes this generally secularising is that the Scots who have no faith (and that is now most of us) do not, as conservative Christians might wish, draw a line between Christianity and other faiths. They are more likely to draw the line between the religious and the secular and conclude that every religion has a similar potential to be disruptive. Especially when conservative Christians join in by claiming that their sensibilities are treated less gently than those of Muslims, the public response is likely to be deeper suspicion of all religion.

Notes

1. S. Crearer, 'The baggage handler who tackled terrorists', *The Times*, 2 July 2007; http://www.timesonline.co.uk/tol/news/uk/article2020607.ece.

2. For a detailed account of early Muslim migrants, see B. Maan, *The Thistle and the Crescent* (Glendaruel: Argyll Publishing, 2008).

3. W. Millar, 'Muslims and multicultural nationalism in Scotland', unpublished paper given at the University of Notre Dame, 18 October 2008.

4. Country of birth of Muslims was as follows: Scotland (40.0 per cent), Pakistan (25.9), England (9.3), Middle East (7.3), North Africa (4.1), India (2.8), Eastern Europe (2.4), Bangladesh (2.3), Far East (1.6 per cent). The remainder were born in other parts of Africa, Asia and the EU; Office of the Chief Statistician, *Analysis of Religion in the 2001 Census: Summary Report* (Edinburgh: Scottish Executive, 2005), Table A3.7.

5. Office of the Chief Statistician, *Analysis of Religion*, Table 1.17.

6. Scottish Government, *Experiences of Muslims Living in Scotland* (Edinburgh: Scottish Government, 2011), para. 3.13.

7. 'Mosque attendance affects integration?', *The Herald*, 22 October 2008; reproduced at http://www.asianimage.co.uk/display.var.2462471.0.mosque_attendance_affects_integration.php.

8. Scottish Government. *Experiences*, para. 3.28.

9. R. Arshad, 'Foreword', Ipsos MORI Scotland, *Muslim Integration in Scotland Final Report* (London: British Council, 2010), p. 2.

10. The exact figures are 79.7 per cent for Muslims, 75.7 per cent for Sikhs and 68.9 per cent for Hindus. Only 42.3 per cent of married Catholics had a Catholic spouse. Office of the Chief Statistician, *Analysis of Religion,* Table A4.7.

11. Miller, 'Muslims', p. 6. As Miller's paper was concerned with attitudes of Scots toward English and Muslim settlers, he distinguishes 'Majority' or native Scots from migrants and Scots from ethnic minority backgrounds. This is purely a pragmatic analytical distinction; Miller is not making any claims about who is a 'true' Scot.

12. Ipsos MORI Scotland, *Muslims*, p. 31.

13. The BNP is trivial, as is the Scottish Defence League.

14. In the 2001 census, 29 per cent of Muslims (as compared to 11 per cent of all people) were self-employed and many of the rest would have been employed by other Muslims: Office of the Chief Statistician, *Analysis of Religion*, Chart 4.8. One-fifth of all working Scots were employed in the G and H categories: wholesale and retail trade and hotels and restaurants; the figure for Muslims was 51 per cent.

15. B. Maan, *Thistle and Crescent*, p. 203.

16. BBC, 'Muslim integration easier in Scotland than England', *BBC News*, 10 August 2010; http://www.bbc.co.uk/news/uk-scotland-10920747.

17. Miller, 'Muslims', p. 16.

18. Miller, 'Muslims', combines a variety of anti-Muslim attitudes into a scale for

'Islamophobia' and finds that while 49 per cent of Scots could be described as Islamophobic, the corresponding figure for England would be 63 per cent. It is arguably harsh to describe some of the attitudes used to form the scale as Islamophobic (or to be more precise, the cut-off lines in sliding scales are sometimes contentiously placed) and so we should not make too much of the actual numbers, but the differences between Scotland and England remain even if we adjust some of the definitions slightly.

19. BBC, 'Man jailed for Muslim veil attack', *BBC News*, 26 July 2010; http://www.bbc.co.uk/news/uk-scotland-glasgow-west-10766880.
20. A. Siraj, 'Meanings of modesty and the hijab amongst Muslim women in Glasgow', *Gender, Place and Culture* 18 (2011), p. 724.
21. *Daily Record*, 11 November 2004.
22. E. Ferguson and B. Wylie, 'Bad blood in the thorns of Labour's rose', *The Herald*, 23 May 1993. Jimmy Dunnachie was a former shipyard and Rolls Royce worker, trade union activist and local councillor best known for resisting the attempts of Militant Tendency to take over the constituency and replace him by Tommy Sheridan. Despite his decade in parliament, his Wikipedia entry correctly says that 'he was not prominent in politics'; http://en.wikipedia.org/wiki/Jimmy_Dunnachie.
23. In 2012 Mohammad Ramzan, Sarwar's brother and a prominent Labour funder, announced that he was now supporting the SNP; http://www.heraldscotland.com/news/home-news/millionaire-labour-party-donor-defects-to-the-snp.17403393.
24. BBC, 'Funderal held for first Muslim MSP', *BBC News*, 7 February 2009; http://news.bbc.co.uk/1/hi/scotland/7876579.stm.
25. There are so few Muslims in Scotland that any representative sample survey (such as the Scottish Election Surveys) will have too few for reliable analysis. Hussain and Miller's work was based on a single survey which boosted Muslim numbers and their data concerns retrospective recollection of voting; A. Hussain and W. Miller, *Multicultural Nationalism: Islamophobia, Anglophobia and Devolution* (Oxford: Oxford University Press, 2006).
26. Hussain and Miller, *Multicultural Nationalism*, makes this argument.
27. For an articulate defence of multi-culturalism, see T. Modood, *Multiculturalism: A Civic Idea* (Cambridge: Polity, 2007).
28. Ibn al-Waleed, 'Scottish Islamic Foundation tightens stranglehold over Scottish Muslims', *Your View*, 26 January 2009; http://hurryupharry.org/2009/01/26/scottish-islamic-foundation-tightens-stranglehold-over-scottish-muslims/.
29. Christian Institute, 'Muslims cash in on Scots equality fund', Christian Institute website, 11 March 2009; http://www.christian.org.uk/news/muslims-cash-in-on-scots-equality-fund/.
30. *Daily Mail*, 'Muslims outraged at police advert featuring cute puppy sitting in policeman's hat', *Daily Mail*, 1 July 2008.
31. Scottish Government, *Experiences*, para. 3.11.
32. 'Mosque attendance affects integration?', *The Herald*, 22 October 2008;

reproduced at http://www.asianimage.co.uk/display.var.2462471.0.mosque_atte
ndance_affects_integration.php.

33. http://en.wikipedia.org/wiki/Murder_of_Kriss_Donald.

34. For example, Campaign Against Racism and Fascism, 'Behind Glasgow's gangs',
CARF 43, April/May 1998; http://www.irr.org.uk/carf/feat12.html.

35. G. Berman, 'Prison population statistics', House of Commons Library standard
note SN/SG/4334, May 2012. It is worth noting that debates about prison populations can take two very different directions. It used to be the case that they were
taken as evidence of criminality. Certainly in the 1930s anti-Catholic agitators
such as Alexander Ratcliffe saw what he believed to be a disproportionate number
of Catholics in prison as proof that Romanism bred crime. Now, with much
greater scepticism about the even-handedness of policing and court decisions, such
statistics tend to be taken as evidence of victimisation.

36. S. Bruce, *Politics and Religion in the UK* (London: Routledge, 2012), p. 143.

37. S. M. Bleher, 'Scottish Islam – does it exist?', *Mathaba*, 13 April 2009; http://www.
mathaba.net/news/?x=619596.

38. Scottish Government, *Experiences*, para. 3.2.1.

SEX AND POLITICS

In February 2013 Cardinal Keith O'Brien resigned. Three priests and one former priest had accused him of 'inappropriate behaviour' in the 1980s. Although he initially denied the charges, the Vatican pushed him to quit a few months before his due retirement at seventy-five. In some ways O'Brien was progressive. He was in favour of priests being allowed to marry. When Steve Gilhooley published his account of having been abused at a seminary in Cumbria, O'Brien defended him against Vatican officials who seemed more concerned about Gilhooley than about what he revealed.[1] But O'Brien had also been such a vocal opponent of gay marriage that in 2012 the gay rights campaigning organisation Stonewall had made him its Bigot of the Year.

Two of O'Brien's colleagues could have made Stonewall's short list. Philip Tartaglia, Archbishop-elect of Glasgow, told a conference on religious freedom at Oxford University:

> If what I have heard is true about the relationship between the physical and mental health of gay men, then society is being very quiet about it. Recently in Scotland, there was a gay Catholic MP who died at the age of 44 or so, and nobody said anything, and why his body just shut down at that age. Obviously he could have had a disease that would have killed anybody. But you seem to hear so many stories about this kind of thing, but society won't address it.[2]

The attack was particularly pointed because the man in question was David Cairns. A former priest who, with no scandal, had resigned his orders to pursue a political career, Cairns was responsible for removing of one of the last Catholic disabilities. Under the 1829 Catholic Relief Act, present and former priests were barred from parliament. Siobhain McDonagh MP introduced a private member's bill which prompted the government to remove restrictions on clergy of whatever denomination from sitting in the House of Commons.³ Instead of mourning the untimely death of a Catholic hero, Tartaglia chose to take a cheap (and medically ill-informed) shot at gay men. This was consistent with the Scottish hierarchy's general boorishness. In a 2008 lecture, Bishop Joseph Devine said:

> In the recent New Year's Honours List, I saw that, to widespread public acclaim, the actor Ian McKellan was honoured for his work on behalf of homosexuals being awarded the same status as heterosexuals. A century ago, Oscar Wilde was locked up in Reading Jail for the kind of sin that was not able to speak its name. That sin was homosexuality. Now we include in the Honours List people who live a lifestyle that is totally at odds with the family and children.⁴

Perhaps Devine drew the contrast between being honoured and being jailed just to show how times have changed but it is clear which era he preferred. What makes the reference to Wilde particularly distasteful is the depth of loathing for homosexuality it displays. Devine must have known that Wilde's chief prosecutor in the libel case which eventually led to his imprisonment was Sir Edward Carson, the Ulster Unionist who did most to keep Northern Ireland out of the Irish Free State. Thus the leader of the despised Ulster Proddies becomes a hero when he prosecutes homosexuals.⁵ O'Brien's predecessor was as malign on the subject. When the Scottish government was moving to repeal Section 2a of the Local Government Act, Cardinal Thomas Winning argued that the gays should be banned from working with children because they were more likely than heterosexuals to engage in 'predatory and abusive' relationships, a claim for which there was no good evidence, not even in the record of abusive Catholic priests.⁶

The Catholic Church is not alone in its homophobia. The amorphous structure of the Church of Scotland makes it harder to identify an official position but there are many Kirk clergy who would qualify for Bigot of the Year if they had the standing of a Catholic cardinal, and the smaller conservative Protestant bodies are similarly opposed to the toleration of homosexuality. The Free Presbyterian Church objected as firmly to gay marriage as it had to every step in the increasing toleration of homosexuality:

> We regard the Scottish Government's stated wish to go forward to legislating on this subject extremely dangerous and subversive of Christian morality and harmful to the foundations of our society which are so intimately bound up with the divinely ordained institution of marriage. We remind the Scottish Government that we have protested against previous decisions relating to Civil Partnerships as also to legislation passed by the Scottish Parliament permitting the advocacy of homosexuality in Schools and other public bodies. We further remind the Scottish Government that we are under oath to preach and declare the whole counsel of God which specifically

> condemns homosexuality which this consultation process pretends to legitimise. Our authority in such matters is only the Word of God and we refer the Scottish Government to its plain statements condemning homosexuality.

Which it then listed as though seriously expecting the Scottish government to check its scripture homework.

Nor was homophobia confined to the Christian churches. One of Scotland's most senior Muslim leaders, Bashir Maan, was asked to resign as president of the Scottish Council for Voluntary Organisations in 2006 after deploring sex education in schools. 'These politicians, through certain elements of sex education in schools, are motivating young, innocent children to indulge in premature sex that is resulting in teenage pregnancies. As if that were not enough, gay sex education is being added to the sex curriculum in schools. This will encourage experiments with homosexuality among young children and add to the growing creed of homosexuality.'[7] In 2012 Maan spearheaded the campaign by the Council of Glasgow Imams to encourage Muslims not to vote for pro-gay rights candidates in the local government elections: 'Every voter will have to make sure the person they are voting for is not in favour of same-sex marriage. It is up to them who to vote for but they should ask every person who comes to them and asks for their support.'[8]

Christian Politics: from Social to Sexual

Religion can be linked with social attitudes through accidentally shared characteristics of voters, through the institutional interests of churches and through their religiously inspired value positions. Where there are regular patterns of association, they often owe more to the social status of the believers than to the religion itself. As we saw in Chapter 10, speaking in tongues does not make people right-wing; the association is simply that the charismatic movement appeals mostly to middle-class people working in the private sector who tend to be right-wing anyway. As we saw in Chapter 3, there is nothing about Catholicism as such that makes Scots Catholics left-leaning. In countries such as France, Italy and Spain, where Catholics are a large majority, churchgoing Catholics are generally right-wing. That Scotland's Catholics have traditionally been Labour voters (as they have been in Australia and the USA) is better explained by class background than by religion. The Irish Catholic example also shows elements of an ethnic link between religion and politics: once the association between the Irish migrants and the labour movement had been created, loyalty to one's people gave an additional reason for voting Labour.

Religion may more directly affect politics through organisational interests and through values. It is important to appreciate that churches have institutional interests. The Catholic Church is doubtless sincere in its stated reasons for insisting on its own schools and for rejecting artificial contraception but it has an additional reason for those policies: maximising the size and commitment of the Catholic population. I offer the Catholic Church as an example not because it is the only self-interested religious organisation but because it is the most effective. As many commentators have pointed out, the loose structure of Protestant churches makes them relatively poor at promoting their interests.[9]

Finally, religious cultures are potent sources of values which can have consequences for individual political preferences, though those values are often so general that the same religious belief system can produce entirely antagonistic political positions. Quite what counts in any time and place as 'loving thy neighbour as thyself' is rarely so obvious as to prevent argument.

There is nothing new about Christian churches trying to control expressions of human sexuality. What is novel about our current context is that they seem little interested in anything else and that is worth explaining.

One change is the loss of church functions to the secular state. In the eighteenth century the Church of Scotland was responsible for education and for social welfare. Kirk sessions and presbyteries managed the provision of schools and schoolteachers, and determined which of the poor were entitled to beg in the parish and to receive support from its poor-relief funds. Some of those funds were raised by fines imposed on parishioners who were found guilty of such sins as the wonderfully named 'houghmagandy' (or extra-marital sexual intercourse). It was only as the Church lost its wider responsibilities that the business of the Kirk session became confined to monitoring the sex lives of parishioners.[10]

Another important long-term change is the rise of representative democracy. One reason why organised Christian groups played a large part in promoting legislation to reform such excesses of the early industrial revolution as the use of child labour in mines and factories was that ordinary people lacked the power to campaign for such legislation themselves. The Reform Act of 1832 (and its Scottish and Irish counterparts) increased the size of the electorate by about 50 per cent and was quickly followed by further expansions until everybody had the vote. Until then, most people had few opportunities for concerted political action. Social improvement involved an enlightened elite acting on behalf of the masses. Once the masses had acquired the ability to act for themselves (through organised labour unions as well as political parties), the space for the churches was correspondingly reduced.

The growth of the secular state and the increasing assertiveness of the common people combined to curtail paternalism in every form. Especially in the late nineteenth century, when their exclusion from paid work denied middle- and upper-class women other outlets for their talents, 'good works' provided a respectable and worthy occupation. The Victorian era saw a massive growth in philanthropy with an explosion of societies for the improvement of this and the reform of that. The more powerful and prosperous the common people became, the less they sought charity from their social superiors and the less those superiors felt obliged to provide it. The scope and the need for Christians to reform the world was drastically shrunk.

In one obvious sense, the current Christian obsession with sex is a product of secularisation eliminating alternative interests. A typical characteristic of modernisation is that ever-larger areas of human life become free from religious governance. The economy and the polity are now entirely devoid of religious influence. Where the Christian Church of the Middle Ages could set the just price of bread, the modern church can pronounce as much as it likes on the economy but it will make no difference. What is left is the home life. Modern society offers religion a compact: religious freedom in the private sphere in return for a secular public space. You can now believe anything you like and be – almost – anything you like in your private lifeworld. But no religion can claim domination of the state or the public arena. That compact has led us to a rather curious place. The remit of Christian ethics has been reduced to sex and a clutch of related matters such as fertility and embryology.

Gay Rights

Dating social change is never easy, but a lazy chat in 2000 sticks with me as a significant marker. A neighbour, Aberdeenshire born and bred, and I were leaning on my field gate having a quiet news and we got round to the subject of the pub at the crossroads a mile or so away. It had recently been sold. 'It's twa pooves have got it noo', Geordie said. He drew on his hand-rolled cigarette and I waited for some rustic expression of homophobia. Instead he added: 'Likely the food'll be improved'.

My mother was a great fan of Liberace and of Larry Grayson but would not believe they were gay. In the early 1960s we ate Sunday lunch to Home Service broadcasts of *Around the Horne* and my parents chuckled over the double entendres of the gay couple Julian and Sandy, played by Hugh Paddick and Kenneth Williams. In one memorable skit, Jules and Sandy are telling Mr Horne about their cruise and about Sandy falling in the water and needing to be rescued. Horne, the straight man, asks 'Were you dragged up on deck?' Jules replies, 'Oh no, Mr Horne! We were dressed very casual!' In retrospect I would love to know what my parents were laughing at because, like much of the British public, they refused to admit that the very thing that made Grayson and Julian and Sandy funny existed. Douglas Byng's risqué cabaret act included lewdly singing *Doris the Wind*: 'I blow through the bedrooms and blow out the light / I blow to the left and I blow to the right / My life's just one blow through morning to night / It's the wind, it's the wind'. He was so popular that during the war he was hired to entertain British troops in battle zones. That he was gay was the key to his humour but, if pressed to confront the issue, he and his audiences would have denied his homosexuality.[11]

Roy Jenkins is probably best known as the patrician elder statesman who led the Social Democratic breakaway from the Labour party in 1981 and finally saw his brand of centre-left politics triumph in the person of Tony Blair, but for those with longer memories he is the reformer who, as Home Secretary from 1965 to 1967, ended capital punishment, relaxed the divorce laws, abolished theatre censorship, and gave government support to a bill for the legalisation of abortion introduced by David Steel. He also decriminalised homosexuality at a time when 25 per cent of people thought it should be punished, 22 per cent thought it should be condemned though not punished, and only 36 per cent thought it should be tolerated.[12] Compared to contemporary politicians, who seemed perpetually terrified of the press, Jenkins was a man of enormous self-confidence: he dismissed criticism of the so-called 'permissive society' by responding that it was in reality the civilised society and that homosexuals paid taxes too.

The march of gay rights has been long and it has suffered setbacks. Most notable was the Conservative government's infamous Section 28 of the Local Government Act 1988 (and section 2a of the corresponding Scottish legislation): a local authority 'shall not intentionally promote homosexuality or publish material with the intention of promoting homosexuality' or 'promote the teaching . . . of the acceptability of homosexuality as a pretended family relationship'. But gay rights triumphed, immeasurably helped by the willingness of popular performers and entertainers to 'come out'. Where Byng and Williams walked the tightrope of building a comedy career on being gay while never actually acknowledging it, John Barrowman, Alan Cummings, Karen Dunbar and Rhona Cameron could be entirely open about their homosexuality. The already-mentioned classical actor Ian McKellen, who late in his career reached new audiences as Gandalf in the *Lord of the Rings* films, came out in 1988 and co-founded Stonewall, an organisation which campaigned for gay rights. In 1984 Chris Smith became Britain's first openly gay MP when during a rally against a possible ban on gay employees by a town council, he began his speech: 'Good afternoon, I'm Chris Smith, I'm the Labour MP for Islington South and Finsbury and I'm gay.'[13] He was later promoted to the cabinet. Eventually even Welsh rugby players and referees were coming out of the closet.

The election of the Labour government in 1997 was a watershed. Same-sex partners were recognised for immigration purposes. The ban on gays serving in the forces was lifted. The age of consent for gay and heterosexual sex was equalised at sixteen. In 2003 Section 28 was repealed and it was made illegal to discriminate against people in the workplace on grounds of sexual orientation. In December 2005 the Civil Partnership Act – which gave gay couples a legal standing similar to that of married couples – came into force.

Those changes were consolidated by homophobes losing their political home. When David Cameron, forty years younger than Thatcher, was elected leader of a Conservative party that had lost three successive elections, he set out to rid it of its image as the nasty party. He appointed gay MP Alan Duncan to his front bench team and in 2008 declared that he was thrilled that Duncan was to become the first Conservative MP to enter a civil partnership. The following year Cameron addressed a Gay Pride meeting and assured his audience that homosexuals could feel at home in the modern Conservative party. By 2013 the governments of both Scotland and the UK were legislating for gay marriage.

In 1983 the British Social Attitudes Survey found that just over half the public thought that homosexuality was 'always wrong' and only one in five respondents said it was 'not at all wrong' or 'rarely wrong'. In 2000 over a third of Britons said that 'sexual relations between same-sex adults' were 'not wrong at all'.[14] A 2007 Scottish poll showed that over two-thirds of Scots now supported civil partnerships. Five years later, Ipsos MORI asked Scots to express the extent to which they agreed or disagreed that 'same-sex couples should have the right to get married'. The poll showed that just under two-thirds agreed while only 26 per cent disagreed.[15]

The Churches' Response

The Catholic Church's outright hostility to gay marriage has already been mentioned, as has that of the Free Presbyterian Church. The Church of Scotland was also opposed. In December 2012, it said:

> The Church of Scotland has already voiced opposition to same-sex marriage. Unless our General Assembly decides otherwise, we cannot support the Government's proposals on celebrating civil partnerships or same-sex marriage. We have also expressed concerns about the speed with which the Government is proceeding with this and what we fear will be inadequate safeguards for religious bodies and ministers and people of faith who view this as being contrary to their beliefs.

The Kirk also faced internal divisions over the ordination of gay clergy. The irony of churches struggling with gay rights is that they may well have more homosexuals in their ranks than other 'establishment' organisations. One senior Church of England cleric reckoned that a quarter of the men he trained with were gay.[16] There has always been a quietly acknowledged presence of gay men at the 'high' or Anglo-Catholic end of the Church of England and in the Catholic Church. Like the theatre and other performing arts, ritualistic churches seem to attract cultured men who are, in the contemporary language, 'in touch with their feminine side' and whose sensitivity makes them excel in the pastoral role. Some manage their sexuality by becoming celibate, while some simply lie about it and maintain discreet relationships.[17]

Quite which of permitting its ministers to marry and being largely devoid of colour and ritual explains why the Kirk has generally not been as attractive to gay men as the Catholic Church and the Church of England is not clear but it does seem to be the case that its clergy have been fairly resolutely heterosexual. Until recently it has balanced its progressive and its conservative wings by saying little about gay rights. But as the Church has shrunk, its congregations have aged, and its ideological centre has followed its age profile rightwards. In 2006 its General Assembly only narrowly rejected a motion to prevent its clergy from conducting religious ceremonies to mark civil partnerships. Three years later there was concerted opposition to an Aberdeen congregation selecting as its new minister an openly gay man. In a classic Presbyterian stall, the General Assembly in 2009 tried to buy time by declaring a two-year moratorium on further gay ordinations. When that expired:

> The church's general assembly, its law-making body, voted . . . to lift that moratorium, officially allowing gay ministers to take on parishes for the first time since its formation 450 years ago. The general assembly also allowed serving gay and lesbian ministers who have kept their sexuality private to openly declare their sexuality – a proposal bitterly resisted by evangelical and conservative ministers.[18]

Just how bitterly resisted remains to be seen. As with all such changes there was much bluster beforehand, with the press headlining reports 'A fifth of elders ready to leave Church of Scotland?' and 'Up to 150 ministers might quit Church of Scotland'.[19] As of May 2013 only three congregations had left: one in each of Glasgow, Edinburgh and Aberdeen.

Clearly many Scottish Christians are obsessed with homosexuality. If that seems an exaggeration, consider how much ecclesiastical attention it occupied at a time when very large parts of North Africa and the Middle East were degenerating into chaos, the European Union was being threatened by recession, and the world's banking system was perilously close to collapse. I have already suggested that the churches' fixation with personal sexual behaviour owes much to the fact that they have lost the battle to influence much else. But that leaves the question of why homosexuality (as compared, for example, with marital infidelity) should arouse so much ire. It is of course condemned by some passages of the Bible but then so is much else: we no longer think it wise to kill any member of our family who suggests worshipping a different God and we do not stone adulteresses to death.

It is generally wise to avoid Freudian psychoanalysis. Even when the explanations are intuitively plausible, there is no way of proving or disproving them, but there is something in Christian revulsion for homosexuality that suggests the psychiatrist's couch: O'Brien's life of hypocrisy and denial is a textbook example. It is hard not to notice that a popular Brethren journal is called *Precious Seed* or that the early charismatic movement called its leadership style 'covering', a euphemism used in stock-breeding circles for the male animal doing its job. And one wonders about the subconscious motivation behind what the Edwardians called 'muscular Christianity'. Noel Palmer became a major figure in Cambridge student evangelical circles in the 1920s. He had been recovering from wounds in a military hospital on the Backs since January 1919 and had fallen in with the students' Christian Union. He wrote: 'I had never before seen such a group . . . They were all *men* and I hated "cissies" and prigs. These men knew and understood men, were natural and wholesome in every way. The church often put me off or left me cold; they attracted me and set me on fire.'[20] Yes, well.

The key is an extension of the last-skittle-standing principle I have advanced to explain the shrinking of Christian ethics to sex. Conservative Christians have usually been puritans. Sex is fun and fun is bad because it distracts us from glorifying God. Were it not required for the continuation of the species, many Christians would ban it altogether and many more permit it only for the purposes of reproduction, which is why the Catholic Church is so firmly opposed to artificial contraception and why spilling one's seed, precious or otherwise, is a sin. Homosexuals, because their sexual activity cannot produce offspring, are therefore very bad. Conservative Christians have lost most of their wars on sex. Easy contraception has allowed the pleasure of sex without the dread of yet another pregnancy and no amount of church criticism has prevented even Mass-taking Catholics making use of it. The prohibition on sex before marriage is a complete washout. In the 1970s the phrase 'living in sin' was still used and not always ironically. Now couples living together, as either a prelude or an alternative to marriage, is unremarkable, as is illegitimacy. In 2012, for the first time since records had been kept, more babies in Scotland were born to unmarried than to married women.[21] Which leaves homosexuality as one of the very few items on the list of battles not yet entirely lost.

The debate over gay rights is important for understanding the Christian churches in contemporary Scotland. It illustrates the very narrow remit permitted by a largely secular society to organised religion. It also illustrates the degree to which the recent rapid decline in churchgoing has left congregations with a skewed age profile. That decline will not be retarded by going to the barricades over a change in attitudes that itself is strikingly influenced by age. In 1983 people aged sixty-five and over were 80 per cent more likely than young adults to believe that homosexuality was always wrong. By 2000 they were 300 per cent more likely to feel that way, not because they had changed but because younger age cohorts had become more liberal and tolerant.[22] The decline in the churches has been a result of them failing to recruit from their own pool of teenagers at the rate needed to replace the elderly as they die. As young people are markedly more tolerant of 'lifestyle' deviation than are the elderly, the homophobic stance of many Christian leaders seems unlikely to change their inability to attract the young.

Christian Parties in Scotland, 1997–2011

One way we can assess the popularity of conservative Christian attitudes and policies is to look at the record of a number of Christian parties that were active in Scotland after 1997. Scotland is unusual in lagging a good century behind its European neighbours in acquiring political parties with the word 'Christian' in the title. In the 1930s some Catholic Labour politicians in Glasgow toyed with the idea of creating a continental-style Christian Democrat party but, especially after the labour movement had proved itself no threat to the Catholic Church's school interests, wiser counsels prevailed.

The great difference with Catholic Europe is that in Britain the rise of democracy did not divide the society into secular left and conservative Catholic blocs. As the unitary Catholic Church was invariably on the side of the old order, radical political movements in most European states were secular and anti-clerical. The French Revolutionary Denis Diderot is credited (as are a few others) with saying: 'Men will not be free until the last king is strangled with the entrails of the last priest'. Britain exhibited no similar abrupt political divide around religion because British Christianity was reformed Protestant: it easily fragmented and working-class people who objected to the state church's support for the status quo could exhibit political dissent while remaining Christian by joining dissenting sects such as the Baptists or Primitive Methodists in England or the United Presbyterians and Free Church in Scotland. From the 1832 Reform Act until the end of the twentieth century, committed Christians could be found in all three British parties. Although the general coincidence of conservative religious and political values meant that the Tory party tended to be slightly more attractive to Christians, there were many dissenting Christians prominent in the Labour and Liberal parties. Indeed, the British labour movement (as we saw with John Wheatley in Chapter 3) probably owed more to progressive Christians than to revolutionary socialists.

The other features of Britain's polity that discouraged the formation of Christian parties were its winner-takes-all election system and its merging of legislature and administration. Where many countries divide the body that makes laws from the body that administers the country – as the USA does this by separating the presidency from Congress – Westminster combines both functions and thus makes the party that wins a parliamentary majority immensely powerful, even when every seat that made up that majority was won by only a slim margin. As the fate of the Liberal party after it split over Ireland showed, there was little space for third parties in the Britain of the twentieth century and, the Tory–Lib Dem coalition notwithstanding, that remains true for Westminster.

When the UK did finally acquire Christian parties it was in response to two socio-moral issues: abortion and gay rights.[23] The first outing of a Christian party was at the 1997 general election when the Pro-Life Alliance (PLA) which, as its name suggests, was primarily concerned with the abortion issue, fielded nine candidates in Glasgow and neighbouring constituencies. Overall its performance firmly placed it among the eccentric deposit-losers.[24] In the nine seats the PLA averaged only 1.5 per cent of the vote, with its best performance in East Kilbride (2.40 per cent) and its worst in Paisley North (0.57 per cent).

The elections for the Scottish Parliament should have been much more fertile. The unpopularity of the Conservative party should have meant that, compared with England, Scotland had a larger constituency of unattached social-moral conservatives. Second, the elections were fought on the 'additional member' system of proportional representation. Each voter has two votes: constituency and region. Constituencies are grouped into regions. The first vote is counted in a winner-takes-all election for a constituency representative. The second votes are totalled to reflect preferences across the large region. Additional members are allocated to parties so as to compensate for the difference between the overall pattern of preferences in the region and the affiliations of the constituency winners. For example, the Conservative vote in Scotland is too small and spread too thin to win any constituency seats in most regions but in most regions there are enough Tory votes to merit 'top-up' compensatory seats in the second round.

Although the system was intended to ensure that the Scottish Parliament better reflected voter preferences than would have been the case with a winner-take-all system, it had the novel consequence of allowing voters to split their votes. For example, someone who voted Labour in a Glasgow seat could be confident of electing a representative. Because Labour would win so many seats in that region, there would be less point in also voting Labour with the second or regional vote. It would not be pointless, because a strong Labour vote on the regional list would justify its constituency successes and reduce the number of additional seats that were given to other parties in compensation. Nonetheless giving people two votes allowed them to behave like the football fan who has his Premier League team but also supports a 'diddy team' in the lower leagues: voters could give their constituency vote to their serious choice but give the regional vote to a less pressing commitment.

The PLA certainly advertised that option widely but in the event it made little difference. In the first election to the Scottish Parliament in 1999 the PLA failed to recruit enough candidates to contest all the regions and in those it did contest, it did less well than in the 1997 Westminster election: only 0.6 per cent of the vote. Only in the West of Scotland region did it reach 1 per cent. It could be that the potential of vote-splitting was swamped by the novelty of voting for the new Parliament but the performance four years later was much the same (details are in the Appendix: Table A12.1).

The third elections to the Scottish Parliament were more promising. The PLA was by then subsumed within a new all-Britain party: the Christian People's Alliance (CPA). This presented itself as a continental Christian

Democrat party with distinctive positions on the full range of political issues. In English elections it increasingly focused on the threat from Islam. In Scotland the PLA influence dominated; almost all its candidates were Catholics and abortion remained its main concern. The CPA was joined by another new party. The Scottish Christian party (SCP) was the Scottish wing of an initiative led by the colourful George Hargreaves, a black pentecostal pastor who in an earlier life had achieved some success as a producer of disco music, and whose gift for self-publicity later saw him star in the 2008 Channel 4 reality TV show *Make Me A Christian*, which was every bit as ghastly as one would expect.

Hargreaves attracted media attention but few votes. In the 2005 general election he stood in the promising seat of the Western Isles. Lewis and Harris are the most conservatively religious parts of the UK and those conservatives had been politicised by losing campaigns to prevent flights and ferries on the Sabbath. Despite those advantages, Hargreaves won only 7.6 per cent of the vote. The following year he contested a by-election in the far less promising industrial lowland constituency of Dunfermline and West Fife where he gained 1.2 per cent of the vote.

The SCP was sufficiently well-funded by its London backers to field candidates in all the regions. However, it struggled to find them. It is clear from their addresses and from their failure to produce any biographical details for local media and election websites that at least half the candidates were purely nominal. Nonetheless the appearance of a robust party was created by the great deal of publicity that Hargreaves attracted by standing on an anti-gay rights platform and by standing against Dr Patrick Harvie, a bisexual Green party activist.

Although neither the CPA nor the SCP came close to winning a regional seat, the combined vote was promising in those areas with a high concentration either of Catholics (Glasgow, Central and the West of Scotland) or of conservative evangelical Protestants (the Highlands and Islands). The overall Scottish total of 2.3 per cent was a combination of lows in Mid-Scotland and Fife (0.9 per cent), the Lothians (1.0) and the North-East and South-West regions (both 1.1). The highs were Highlands and Islands (3.9), Central (3.6), Glasgow (2.7) and West of Scotland (2.5 per cent).

But 2007 proved to be a false dawn. Far from building on its performance, the CPA struggled to find money for deposits and activists and could contest only two regions in 2011. The SCP contested all eight regions but still had to field nominal candidates to make up numbers. The replacement of George Hargreaves by an Inverness doctor as party leader may have answered the criticism that the SCP was a foreign import but it also removed the party's main source of publicity. Overall the vote was less than half of its 2007 level, which must mean that many of those who voted Christian then did not repeat the experience in 2011.

Contesting only the regional vote reduced the costs of lost deposits and made minimal demands on potential supporters but it denied the CPA and SCP an important source of publicity. Local media gave a great deal of attention to the election but they did so by profiling their constituencies and the candidates standing in them. As a result, of the seven north and north-east of Scotland weekly papers that I surveyed in the three weeks before the election, only one carried any discussion of the SCP and that was in the one area where a Christian candidate did contest a constituency: Inverness and Nairn. That was also the Christians' best performance, with 2 per cent of the regional vote. But even here the vote was down by almost 50 per cent from the 2007 level and similar falls were recorded across Scotland.

The Candidates of Marginality

A close look at what sorts of people stood as candidates for the various Christian parties is useful because it both shows their narrow appeal and explains their inability to broaden it. Of the nine people who stood for the PLA in 1997, four were Muslim, three were Catholic and one was an evangelical Protestant. The three Muslims all had identifiably foreign surnames, as did two of the Catholics. An election on a single socio-moral issue is unusual enough; that this was very much a minority interest was reinforced by the candidates' minority backgrounds.

In the 2007 election to the Scottish Parliament, the SCP fielded seventy-six candidates and the CPA fielded fifteen. All the CPA candidates were sufficiently involved to provide personal details on the party's website and in election literature, but a large proportion of the SCP candidates were purely nominal and nothing could be learned of them beyond names and addresses. Unlike those of the sister parties in England (which depended heavily on ethnic minorities), almost all the Scottish candidates were 'white British'. I decided to leave three London residents out of the SCP calculations. Of the remaining seventy-three, all but two were White British, the vast majority of them Scots. The story is the same for the CPA: all White British apart from one Rhodesian and one Glaswegian of Pakistani parentage.

It was only possible to identify the occupations of 42 per cent of the sample so we should be wary of making too much of what is known but, for the SCP, about 10 per cent were senior managers and professionals, with retired doctors and headteachers making up a large part of that group. Some 43 per cent were skilled white-collar workers, with teachers again being prominent. There were proportionately fewer self-employed business people. There were also a lot of clerics: 29 per cent of those whose occupations could be identified.[25]

The CPA social class profile was interestingly different. Over 40 per cent were senior professionals and managers, a quarter were skilled white-collar workers (with teachers again being prominent) and a similar proportion were self-employed business people. However, there was only one religious official: an

ordained Catholic deacon. The lack of clergy in the CPA is a reflection of the differing religious profiles of the two parties. Again one has to be cautious of the low
numbers, but of twenty-one SCP activists whose church connection is known, a
disproportionate nine were members of charismatic fellowships. There were four
independent evangelicals, two Free Church, one Baptist, one Episcopalian and
three Catholics. There were no members of the mainstream Church of Scotland.
The CPA had no clergy candidates because it was overwhelmingly Catholic, a
reflection of the centrality to the CPA in Scotland of the abortion issue.

In the 2001 Scottish Social Attitudes Survey, 15 per cent claimed to attend
church 'weekly or more often'. Those figures are doubtless an exaggeration but
even the more likely figure of 7 per cent gives us seven times as many churchgoers as voters who opted for a Christian party in the 2011 election. There are, of
course, many reasons why a serious Christian who shared Cardinal O'Brien's
fears of secularity might not vote for the CPA or SCP, but all the qualifications one can imagine do not substantially undermine the obvious conclusion.
Devolution and a proportional representation voting system gave conservative
Christians in Scotland a novel opportunity to make their protest. The number
who chose to do so in 2007 was trivial and only half of them repeated the
action in 2011.

Do Scots want Religion to be More Influential?

We need to be cautious in interpreting the failure of the CPA and SCP. One
may like a party's platform and still not vote for it because one dislikes something else about the party, because one gives other values greater priority, or
because one sees little chance of success. My casual questioning of voters in
1997 suggested that some people who might have voted against abortion were
put off by the foreign surnames of candidates. One man said, 'Is this some kind
of Eastern outfit?' I have also been told that the exotic George Hargreaves – a
Black Pentecostal pastor with a London accent – discouraged potential supporters who saw him as an opportunist who 'had no place poking his nose into
other people's business', as one Lewisman put it. And as with any new party,
the CPA and SCP were so short of candidates that they could not select only
those who would make creditable presentations of party policy and thus were
periodically embarrassed by clumsy novices. But even allowing for the CPA
and SCP performing badly as parties, one might have thought that a greater
proportion of churchgoing Scots would have split their vote in their favour.

That they did not brings us to the second reason: relative priorities. As
experienced pollsters know, it is hard to predict behaviour from stated value
preferences without also exploring how people rank their values. One may
well dislike abortion but feel more strongly about other issues. And although
we often treat voting patterns as evidence of people's attitudes, elections are
not opinion polls. One might feel very strongly that abortion is a bad thing

Table 12.1 Acceptability of Religious Leaders 'Speaking Out' and Church Attendance, Scottish Social Attitudes Survey 2001

% who think it is right for religious leaders to speak out on . . .	Church attendance		
	No religious background or never regularly attended	Used to attend regularly but stopped	Regularly attends
World poverty	76	85	91
Environment	61	66	73
Education	45	47	72
Abortion	32	35	62
Sexual behaviour	30	35	58

but not believe that it is a matter to be determined by legislators. It is quite possible that some conservative Christians shared the values of the CPA or SCP but did not agree that these should be politicised. Finally, how values shape voting is much influenced by the political climate. So long as Scotland's politics are dominated by the national question, and so long as the SNP and Labour have similar stances on the socio-moral issues that concern conservative Christians, opportunities to raise them are limited and anyone who does so runs the danger of appearing eccentric and out of touch; something implicitly recognised by the CPA and SCP trying to present themselves as 'full spectrum' parties rather than as special interests.

All of this is a long introduction to evidence that even Christians are not persuaded by the argument that religious values should have more influence on politics. In the 2001 Social Attitudes Survey we asked if respondents thought it right for religious leaders to speak out on a variety of issues (see Table 12.1). Whereas other surveys have used a long list of such topics, we elected to use a small number of items from the global to the intensely personal. A large majority of respondents were happy to have church leaders speak out on such large abstractions as world poverty and the environment, while views on education were more divided, and only a minority thought it proper for church leaders to pronounce on abortion or personal sexual behaviour. Yet the churches spend a great deal of their time instructing us on personal sexuality. When we divide respondents into three groups by church attendance we find that churchgoers are more likely than those with no religious background to approve of church leaders taking public stands: the range of percentages of respondents approving runs from 91 to 58 per cent for churchgoers but from 76 to 30 per cent for those who have no religion or never attended church regularly. But the ordering of the issues is the same for each group. Unchurched Scots thought it most appropriate that the clergy pronounce on world poverty and the environment and least appropriate that they tell people how to behave in private. And the regular churchgoers took the same view.

There is much evidence that the Scots are sympathetic to religion in principle – it is a good thing because it is about morality and morality never hurt anyone – but are hostile to it in the particular, especially when it involves constraining people's behaviour, especially their own. So no one minds clergymen badgering the government about world poverty but very few people want to be told what they cannot do in their private lives.

Other survey data allow us to look more closely at public attitudes to the general principle that religion should have more influence on public life. Unfortunately the surveys sampled Britain as a whole rather than just Scotland but there is little reason to think that Scots are unusual in these views. The surveys, conducted in 1998 and 2008, contained six questions or statements which relate to the public presence of religion:

> 'Religious leaders should not try to influence how people vote in elections';
> 'Religious leaders should not try to influence government decisions';
> 'Looking around the world, religions bring more conflict than peace';
> 'People with very strong religious beliefs are often too intolerant of others';
> 'How much confidence do you have in churches and religious organizations?'; and
> 'Do you think that churches and religious organizations in this country have too much power or too little power?

The responses to the six items were combined to form a single 'attitude' toward the influence of religion. Each item invited responses thath can be scaled from 1 to 5, so that 2.5 marks the mid-point of relative neutrality, scores of 2.6 and above represent being 'pro-public religion', and scores of 2.4 and below show opposition to religion enjoying greater influence. The associations between church attendance and being pro-public religion are detailed in Table A12.2 in the appendix but there are two clear conclusions.

First, most Britons are opposed to religion enjoying any great public influence: the average score is 2.32, well below the neutral mid-point. Only for the 11.8 per cent of respondents who claim to attend church weekly or more often is the score above the mid-point and, at 2.92 in 1998 and 2.91 in 2008, it is not far above. Second, the only discernible change between 1998 and 2008 – a decade which saw the destruction of the World Trade Center, the London Undergound bombings, and a slew of disputes over the rights and privileges of religion – is a slight hardening of attitudes against religion. That the shift is across the board suggests that even British churchgoers see virtue in the privatisation of religion.

Conclusion

Conservative Christians are fond of language which suggests they have been cheated. Church leaders talk of Christianity having 'been marginalised', the verb suggesting that some unrepresentative minority has deprived them of their rightful position in society. That rather misses the point that the churches have lost influence because they have lost size. Had the churches remained as popular in 2001 as they were in 1851 or even 1951 they would be considerably more influential. That the Christian churches are now minority-interest groups rather than the conscience of the nation is not the work of some secular agent that has cheated them. It is a consequence of their inability to retain the allegiance of the population.

Arguably, far from being marginalised, the Christian churches still enjoy a degree of access to channels of persuasion appropriate to the popularity they enjoyed a century ago, not their current standing. It remains standard procedure for news outlets, for example, to solicit the views of church leaders not just on religious matters but also on scientific and medical developments that (often at a stretch) can be thought of as challenging our thinking about the nature of life. The example that I still find striking is the respectful attention that was given to church voices when the successful cloning of adult somatic cells through nuclear transfer led to the birth of Dolly the Sheep in 1996. In a number of radio and television interviews, conservative Christians objected strenuously, though they often struggled to explain to what they objected or why. The churches are still invited, as they were in the Middle Ages, to provide divine approval for public bodies by leading religious ceremonies. And of course the Catholic Church still manages 14 per cent of Scotland's schools. None of this suggests a secularist conspiracy to deprive the churches of the opportunity to influence people.

What this chapter has demonstrated is that most Scots are not persuaded by the conservative sexual mores of the churches. Their general puritanism has been comprehensively rejected and recent struggles over gay rights suggest that most Scots regard sexual orientation as a private matter which should no longer result in any public disabilities. Moreover, there is no popular support for the proposition that society would be improved by religious leaders enjoying greater influence.

Some Christians may find this disheartening but it is worth reminding them of the protection that a largely secular society offers religious people (especially those who belong to any body other than the national church). The UK state fumbled its way slowly to the position adopted by the drafters of the American constitution: the state will not promote any particular religion but it will also not prohibit any religion. What Thomas Jefferson called a 'wall of separation' between church and state was not the work of secularists. It was devised by Protestant dissenters who appreciated that the best way to protect their religious freedom was to ensure that no religious group, not even a religious majority, could use the power of the state to impose its views on the rest of the population.

In one sense the churches know that they have lost the right to claim God trumps. As they can no longer expect that announcing that God wishes this or that will be terribly effectual, conservative Christians have to offer secular justifications for their policy positions. They present partial histories: the world was a better place when they held sway, which may be true for a majority conformist but patently untrue for minorities. They offer dubious social analysis: with remarkable chutzpah Pope Benedict argued that Catholic priests sexually abused children because they had been corrupted by the sexual permissiveness promoted by liberals.[26] And they threaten us with implausible dystopias: permit gay marriage and bestiality will be next. What the evidence presented in this chapter shows is that most Scots share neither the conservative Christian view of the past nor its bleak view of the future.

Notes

1   S. Gilhooley, *The Pyjama Parade* (Edinburgh: Lomond, 2001).

2. 'Anger as archbishop suggests MP died from organ failure "because he was gay"', *Daily Mail*, 25 July 21012.; http://www.dailymail.co.uk/news/article-2178762/Archbishop-Philip-Tartaglia-suggests-MP-David-Cairns-died-44-gay.html. Instead of apologising, the Catholic Church's director of communications tried to defend the claim.

3. Anglican bishops are still excluded because they have twenty-six reserved places in the House of Lords.

4. J. Devine, 'Gonzaga lecture', 2008; http://www.catholicculture.org/culture/library/view.cfm?recnum=8079.

5. I should confess a degree of personal animus here. Bishop Devine was one of the Catholic church leaders who mis-represented the evidence on religiously aggravated offences so as to present Scots Catholics as victims of Protestant abuse. I wrote to him to explain his mistake. He ignored my alternative reading of the data.

6. L. MacLaren, 'Cardinal challenged on careers ban on gays', *The Herald*, 8 November 1999.

7. A. McDermid, 'Bashir Maan forced to quit charity post over anti-gay stance', *The Herald*, 15 June 2006; http://www.heraldscotland.com/sport/spl/aberdeen/bashir-maan-forced-to-quit-charity-post-over-anti-gay-stance-1.17397.

8. G. Braiden, 'Muslims urged to take gay marriage poll stand', *The Herald*, 19 April 2012; http://www.heraldscotland.com/news/home-news/muslims-urged-to-take-gay-marriage-poll-stand.17348741.

9. This is a major theme of H. Reid, *Outside Verdict: an Old Kirk in a New Scotland* (Edinburgh: Saint Andrew Press, 2002).

10. The interest of Kirk sessions in sexual misdemeanour was not merely prurient. Until 1845 the Kirk had responsibility to care for the destitute and hence had a strong interest in identifying fathers of children born out of wedlock. For a detailed illustration of the system's operation, see R. Sandison, *Christopher Sandison of Eshaness (1781–1870): Diarist In An Age Of Social Change* (Lerwick: Shetland

Times, 1997), pp. 101–5. For the history of the Kirk's attempts to control sexual behaviour, see S. J. Brown, 'The decline and fall of kirk session discipline in Presbyterian Scotland, c.1830–1930' (unpublished conference paper, Association of Scottish Historical Studies, 1991).

11. P. Newley, *Bawdy but British: the life of Douglas Byng* (London: Third Age Press, 2009).
12. Social Surveys (Gallup Poll) Ltd, *Television and Religion* (London: University of London Press, 1964).
13. D. Campbell, 'The pioneer who changed gay lives', *Observer*, 30 January 2005.
14. These data come from the analysis of the British Social Attitudes Survey in A. Crockett and D. Voas, 'A divergence of views: attitude change and the religious crisis over homosexuality', *Sociological Research Online* 8 (2003); http://www.socresonline.org.uk/8.
15. Ipsos MORI, *Statement On Same-Sex Marriage Poll In Scotland*, 18 June 2012; http://www.ipsos-mori.com/newsevents/latestnews/1098/Ipsos-MORI-statement-on-samesex-marriage-poll-in-Scotland.aspx. Accessed July 2012. An ICM poll for the *Guardian*, where the question was the more specific 'Do you support the move to legalise gay marriage?', produced almost identical proportions; http://www.guardian.co.uk/society/2012/dec/26/voters-back-gay-marriage-poll.
16. R. Gledhill, 'Friend of Dr Rowan Williams feels "betrayed" by his stance on gays', *The Times*, 8 December 2009; http://www.thetimes.co.uk/tto/faith/article2100871.ece.
17. Kevin McKenna raises the interesting possibility that the Catholic Church might itself have inadvertently encouraged gay young men to join the clergy. The Church treats homosexuality as a vile sin. Young Catholic homosexuals are told to control their urges. The celibacy of the clergy appears to offer an attractive career which also resolves, through suppression, the gay man's identity problems. See K. McKenna, 'Unfit for purpose and in denial: a church that has lost all authority', *Observer*, 2 March 2013.
18. S. Carrell, 'General assembly opens up prospects of church recognising civil partnerships for same-sex couples', *Guardian*, 23 May 2011.
19. 'A fifth of elders ready to leave Church of Scotland?', *British Church Newspaper*, reprinted in *Scottish Protestant View*, June 2011; S. Carrell, 'Church braced for mass walkout over gay clergy', *Guardian*, 15 November 2011.
20. O. R. Barclay, *Whatever Happened to the Jesus Lane lot?* (Leicester: IVP, 1977), p. 85.
21. The proportion of births to unmarried parents (including those registered only in the mother's name) was 29.1 per cent in 1991, 43.3 per cent in 2001 and 51.0 per cent in 2011. M. Wade, 'More children born to unwed women than to married ones', *The Times*, 18 December 2012.
22. These data come from the analysis of the British Social Attitudes Survey in Crockett and Voas, 'A divergence of views'.
23. The English arms of the parties, especially in London elections, became increasingly

focused on fears about resurgent Islam but, with its very small Muslim population, Islamophobia was not a politically attractive option in Scotland.

24. To discourage frivolous interventions, election candidates are required to lodge a 'deposit' (currently £500 per seat for Westminster elections) which is returned if the candidate gets more than 5 per cent of the votes cast. That is not enough to discourage single-issue candidates who wish to campaign on some local issue such as hospital or school closures or who simply seek publicity for themselves.

25. Such a high proportion may well be a result of the large number of unknowns. Because pastors tend to be named on their church websites, Google searching probably identified all of those who were religious officials while it failed to identify those with more humble or private occupations. However, even if there were no clergy among those I could not identify and we expressed the clergy presence as a proportion of the entire cadre, at around 12 per cent it would still be vastly greater than in the Scottish population at large.

26. J. Martin, 'Benedict Addresses the Bishops on Abuse', *New York Times*, 6 April 2008: http://thepope.blogs.nytimes.com/2008/04/16/benedict-addresses-the-bishops-on-abuse/?_r=0.

ADDENDUM: SCOTLAND'S RELIGION, 2011

As of the autumn of 2013 only the most basic data on religious identity from the 2011 census are available and it is not yet possible to explore the correlations (for example, place of birth and religion) that would help explain changes since 2001. The 2011 census asked only for current religious identity. Dropping the 'religion of upbringing' question means that some reasons for changes are obscured. It also means that even when all the data is released we will not be able to address questions (such as the links between religion and social mobility) where how people were raised may be more important than what they became possibly half a century later. A further problem is that a small but vital part of the 2001 data – the 'Other religion' and 'No religion' categories – has been recoded so that some responses which were then coded as 'Other religion' have now been shifted to the 'No religion' set. A final reason for not replacing the 2001 figures in the text with those for 2011 is that the 2001 census coincided with an edition of the national Scottish Social Attitudes Survey and a large survey of Glasgow, both of which were concerned primarily with religion and supposed associated characteristics. The three sources together allow for considerable depth of analysis and adding the 2011 census figures would have made parts of them even more complex than they are now.

Such an imposition on the reader would be justified if the 2011 census revealed anything which challenged my arguments. Fortunately for my claims to expertise, such of the new census data as have been released show no surprises: indeed, much of what was reported as 'change' is merely the working through of age-related differences that were visible in 2001. As Scots aged 18 to 34 in 2001 were much less likely than those 55 and older to claim a religious identity, an increase in the 'No religion' category was to be expected. However, the growth of the Nones is symbolically important because the most popular religion in Scotland now is 'No religion'. As the table below shows, at 36.7 per cent (or 43.7 per cent if we add those who did not answer the question), it over-took Church of Scotland (32.4 per cent in 2011). The growth in 'No religion' was also larger than is explained simply by the working through of existing age cohort differences: that is, there has been a net growth in 'No religion'. Until we can correlate current religion with place of birth we cannot be entirely certain that the change is not a result of migration but it seems highly likely that over the decade between the two censuses, a non-negligible number of Scots either 'lost' their faith or, more likely, decided to stop claiming a purely nominal attachment.

Although the percentage of Scots who described themselves in 2011 as Catholic remains the same as it was in 2001, the number of such people increased by 37,000, largely as a result of Polish migration. There have also been gains for Muslims, Hindus, Sikhs and Buddhists. Again we cannot be certain until more detailed data is released but these changes are almost cer-tainly a consequence of immigration and larger than average-sized families. There is no other evidence to support the view that Scots who in 2001 did not claim a non-Christian religious identity have converted.

Finally, it is worth noting the fate of the 'Other Christian' category. It shows net loss of 56,000 people and a relative decline from 6.9 to 5.5 per cent. Again we cannot be sure what this means until a detailed breakdown is released but it is consistent with my view that charismatic and independent evangelical churches have not proved (as their promoters hoped) to be the salvation of Christianity.

Table Addendum 1: Religion, Scotland, 2001 and 2011

	2001		2011		
	Number	Percentage	Number	Percentage	Change in number: 2001 to 2011
All people	5062000	100.0	5295000	100.0	233000
Church of Scotland	2146000	42.4	1718000	32.4	−428000
Roman Catholic	804000	15.9	841000	15.9	37000
Other Christian	347000	6.9	291000	5.5	−56000
Buddhist	7000	0.1	13000	0.2	6000
Hindu	6000	0.1	16000	0.3	11000
Jewish	6000	0.1	6000	0.1	−1000
Muslim	43000	0.8	77000	1.4	34000
Sikh	7000	0.1	9000	0.2	2000
Other religion	8000	0.2	15000	0.3	7000
No religion	1409000	27.8	1941000	36.7	532000
Religion not stated	279000	5.5	368000	7.0	89000

Source: National Records of Scotland, *Census 2011: Release 2A* (Edinburgh: The Scottish Government, 2013), p. 32; http://www.scotlandscensus.gov.uk/en/news/articles/release2a.html. Accessed 26 September 2013.

STATISTICAL APPENDIX

Table A1.1 Religious Upbringing and Current Religion, Scottish Social Attitudes Survey 2001

	Religious upbringing				
	No religion %	Christian of no denomination %	Roman Catholic %	Protestant mainstream %	Protestant conservative %
Current Religion					
No religion	89	54	20	31	35
Christian of no denomination	3	44	2	3	4
Roman Catholic	–	2	75	2	–
Protestant mainstream	6	–	2	63	28
Protestant conservative	1	–	–	–	32
Other Christian and other religions	–	–	–	–	1
Total	99	100	99	99	100

Table A1.2 Belief in God, Scottish Social Attitudes Survey 2001

	%
There is a personal, creator God	25
There is some sort of spirit or life force	28
There is something there	24
I don't really know what to think	11
I don't think there's any sort of God, spirit or life force	6
None of the above	6
Total	99

Table A1.3 Church Attendance and Non-Materialist Beliefs, Scottish Social Attitudes Survey 2001

	Church Attendance					
	Non-religious	Never attended regularly	Attended regularly; definitely stopped	Attended regularly; stopped but might go again	Regular churchgoer	All Scots
Percentage of those in each attendance category which . . .						
Has had answer to prayer	8	18	28	43	68	34
Has sense of having lived previous life	19	17	16	27	14	17
Has had actual contact with someone dead	20	23	23	32	21	23
Thinks there is another existence after death	33	37	37	63	68	46

Scottish Gods

Table A1.4 Sympathy for Religion by Age Cohort, Scottish Social Attitudes Survey 2001

	Yes	No	Don't mind	Total
18–34 years				
There should be daily prayers in state schools (%)	24	62	14	100
The BBC and ITV should be legally required to show religious programmes^ (%)	21	10	69	100
34–54 years				
There should be daily prayers in state schools (%)	41	48	11	100
The BBC and ITV should be legally required to show religious programmes^ (%)	36	7	57	100
55 or over				
There should be daily prayers in state schools (%)	70	20	10	100
The BBC and ITV should be legally required to show religious programmes^ (%)	55	3	42	100

^ For this item, 'Yes' means 'should continue' and 'No' means 'should be phased out'.

Table A7.1 Free and Free Presbyterian Church Membership, 1980–2010

	1980	1990	2000	2010
Free Church	21270	20000	13505	9140
Free Church Continuing	–	–	1500	1500
Free Presbyterian	6280	4020	4000	2600
Associated Presbyterian	–	1250	1200	400
	27550	25270	20205	13640

Note: Data are from P. Brierley, *UK Religious Trends 7* (Swindon: Christian Research, 2008), Table 8.12 and P. Brierley, *UK Religious Trends 2* (London: Christian Research, 1999), Table 8.14. Figures in italics were estimated by projecting previous trend lines.

Table A8.1 Distribution of Charismatic 'New Churches', 2005

	England	Scotland	Wales	N. Ireland	%
% of population	84.0	8.6	4.9	2.9	100
% of New Churches	94.8	3.1	1.9	1.3	100

Notes: Population as per 2001 census; distribution of New Churches is from projections to 2005 of 2003 data in P. Brierley (ed.), *UK Religious Trends 4* (London: Christian Research, 2003), Table 9.9.1.

Table A12.1 Christian Parties in Scottish Parliament Elections, 1999–2011, Regional Vote (% of votes cast)

Region	1999 %	2003 %	2007 %	2011 %
Central	0.8	–	3.6	1.4
Glasgow	0.9	1.3	2.7	0.7
Highlands and Islands	–	–	3.9	2.0
Lothians	0.3	0.2	1.0	0.5
Mid-Scotland and Fife	0.2	0.4	0.9	0.6
North-East Scotland	–	–	1.1	0.8
South of Scotland	–	–	1.1	0.7
West of Scotland	1.0	1.4	2.5	0.9
Scotland total	0.4	0.4	2.3	0.9

Table A12.2 Religiosity and Pro-Public Religion Attitudes, British Social Attitudes Survey 1998 and 2008

Church attendance	Mean score on 6-item scale; range 1–5	
	1998	2008
Not religious / Never attend	2.14	2.08
Less often than monthly	2.41	2.37
Monthly but not weekly	2.59	2.47
Weekly or more often	2.92	2.91
All respondents	2.32	2.24

INDEX

EU Authorised Representative:

Easy Access System Europe Mustamäe tee 50, 10621 Tallinn, Estonia

gpsr.requests@easproject.com

Printed and bound by CPI Group (UK) Ltd, Croydon, CR0 4YY

26/05/2025

01882762-0001